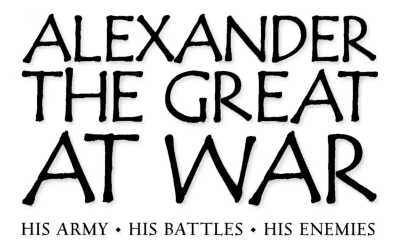

ALEXANDER THE GREAT AT WAR

HIS ARMY · HIS BATTLES · HIS ENEMIES

OSPREY
PUBLISHING

ALEXANDER THE GREAT
AT WAR

HIS ARMY · HIS BATTLES · HIS ENEMIES

EDITOR RUTH SHEPPARD

First published in Great Britain in 2008 by Osprey Publishing, Midland House,
West Way, Botley, Oxford OX2 0PH, United Kingdom.
443 Park Avenue South, New York, NY 10016, USA.
Email: info@ospreypublishing.com

Material from Duncan B. Campbell, Elite 121: *Ancient Siege Warfare*; Duncan B. Campbell, New Vanguard
78: *Greek and Roman Siege Machinery*; Duncan B. Campbell, New Vanguard 89: *Greek and Roman Artillery*;
Jack Cassin-Scott, Men-at-Arms 69: *The Greek and Persian Wars 499–386 BC*; E. V. Cernenko,
Men-at-Arms 137: *The Scythians*; Nic Fields, Fortress 40: *Ancient Greek Fortifications 500–300 BC*;
Nic Fields, New Vanguard 132: *Ancient Greek Warship*; Waldemar Heckel, Essential Histories 26:
The Wars of Alexander the Great; Waldemar Heckel, Warrior 102: *Macedonian Warrior*; Nicholas Sekunda,
Elite 7: *The Ancient Greeks*; Nicholas Sekunda, Elite 42: *The Persian Army 560–330 BC*; Nicholas Sekunda,
Elite 66: *The Spartan Army*; Nicholas Sekunda, Men-at-Arms 148: *The Army of Alexander the Great*;
Nicholas Sekunda, Warrior 27: *Greek Hoplite*; Philip de Souza, Essential Histories 27: *The Peloponnesian
War 431–404 BC*; Philip de Souza, Essential Histories 36: *The Greek and Persian Wars 499–386 BC*;
Michael Thompson, Campaign 182: *Granicus*; John Warry, Campaign 7: *Alexander 334–323 BC*;
Christopher Webber, Men-at-Arms 360: *The Thracians*.

A CIP catalogue record for this book is available from the British Library.

ISBN-13: 978 1 84603 328 5

Page layout by Ken Vail Graphic Design, UK
Index by Alison Worthington
Typeset in Truesdell and Centaur MT

Maps by The Map Studio
Originated by PPS-Grasmere Ltd, Leeds, UK
Printed in China through Bookbuilders

08 09 10 11 10 9 8 7 6 5 4 3 2 1

For a catalogue of all books published by Osprey please contact:

NORTH AMERICA
Osprey Direct c/o Random House Distribution Center
400 Hahn Road, Westminster, MD 21157, USA
E-mail: info@ospreydirect.com

ALL OTHER REGIONS
Osprey Direct UK, P.O. Box 140, Wellingborough, Northants, NN8 2FA, UK
E-mail: info@ospreydirect.co.uk

www.ospreypublishing.com

Osprey Publishing is supporting the *Woodland Trust*, the UK's leading woodland conservation charity,
by funding the dedication of trees.

Front cover: akg-images/Erich Lessing. Back cover: Topfoto. Back cover flap: Werner Forman Archive/
Schimmel Collection, New York. Endpapers: akg-images/Erich Lessing. Title page: akg-images/
Nimatallah.
Pages 6–7: akg-images/Erich Lessing.

CONTENTS

CHRONOLOGY

All dates are BC unless otherwise indicated

GREECE AND PERSIA IN THE 5TH CENTURY

When Alexander ascended the throne of Macedon following the death of his father in 336, the city-states of Greece and the huge empire of Persia had already been in conflict for hundreds of years. Ancient Greece was divided into hundreds of city-states (*poleis*, singular *polis*). The size of these states varied considerably but most comprised an urban centre, where much of the population lived, and where the principal public buildings were located, plus a surrounding rural territory. Although there were many differences in the ways that each state was organized and governed, broadly speaking they came in two types: democracy, where decision making was in the hands of the majority of the citizens, or oligarchy, in which effective control of decision making was limited to a minority of the citizens.

Armed conflict between the city-states was common. In his *Laws* Plato argued that peace is but a word, and that every state was, by nature, engaged in a permanent undeclared war with every other state (*Laws*, I.626a). Warfare pervaded all spheres of political, cultural and intellectual endeavour in Greece: it was the subject of most of the surviving Greek tragedies and comedies and warriors and warfare are the most common subjects of Greek sculptures and vases, while Classical Greek philosophy also addressed the role of the hoplite: the citizen-soldier.

Conflict was also common within the Achaemenid Empire of Persia. At its greatest extent, the empire covered a huge area, from Asia Minor to India, and its subjects included numerous peoples. The kings of Persia expanded their rule over several centuries, and were constantly challenged by the huge distances involved in ruling and administering the provinces of their empire, known as satrapies. In the late 6th century, King Darius I had a trilingual inscription carved into a rockface at Bisitun in Iran to record his actions as king. After taking the throne, he had put down a number of rebellions across his empire over several years; the carving includes a representation of nine of the defeated rebel leaders tied together. Revolt or rebellion among the peoples of the empire

OPPOSITE
This Greek vase shows a Greek hoplite and a Persian warrior fighting. (C. M. Dixon/Ancient Art & Architecture Collection)

THE GREEK AND PERSIAN EMPIRES, C.400

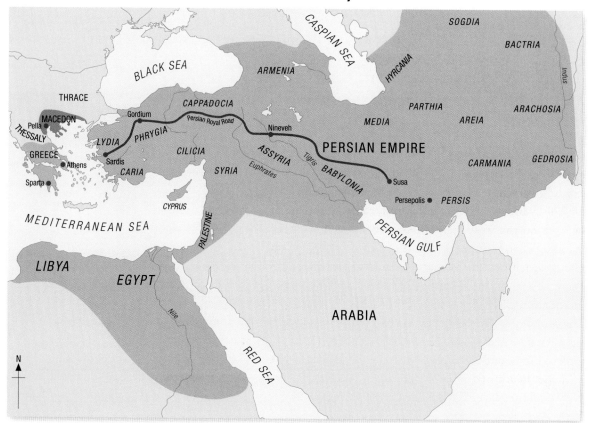

CHRONOLOGY OF THE GREEK AND PERSIAN WARS

499–493	Ionian Revolt
499	Persians attack Naxos
494	Persians defeat Ionians
493	Persian rule extended to Ionia
490	Darius I launches military expedition against Greece; Greeks defeat Persians at the battle of Marathon
486	Death of Darius I; Xerxes becomes king of Persia
480	Xerxes invades Greece; Persians win battle of Thermopylae and sack Athens; Persian navy suffers heavy defeat at Salamis
479	Greeks defeat Persians at battles of Plataea and Mycale
478/477	Formation of the Delian League, headed by Athens
449	Peace of Callias between Athens and Persia
431–404	Peloponnesian War between Athens and Sparta

and the men who ruled the satrapies in the name of the king, and even involving members of the king's own family, were common throughout the empire's history. The Greek and Persian Wars grew out of what was originally classed as one of these revolts.

THE GREEK AND PERSIAN WARS

Throughout the 5th century and into the 4th century a state of war existed between the city-states of Greece and the mighty Achaemenid Empire of Persia. These wars probably began with the rise to power of the Persian Empire under the first Achaemenid king, Cyrus the Great. Soon after ascending the throne of western Persis in 559, Cyrus conquered eastern Persis, then continued to expand his empire by conquering the Median Empire, Lydia and Babylon. The king of Lydia, the legendary Croesus, had brought the prosperous Greek cities of Ionia on the west coast of Asia Minor under his rule and made them pay tribute. When he was defeated, these cities acknowledged the rule of Cyrus, but many participated in a revolt of the Lydians and had to be brought back under Persian control by force. Some of the islands off the coast of Ionia retained their independence for some time, but by 518 the Persians controlled all of Asia Minor and most of the east Aegean islands. As with elsewhere in their empire the Persians installed or sponsored local aristocrats as rulers of the Greek cities in Asia Minor and the nearby islands, and exacted tribute from the Ionians.

In 499, following a failed naval expedition by the Persians against the island of Naxos, off the coast of Ionia, the Ionian Greeks revolted against the Persians. The Ionians realized that they could not throw off the yoke of Persian rule unaided, so they sought assistance from their kinsmen in mainland Greece. They were unsuccessful in seeking the help of Sparta, the strongest Greek city-state, or several other leading states, but they did persuade Athens and Eretria to send military expeditions on warships, stressing the ease with which they would defeat the Persians. By sending ships, the Athenians and Eretrians may have hoped to dissuade the Persians from further expansion westwards. With the benefit of hindsight, the historian Herodotus stated in his history that 'These ships were the beginnings of evils for Greeks and barbarians' (*Histories*, 5.97.48). The first target for the revolt was Sardis. When the Ionians were heavily defeated by Persian cavalry, the Greek contingents realized that the easy pickings they had been promised were unlikely to materialize and so returned home, leaving the Ionians to fight on alone. Despite renewed efforts to incite wider rebellion among the subjects of King Darius I, including supporting a short-lived revolt on Cyprus, the Ionians were eventually crushed in 494, and Persian rule was restored in Ionia by 493.

A year after Thermopylae, the Greeks and Persians met again, at Plataea. The Greek army decided to retreat from the plain of Asopus, so after nightfall the contingents of the army began to withdraw, except for the Spartans. Amompharetos, the lochagos of the Pitanate lochos, refused to retreat and disgrace Sparta. As this threatened the survival of the Greek forces, Pausanias, the commander of the Spartan army, attempted to persuade Amompharetos to lead his lochos to the rear, threatening to leave them to die. At this point, the Athenian herald arrived to see what was happening. In an imitation of the Athenian voting system which used small pebbles as ballots, Amompharetos threw a huge rock down at Pausanias' feet declaring that it was his vote against fleeing before the enemy. At daybreak, the army began to retreat, without the Pitanate lochos. Amompharetos reluctantly followed. The untidy retreat of the Greeks encouraged the Persians to pursue them incautiously which brought about the Persian defeat. (Richard Hook © Osprey Publishing Ltd)

In 490 Darius launched a military expedition against Greece. He sought revenge against those mainland Greek cities that had supported the Ionian Revolt. An invasion force landed on the plain of Marathon, roughly 20 miles north of Athens, where it was met and defeated by a combined force of Athenian and Plataean hoplites.

Ten years later, Darius' successor, Xerxes I, led another, larger expedition against Greece and the Athenians in particular. Crossing the Hellespont in 480, he accepted Macedon's surrender and marched south through Thessaly towards central Greece and Attica. Despite the legendary resistance of the Spartan warriors at Thermopylae, the Persians took the pass, leaving the road to Athens and the Peloponnese open. Unable to confront the massive Persian army, the Athenians abandoned their city and looked to their powerful navy to face the Persians. The city of Athens was duly sacked and burned but the Persian navy suffered a heavy defeat off Salamis. The following year the Persians returned. Having persuaded the Spartans to confront the Persians, the Greeks engaged and defeated the Persian army at Plataea. In the same year the Persian navy was defeated again at Mycale, ending Persian military adventures in Greece. However, although the kings of Persia would not return to Greece with a military force, they constantly meddled in her internal affairs through diplomatic and other means. Persian financial support and the prospect of military intervention in favour of one city-state or another continued to be a destabilizing factor in Greek internal relations until the mid-4th century.

THE DELIAN LEAGUE

Athens and Sparta had been the two leading states in the alliance formed to combat Xerxes' invasion in 480, and both could claim to have been instrumental in saving the Greeks from conquest: the Athenians had taken a leading role at Salamis and Sparta had led the Greek army that had defeated Xerxes at Plataea. The alliance began to break up after their victory over the Persians. The Athenians formed a new alliance in 478/477 to ravage the territory of the Persians in compensation for the subjugation of Ionia and the invasion of Greece. Each ally contributed men, ships or money, and the effort was administered and commanded by the Athenians. This alliance is known as the Delian League. The Spartans already had their own alliance known as the Peloponnesian League, made up of the small city-states in the Peloponnese, and some larger ones. The cities had more autonomy than in the Delian League, and the league was essentially a defensive alliance which was activated upon the presentation of a clear threat to a member.

The Delian League successfully waged war against the Persians, and in 449 the Athenians negotiated a formal peace treaty with Persia, known as the Peace of Callias, in which Persia disavowed any formal ambition of conquering Greece

The tombs of the Persian kings at Nagsh-e-Rustam near the city-palace of Persepolis in modern Iran. It was already a place of importance when Darius I ordered his tomb to be carved into the cliff. There are three other Achaemenid tombs at the site which are careful copies of Darius' tomb. It is thought that these are probably the tombs of Xerxes I, Artaxerxes I and Darius II. The site also has a number of reliefs dating from the later Sassanian dynasty. (akg-images/Bildarchiv Steffens)

THE FATHER OF HISTORY

The events of the Greek and Persian Wars are recorded in one of the most important works of Classical Greek literature, the *Histories* of Herodotus. Herodotus was born in the first half of the 5th century in the Greek city of Halicarnassus in Asia Minor. He travelled extensively, collecting information from people about themselves and their ancestors. He was able to talk to many eyewitnesses of events or read accounts from people who had been there. The idea of recording great achievements for posterity was not in itself a new one. Egyptian, Babylonian and Assyrian rulers had long been accustomed to set up memorials to their own greatness, inscribing them with official versions of events. Herodotus' work is special because he sought to go beyond the mere collection of these records and to enquire into their origins and causes. He was consciously looking for explanation of the events. This is how he introduces his work:

Herodotus of Halicarnassus here displays his enquiry, so that human achievements may not become forgotten in time, and great and marvellous deeds – some displayed by Greeks, some by barbarians – may not be without their glory; and especially to show why the two peoples fought with each other.

In this respect Herodotus can be seen as part of a much wider intellectual and cultural tradition of philosophical and scientific speculation and enquiry. There is also an element of learning from the events. Herodotus offers his readers his investigations into the origins and causes of the events he narrates, as well as his interpretations of their wider significance. He invites his readers to learn from his *Histories* although some of his lessons can seem strange to a modern audience.

in return for a similar respect for the Persian sphere of influence in western Asia, Palestine and Egypt. The Delian League had proved a successful alliance, but over the years it had changed from a league of states under Athenian leadership to more of an Athenian empire. By the time of the peace Athens was receiving annual tribute from other states in the league, dominating the economic life of the subject allies, and putting down revolts by them with considerable ferocity.

THE PELOPONNESIAN WAR

During the first half of the 5th century, Athens and Sparta had become the two major powers in Greece. Athens was the main sea power, and Sparta was the main land power. A major turning point in the relations between the two states and their allies came in 462. In 462, Sparta appealed to all her allies for help putting down a helot revolt. A small army of Athenians was among those who answered the call. However, shortly after arriving in Messenia, the Athenians, alone of the allies, were dismissed, apparently due to a growing sympathy for the rebelling helots among the Athenians. This humiliated and insulted Athens, and following

GREECE AND WESTERN ASIA MINOR, C.350

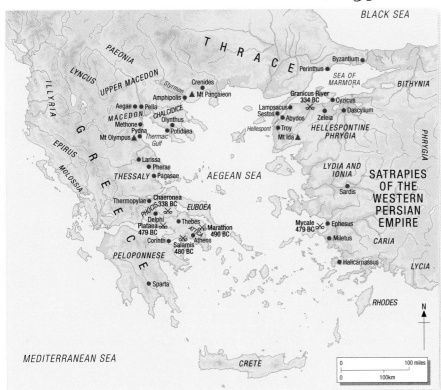

this date there was considerable political tension between the two sides, with both Athens and Sparta forming alliances with each other's enemies. Eventually this escalated into the Peloponnesian War, which erupted in 431 and ended with the surrender of Athens in 404. Although, after the Peace of Callias, Persia had left Greece alone for 30 years, the lure of intervention in the Peloponnesian War proved too difficult to resist. The peace agreed with Persia by Athens had not been formally renewed with Artaxerxes I's successor. Darius II allowed his satraps to distribute funds to Sparta and her allies and then, following a devastating defeat of the Athenians in Sicily, he agreed a treaty with the Spartans. This was undoubtedly militarily expedient, but it was also politically harmful to Sparta's reputation with the Greeks: in return for help in defeating the Athenians, Sparta was agreeing to hand back Greek city-states in Asia Minor to Persia. Darius sent one of his younger sons, Cyrus, to supply the Spartans with the resources to defeat their enemies. Along the way, Cyrus formed a strong friendship with the Spartan admiral Lysander. Lysander had political ambitions, while Cyrus was eager to bring about a Peloponnesian victory in the war so that

he could, in the near future, draw upon their soldiery, which he regarded as the best in the ancient world. Cyrus' elder brother, Artaxerxes II, was the heir to the throne of Persia, and although Cyrus had the support of a faction at court, he would need troops to challenge his brother when the time came for the accession.

Shortly after the collapse of Athens, Darius II died, Artaxerxes II ascended the throne and Cyrus set in motion his scheme to overthrow his brother. A force of some 11,000 mercenaries – which was to become known (after some defections and casualties) as the 'Ten Thousand' – accompanied a much larger Persian force from Lydia to Mesopotamia.

Not far from Babylon, at a place called Cunaxa, the armies of the feuding brothers met in 401. Although the Greeks won an easy victory against the Persians stationed opposite them, the effort was meaningless, since Cyrus himself was killed in an attack on his brother in the centre of the line. With Cyrus' death, the revolt collapsed. But it was not entirely in vain, at least as a lesson to the Greeks: for the ease with which a relatively mobile and efficient army could strike at the heart of the empire exposed the weaknesses of Achaemenid Persia.

OPPOSITE
Two Spartan hoplites and a Tegean ally during the Peloponnesian War. (Angus McBride © Osprey Publishing Ltd)

The Acropolis in Athens. The Parthenon, a temple to Athena, was built in the 5th century to replace an older temple of Athena that was destroyed in the Persian invasion of 480. (akg-images/ Rainer Hackenberg)

GREECE IN THE 5TH AND 4TH CENTURIES

Greek land warfare before the age of Alexander the Great was primarily, and often exclusively, infantry warfare. Chariots had been used in the Bronze Age – either as moving and elevated platforms for archers or as vehicles that simply delivered prominent warriors to the battlefield – but in the Near East and Anatolia the effectiveness of the chariot was negated by new tactics and weaponry, and in the Greek peninsula it had always been of limited value because of the nature of the terrain. The difficulties of topography created similar problems for the unshod horse. Although some regions, such as Thessaly and Boeotia, were more conducive to cavalry warfare, the numbers of mounted troops were limited by the expense of maintaining horses, and few 'horsemen' were actually trained to fight in cavalry formation. Therefore, nature and economics made the Greeks infantrymen – 'men of the spear'.

By the mid-7th century, the Greeks had begun to develop the weaponry and style of close-ordered combat known as 'hoplite warfare'. Although changes did occur in armour and equipment, the appearance and operations of hoplite armies did not alter dramatically over the centuries, nor did the Greeks, despite their overall reputation for inventiveness, show much interest in deviating from a tried and trusted method of warfare. It was only when the goals of war and the attempts to extend power significantly – as in the case of the Peloponnesian War – brought the Greeks to a state of what approximated 'total war' that lasting changes in the manner of waging war began to be made.

HOPLITE WARFARE

Hoplites, heavily armoured Greek infantry, dominated Greek warfare for some three centuries. The Greek word for 'weapon' is *hoplon*, and so a hoplite was literally a 'man at arms'. Hoplites fought in a close formation called a phalanx, which in Greek has a general meaning of 'battle-formation', but which historians frequently apply exclusively to the heavy infantry formation.

OPPOSITE
The Treasury of the Athenians at the sanctuary of Delphi, which was the location of the most famous oracle in ancient Greece. A small building, the Treasury contained trophies from important Athenian victories, and votive objects dedicated to the sanctuary. Athens built the Treasury in the late 6th or early 5th century. It is thought to express the victory of democracy over tyranny, although a different interpretation is that the Treasury commemorates the victory at Marathon. (akg-images/Erich Lessing)

This relief sculpture comes from a large tomb built for a local aristocrat in south-western Asia Minor around 400. It shows hoplites fighting in a phalanx formation. If the discipline and cohesion of the formation was maintained it was very difficult to overcome. An unexpected attack, or one coming from the flank or rear, could however panic the hoplites and break up their formation. (C. M. Dixon/Ancient Art & Architecture Collection)

The hoplite was, in essence, a citizen-soldier. The armies of the Greek city-states were based on a levy of those citizens prosperous enough to equip themselves as hoplites. Except for Sparta, whose warriors devoted their entire lives to military training, and a few state-sponsored units such as the Sacred Band of Thebes, the armies of the city-states were composed of citizens who saw it as their moral, social and political duty to fight on behalf of their city-state. Conscription and mobilization were effectively universal, citizens enjoying the benefits of freedom in exchange for their obligation to defend the state. Any assembly of citizens was by definition a gathering of warriors past and present. Fundamentally, every Greek citizen was a hoplite. They went into battle not from fear of punishment or in hope of plunder and booty. They fought alongside neighbours, brothers, fathers, sons, uncles and cousins. This meant that they did their utmost to demonstrate courage, side-by-side with their comrades, and that they had a vested interest in the outcome. This was the unseen glue that bound the phalanx, and the city-state, together. Only those who clashed with spear and shield, defying death and disdaining retreat, were deemed worthy.

It may seem surprising that Greek warfare was dominated by close-packed, heavily armoured amateurs for so long. The situation endured because, as time passed, the system was maintained for the sake of tradition, shared values and social prejudice. Since hoplites were expected to provide their own equipment, the majority of the population in any given city-state was necessarily excluded. But the full rights of citizenship were only accorded to those who could afford to take their place in the phalanx, so that the hoplites effectively were the 'nation in arms'. It was only in Athens, where the navy became important, that the poorest citizens, the *thetes* who rowed the triremes, came to have a significant military role – hence Athenian democracy, a term derived from the words *demos* (the people) and *kratei* (rule), or what Aristotle aptly called 'trireme democracy'. As the events of the two Persian invasions of Greece showed, hoplites could be extremely formidable. However, during the Classical period the hoplite lost his monopoly of the battlefield, and increasing use was made of cavalry and light infantry.

Training and mobilization

In most states military training began for all young men when they were 18. Most Greek city-states were organized on a territorial basis, and citizen registers were kept in the smallest sub-division of the tribe, originally the *phratry*. The commander of each of the tribal regiments maintained his own list of all citizens available for hoplite service on the basis of these registers. Upon 'coming of age' the claims of a youth to citizenship would be checked against these lists and the names of new members entered upon them. The new soldier-citizens would be gathered together and would swear a common oath. These young men were now called *epheboi* (ephebes or 'youths'), and for the next two years they underwent a programme of physical and military training, the *ephebate*. Some form of ephebate is attested in most Greek states, but practice varied greatly. In Athens the first year of ephebic training was taken up with a cycle of athletic contests, mainly running races, organized by tribe. The second year of ephebic training was generally more intensive and military in character. In many states the ephebes lived together, away from home, in barracks. They provided permanent garrisons for the city-state's key defensive points: the fortified citadel (*acropolis*) of the city and the forts and watch-towers along the border, guarding against surprise attacks by neighbouring states. Since the hoplite was not a warrior who fought individually, ephebic training concentrated on group tactics. There was far less stress on individual weapon skills, such as sword fencing.

Ephebes would rarely be called on to fight before their training was completed, and usually only if the state was invaded and in the greatest danger. Likewise,

HOPLITE ARMOUR AND EQUIPMENT 5TH–4TH CENTURY

On the left is a hoplite of the Peloponnesian War, on the right is a hoplite of the late 4th century. The lightening of hoplite armour through the 5th century was accompanied, and possibly caused, by developments in tactics that required more speed on the battlefield. By the Peloponnesian War sometimes the only armour carried was a shield. The shield was the most important item of hoplite equipment. Weighing about 13.5lb (6.2kg), the hoplite shield was capable of turning a spear- or sword-thrust. The main component of the shield was its wooden base, which was covered in a thin layer of bronze. Blazons were painted directly onto the shield's bronze surface. The rim provided rigidity to the bowl of the shield, preventing it from buckling easily in battle. In place of the close helmets worn earlier in the century the hoplite wears only a felt cap of the type previously worn underneath a helmet for comfort.

Developments in warfare in the 360s instigated more changes in the equipment of the hoplite, and this hoplite of the late 4th century wears a muscle-cuirass and a Phrygian helmet. The helmet was not expected to ward off all blows: strength was sacrificed for lightness and reasonable all-over protection. The inside was sometimes lined with fabric. Blows to the head must have frequently resulted in injury. The brightly dyed horsehair crests attached to Greek helmets were mainly designed to make the hoplite appear taller and more imposing and also served as a badge of rank.

The principal offensive weapon of the hoplite was his spear (dory). Conquered territory was said to be 'spear-won'. In his play, *The Persians*, Aeschylus vividly portrays the Greek and Persian Wars as a contest between the oriental bow and the Greek spear. On vase-paintings the hoplite spear is normally shortened for artistic convenience, but is occasionally shown at its true length of up to 9ft. Only ash could provide strong shafts of this length that were light enough to handle. Ash trees could be found in the mountains of Greece, but many cities imported their supplies from Macedon or other Balkan regions.

Spear-makers would split straight seasoned ash logs down into shafts, then shape them until they were round and smooth. Bronze or iron spear-heads and butts were produced in separate workshops and fitted to the narrower and thicker ends of the shaft respectively. The final stage of production was to fit the spear with a hand-grip at its centre of balance. As well as his spear, the hoplite of the Peloponnesian War carries the most common type of sword (xiphos) which had a cruciform hilt and a straight, double-edged, leaf-shaped blade, broadening towards the tip. (Adam Hook © Osprey Publishing)

citizens were not liable for foreign service after a certain age. In Athens the maximum age for mobilization for foreign service was 50, but citizens could be summoned to serve at home until the age of 60. This means that at any time there were up to 42 age classes liable for mobilization.

In all Greek states with a constitutional government matters of war and peace were debated by an assembly of all male citizens who had completed their military training. If war was decided on, the assembly then had to decide how many men would be required, for how many days and how the army was to be mobilized. There were several levels of mobilization, from entire mobilization, through certain age classes of all the tribes, to just certain age classes of some tribes.

Battle

Hoplite battle was, by its very nature, ritualistic – the idea was to defeat rather than to annihilate. The Greeks had developed what has been called the 'Western way of war' – a head-to-head collision of seasonal soldier-farmers on an open plain in a brutal display of courage and physical prowess. Their battlefields were scenes of furious fighting and carnage that usually lasted not more than an hour or two. Every man was pushed to the limits of his physical and psychological endurance – and then it was over, not to be repeated for a year or more.

That hoplites fought on the flattest piece of terrain was a point made by Mardonius in a speech to his master, Xerxes, the king of Persia (Herodotus, *Histories*, 7.9.1): 'When they declare war on each other, they go off together to the smoothest and flattest piece of ground they can find, and have their battle on it'. Although Mardonius believed that the Greeks pursued their unique style of warfare out of ignorance and stupidity, what he says here is incontrovertible. Any unexpected obstacle could bring the phalanx to a complete halt or break its formation, and Aristotle reminds us that it would break up if it were forced to cross even the smallest watercourse. As a result generals selected level plains on which to fight their battles.

Once a general (*strategos*) had deployed his hoplites and battle had been joined, there was little or no room for command or manoeuvre, and the individual general took up his position in the front rank of the phalanx and fought alongside his men for the duration. Consequently, many generals perished in the fray. It was for the most part outward displays of courage, not strategic or tactical skills, which were all-important for a general.

Greek hoplites were mostly farmers, and were understandably reluctant to leave their land unattended for long periods. Most states were in no position to provide cash to buy food and to compensate the hoplite for his absence from the farm. Consequently the hoplites would not vote for long campaigns. Greek generals were therefore forced to adopt military strategies that would achieve the political objectives in as short a time as possible. This meant that prior to the introduction of efficient siege artillery in the mid-4th century, most Greek states generally lacked the resources to besiege enemy cities for the necessary months or years. Also, the ethics of hoplite warfare and the practical restrictions imposed by the heavy equipment meant the hoplite was ill-equipped to deal with the difficulties of cracking fortified positions. (For more information on siege warfare see Chapter 10.)

Phalanx

It was the hoplite shield that made the rigid phalanx formation viable. Half the shield protruded beyond the left-hand side of the hoplite. If the man on the left moved in close his uncovered side was protected by the shield overlap. Hence, hoplites stood shoulder to shoulder with their shields locked. Once this formation was broken, however, the advantage of the shield was lost – as Plutarch says (*Moralia*, 220a2), the armour of a hoplite may be for the individual's protection, but the hoplite's shield protected the whole phalanx. Thus the injunction of a Spartan mother to her son 'either with this or on this' (*Moralia*, 241f16), that is, he was to return home either alive and victorious carrying the shield, or lying dead upon it after a fight to the finish.

As the phalanx itself was the tactic, two opposing phalanxes would head straight for each other, break into a run for the last few feet, collide with a crash and then stab and shove till one side broke. Thucydides says that an advancing phalanx tended to crab to the right (*Peloponnesian War*, 5.71.1) – phalanx drift, a phenomenon also seen in Macedonian armies. The men on the extreme right tended to drift further to the right, either in fear of being caught on their unshielded side, or to give themselves space to wield their spears, or possibly a combination of the two. The rest of the phalanx would then naturally follow suit, each hoplite edging into the shelter of the shield of the comrade on his right, trying to maintain the line and prevent a gap developing. Thus each right wing might overlap and beat the opposing left.

A phalanx was a deep formation, normally composed of hoplites arrayed eight to 12 shields deep. In this dense mass only the front two ranks could use their spears in the mêlée, stabbing at the vulnerable parts of the enemy, those in the third rank and beyond adding weight to the attack by pushing to their front. This was probably achieved by pressing the shield squarely into the hollow of the man in front's back, seating the left shoulder beneath the upper rim, and heaving, digging the soles and toes into the ground for purchase. Both Thucydides (*Peloponnesian*

THE AFTERMATH OF A HOPLITE BATTLE

This plate shows the aftermath of a hoplite battle in the 360s when the equipment of the hoplite changed dramatically in response to the new type of warfare first developed by the Theban general Epaminondas and then perfected in Macedon. The muscle-cuirass dips at the abdomen to cover the groin, which must have made sitting or bending extremely difficult. The monograms painted on the shields are the emblems of the Achaean and Arcadian Leagues.

The victors are looking after their wounded, carrying off the dead and stripping the enemy corpses of armour, clothing and rings. Booty was normally pooled. Generals often vowed to dedicate a tenth of the booty to a particular god if he granted victory. The rest might be given to 'booty-sellers' who auctioned it to raise money for the state, or was simply divided among the troops. Some of the captured armour would be used to erect a trophy (tropaion) at the point where the 'turn round' (trope) of the enemy had first occurred. Usually it was nailed to a nearby tree as a monument to the battle. Some of the balance would be dedicated to the gods, either at a local sanctuary or at one of the great pan-Hellenic centres.

The defeated city would send out its herald to request a truce to bury their dead. According to the customs of war this constituted an admission of defeat, and so was rarely refused. The request was made as quickly as possible so the bodies could be buried before they began to putrefy or were eaten by scavenging animals. Normally the bodies were buried together in a mass grave on the battlefield.

The fallen were listed by tribe alongside their relatives and neighbours in a casualty list commissioned by the state and erected in the centre of the city. Sometimes an elaborate empty tomb, or cenotaph, was erected in the city to commemorate the sacrifice of its citizens, and a funeral oration was commissioned to celebrate their patriotism.

The wounded could take a long time to die. Greek medical writings contain descriptions of death from battle wounds. The Hippocratic treatise *On Wounds in the Head* describes the grim stages in which the victim of a head-wound dies over 14 days in winter or just seven in summer. Elsewhere the stages of death from peritonitis over five days after an abdominal wound are described in agonizing detail. Casualties sometimes lingered on for considerably longer. It has been suggested that this may be why names are occasionally added in different handwriting to the inscribed lists of the fallen. (Adam Hook © Osprey Publishing)

War, 4.43.3, 96.2, cf. 6.70.2) and Xenophon (*Hellenika*, 4.3.19, 6.4.14, cf. *Memorabilia*, 3.1.18) commonly refer to the push and shove of a hoplite mêlée. Once experienced, such a thing was never easily forgotten and Aristophanes' chorus of veteran hoplites is made to say: 'After running out with the spear and shield, we fought them … each man stood up against each man … we pushed them with the gods until evening.' (*Wasps*, ll.1081–85) The pushing with the shields explains the famous cry of Epaminondas, who had introduced a 50-deep phalanx, 'for one pace more' at Leuctra (*Polyaenus*, 2.3.2, cf. 3.9.27, 4.3.8).

Once a hoplite was down, injured or not, he was unlikely ever to get up again. This short but vicious 'scrum' was resolved once one side had practically collapsed. The phalanx became a mass, then a mob. There was no pursuit by the victors, and those of the vanquished who were able fled the battlefield.

Greek armies in the 4th century

By the 4th century, the traditional clash of hoplite phalanxes had given way to more sophisticated combat involving combined arms, using lighter-armed peltasts, specialist skirmishing troops and, ever increasingly, cavalry. The equipment of the hoplites themselves was adapted during the 4th century to enable them to execute their tactical evolutions on the battlefield at speed and without too much fatigue.

Peltasts were armed with javelins and daggers, or sometimes a thrusting spear or sword. They had little or no armour, and their only protection was the eponymous small shield, the *pelte*. After fighting against the lightly armed and exceptionally mobile Thracian peltasts, the Greeks had created their own peltasts and developed special hoplite tactics. Consequently, Greek states hired fewer Thracian mercenaries, and the Thracians had to face more balanced Greek forces. The much-debated reforms of the Athenian general Iphicrates, in the early 4th century, seem to have improved the equipment of peltasts, lengthening their spears and swords, changing their armour and introducing special footwear, altogether increasing speed and mobility.

Until the 5th century only the armies of the Boeotian and Thessalian Leagues possessed anything more than a token force of cavalry. These two lowland areas were the only ones with landowners rich enough to maintain horses, and land suitable for cavalry warfare. Before the medieval invention of the horse-collar, the motive power of the horse was not put to agricultural use: ploughing fields and pulling wagons were jobs for yoked oxen. Horses were an indecently expensive form of transport and a means of social display. Athens was able to develop a cavalry force in the later 5th century thanks to the revenues of her growing empire. The Athenians enacted legislation to compensate cavalrymen if their horses were

THE GREEKS IN PERSIA

Xenophon's *Anabasis* tells the story of the rebellion of Prince Cyrus against his brother Artaxerxes II, his defeat at Cunaxa in 401, and the fate of the Greek mercenaries in his army, the 'Ten Thousand'. Xenophon, a young Athenian, joined the expedition as a volunteer and was elected commander by the mercenaries themselves after the battle. The mercenaries decided to march 1,000 miles through the western satrapies of Persia back to Greece rather than submit to the victorious Persian king, and Xenophon describes their arduous journey. He discusses how they dealt with the Persian forces who attacked them, and draws sharp contrasts between the Greeks and the Persians through whose 'barbarian' land they were travelling, finding the Persians weak and no match for Greek valour.

Xenophon was a supporter of the concept of the pan-Hellenic crusade. In the council of war he made a speech to the Greeks, persuading them not to trust the Persians, but to act: 'If our purpose is to take our arms in our hands and to make them pay for what they have done and for the future to fight total war against them, then, with the help of heaven, we have many glorious hopes of safety.' (3.2.10) He roused the men saying 'Do not imagine that we are any the worse off because the native troops who were previously in our ranks have now left us. They are even greater cowards than the natives which we have beaten, and they make this clear by deserting us and fleeing to the other side.' (3.2.17) Though he was probably exaggerating to build the confidence of the Greeks, these comments also show the way that many Greeks viewed the Persians at this time.

To men like Isocrates, the march of the Ten Thousand exposed the truth about the Persian Empire: it was crumbling and a concerted effort from the Greeks would bring it crashing down in ruins, even though the truth was that the Ten Thousand had been mixed up in what was essentially a domestic wrangle. Persian forces did not really attempt to stop the Greeks leaving Persia, but they would react very differently to a Greek invasion. The revolt of Cyrus divided Persian sympathies, but the unity of the empire against outside attack was, in 401, unimpaired.

killed on campaign, and the state paid an allowance for fodder, not just in time of war, but on a permanent basis. Sparta and Corinth are the only other Greek states known to have possessed forces of cavalry before the close of the 5th century. Most states established cavalry contingents only in the 4th century.

The advent of larger, more permanent federal entities in Greece also led to permanent armies raised from the citizens of the member cities. These troops, many of them peltasts, had to be paid regularly, a new development for which the states were not necessarily prepared. To solve this problem contingents of Greek mercenaries were offered for service, particularly to the Persians. These contingents were no longer paid individually; rather the Greek state was paid for the loan of its army during times of peace.

THE RISE OF THEBES

The victory of Sparta in the Peloponnesian War and the destruction of the Athenian Empire ended the balance of power in the Greek world. Nevertheless, the price of victory had been great and domination of Greece made demands on Sparta that she could not easily meet. Sparta was notoriously short of manpower and the needs of empire – maintaining garrisons and fleets, and providing Spartiate officials abroad – strained her resources and undermined the simple but effective socio-economic basis of the state and its military power. But the problems were not only domestic. Spartan power had already provoked hostility in Greece, and so when the Spartan king Agesilaus took up the cause of freedom for the Greeks in an expedition against the western satrapies of Asia Minor in 396, Persia supported a coalition of Thebes, Corinth, Argos and a resurgent Athens in a war against Sparta, which was known as the Corinthian War. The Athenian general Conon was put in charge of the Persian fleet that destroyed the Spartan navy in 394 and removed many Spartan garrisons from the Ionian cities and islands. Following this however, the Athenians began to rediscover their own imperial ambitions, so in 387/386 a Spartan envoy called Antalcidas was able to negotiate a treaty with the Persian king, Artaxerxes II. Under the terms of the King's Peace, a general truce was agreed between all the Greek states, with limited autonomy for the Ionian Greeks. Peaceful relations were thus guaranteed by the power of the Persian king. Although Sparta had withstood the Corinthian War, the bitter confrontations of this war were the forerunners of a life-and-death struggle that would see the brief emergence of Thebes as the dominant hoplite power.

The famous Theban wedge, where instead of meeting the enemy line in parallel, the infantry formed an oblique wedge targeting just one area of the opposing army, began to be used as a defensive measure in 394. Soon, however, it became clear that it had tremendous offensive potential and, as a result of the successful execution of Theban tactics by the renowned Sacred Band, Thebes replaced Sparta as the leader of Greece, at least on land. Sparta's defeat at Theban hands in the battle of Leuctra in 371 was catastrophic and it was followed by Theban invasions of the Peloponnese, the foundation of Megalopolis as a check on Spartan activities in the south, and the liberation of Messenia, which had hitherto provided Sparta with slaves (helots) and its economic underpinnings.

Meanwhile, Athens attempted to revive its maritime power by creating the Second Athenian League. This fell far short of the Delian League of the 5th century, for the member states were wary of Athenian imperialistic ambitions and the Athenians themselves were incapable of asserting their domination by

force. The Social War of 357–55 began after several cities broke away from the league. All these debilitating wars of the city-states had diverted Greek attention from the growing danger in the north: Macedon, whose king, Philip II, used the Social War to further his interests in the Aegean region.

During these power struggles in Greece, Persia maintained her interest in a divided Greece by playing the city-states against each other. The allure of Persian gold often proved a temptation too great amongst the warring city-states in their struggles for hegemony.

A PAN-HELLENIC CAMPAIGN

These internal divisions did not go unnoticed by some in Greece, such as the rhetorician Isocrates, who lamented the exhausting and fruitless feuding amongst Greeks. This, he thought, could best be overcome by their uniting in a crusade of retribution against Persia for the sacrilegious crimes which had been committed against Greece a century earlier, a theme expressed in his *Panegyricus* of 380. The theory of pan-Hellenism in his rhetoric did not always match the reality of conflicts between the Greek states. Sparta had accepted Persian support during and after the Peloponnesian War, and Macedon, perhaps out of necessity, had gone over to the Persians during the invasions of the early 5th century; however, the ideal of pan-Hellenism remained a powerful intellectual construct. A commitment to 'freedom', what we might today call a right to self-determination, was deeply valued throughout Greek society, despite the apparently contradictory fact that city-states were not averse to sacrificing the freedom of fellow Greeks if it was in the interests of their own city-state. The Greek city-states in Asia Minor had found their independence under threat on several occasions when they had been sold out by fellow Greeks on the mainland who were attempting to curry favour with the Persians. This happened again with the King's Peace, when Sparta accepted Persian dominion over the cities of western Asia Minor in return for Persian support of Spartan hegemony in Greece. Despite this apparent inconsistency, 'liberation' of Greeks from the yoke of Persian rule was a concept and project often lauded. If not exactly wrath, Sparta did incur some shame from fellow Greeks in what could be portrayed as her treacherous dealings with the old enemy, Persia.

Nevertheless, by the middle of the 4th century, after a half-century of internal struggles, no one city-state in Greece was in a position to undertake leadership in the endeavour, nor, it seems, did any have the will to do so. A new power to the north of the heartland of Greece, however, was soon to be in such a position and under the leadership of its king, Philip II, Macedon was gradually to take up the call.

OPPOSITE

Desperate fights to the death, with massive casualties on both sides, were relatively rare in hoplite warfare. One exception was the battle of Coroneia in 394. With the outbreak of the Corinthian War, the Spartan king Agesilaus was recalled to Europe after his successful campaign against the Persians in Asia Minor. On his march back through Boeotia he was opposed by an army of Argives and Thebans. Xenophon, an eyewitness of the battle, described the action in detail 'as there has been none like it in our time'. Agesilaus was victorious on the right where the Argives fled before Agesilaus' army came into contact. The other allies on this flank fled. The Argives took refuge on nearby Mount Helicon. On the other flank the Theban phalanx broke through and reached the Spartan baggage train. Alerted to this, Agesilaus wheeled his phalanx around, prompting the Thebans to turn about in an attempt to reach the Argives on Mount Helicon and a desperate struggle ensued. (Adam Hook © Osprey Publishing)

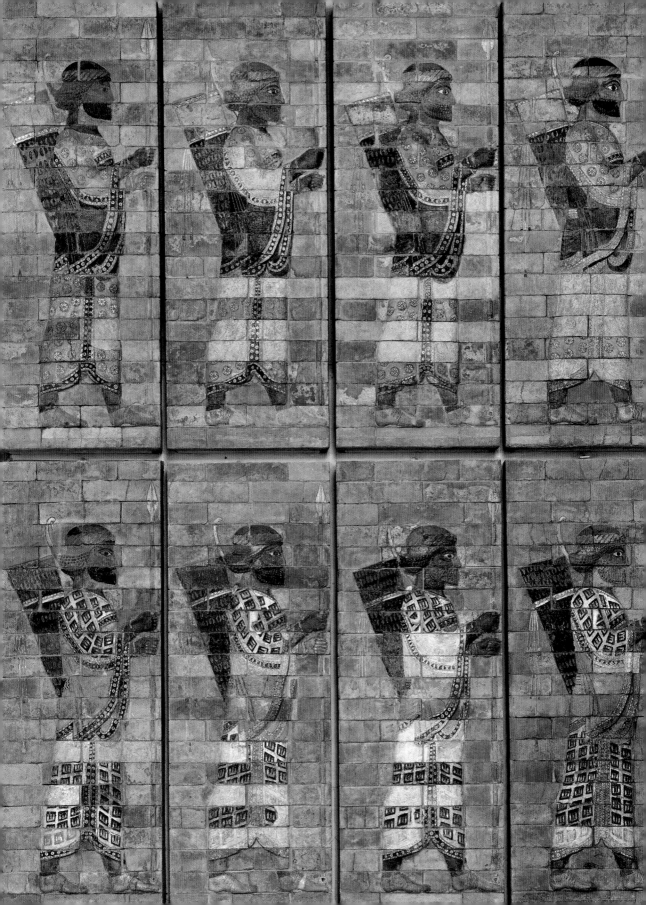

PERSIA IN THE 5TH AND 4TH CENTURIES

In the 4th century, the Persian Empire was the largest ever seen in the ancient Near East. The ruler of this vast realm was the Great King, known to the Greeks as *megas basileus*. By the time of Alexander's invasion, the Persian Empire extended from the shores of western Anatolia to the Indus Valley in the east and from Bactria (modern Afghanistan) in the north to the southern cataracts of the river Nile in Egypt. The inhabitants of Egypt had staged a successful revolt in 405, and from then until just before Alexander's invasion a main aim of the empire was to reconquer the province. The constant revolts within the empire over many years had taken their toll on its economy, as putting down each revolt incurred huge costs, and the loss of Achaemenid control over areas such as Anatolia, India and Egypt also meant the loss of revenues.

From the time of Darius I (521–486), the Persian Empire was divided into administrative units known as satrapies, each under the governership of a Persian noble satrap. In return for protecting the empire they were granted a great degree of autonomy. The Persian king was reliant on the support and co-operation of the satraps. However, at times they proved less than loyal to the king. Rebellions occurred, particularly in the 360s in Asia Minor when a number of now virtually hereditary satraps attempted to carve out essentially independent kingdoms. In addition, rivals and usurpers to the throne, like Cyrus the Younger, also emerged from the satrapal ranks.

Persian nobles had a long tradition of being fierce warriors and independent aristocrats, so they did not accept a minor role in the hierarchy of the empire. Individuals who were closely related to the king were often made the satraps of large or strategically important provinces, while others were given command over armies or other positions of responsibility. They lived in magnificent palaces and enjoyed the use of large estates in the provinces. The public distribution of prestigious gifts, particularly items of gold and silver, was a method used by the kings to indicate who were the most favoured nobles. The Persians maintained their cohesion and distinctiveness in several ways, including their dress, their use of the Persian

OPPOSITE

Enamelled brick relief showing a procession of archers from the palace of Darius I in Susa. (akg-images/Erich Lessing)

language and the education of their sons. Persian boys spent the first five years of their lives away from their fathers in the company of their mothers and other women of the household, but thereafter were taught to be soldiers and rulers. Herodotus claimed that from the age of five to 20 young men were taught only three things: riding, archery and honesty (*Histories*, 1.136). Expertise at the hunt and its

ACHAEMENID CULTURE

Zoroastrianism was the main religion of the Achaemenids, and the main principles of the Zoroastrian religion, with its emphasis on truth and justice, shaped the way that the Achaemenid kings ruled the nations of their great empire. Herodotus recorded that the most disgraceful thing in the world to a Persian was the telling of a lie, and indeed the telling of a lie was punishable by death in some extreme cases.

As Zoroastrianism spread across the Empire, it was subject to syncretic influences from the different nations and religions. Conquered nations were allowed to continue observance of their own religions and languages. For example, Cyrus the Great freed the Jews from their Babylonian captivity, and aided them in their rebuilding of the Temple in Jerusalem. The language of the empire under Cyrus and Darius was Elamite, though in inscriptions the Elamite texts are accompanied by Akkadian and Old Persian versions. Following the conquest of Mesopotamia, Aramaic became the most used language in the empire, although debate continues over whether it was the 'official' language.

Just as Achaemenid religion was subject to many influences, so Achaemenid art and architecture was a blend of many elements. The inclusion of local styles and motifs was acceptable so long as the overall effect was Persian, and it can be seen in Persian artefacts and architecture, such as at the palaces of Pasargadae and Persepolis. (6th-century Achaemenid bowl, Werner Forman Archive/Schimmel Collection, New York)

CHRONOLOGY OF THE PERSIAN EMPIRE

559	Cyrus the Great becomes king of Persia		499–386	Greek and Persian Wars
550	Cyrus takes control of the Median Empire		499	Persians attack Naxos
			499–493	Ionian Revolt
547	Cyrus conquers Lydia and captures king Croesus		494	Persians quell Ionians
			491	Darius demands all Greek states submit to Persian rule
539	Cyrus conquers Babylon			
530	Death of Cyrus; accession of Cambyses		401	Artaxerxes defeats Cyrus at battle of Cunaxa
525	Cambyses invades Egypt			
522	Death of Cambyses; Darius becomes king of Persia		396–394	Agesilaus establishes Persian bridgehead in Asia Minor
520/519	Darius campaigns against Scythia		394–387	The Corinthian War
519–518	Darius extends Persian control over the Ionians		387/386	The King's Peace

associated skills of archery and spear-throwing transferred easily to the military sphere. On a rock inscription at Nagsh-e-Rustam, Darius the Great proclaimed the values of the Persian nobility: 'As a horseman I am a good horseman. As a bowman I am a good bowman both afoot and on horseback. As a spearman I am a good spearman both afoot and on horseback.' After the age of 20, men were liable for military service until they were 50.

The ruling Persian elite did not remain completely apart from the subject peoples of the empire. Intermarriage between Persians and non-Persians did occur, with the daughters of Persian nobles marrying local princes and the Persians taking local aristocratic women as wives or concubines. Cyrus the Great had a policy of respecting local traditions and retaining some local aristocrats and religious leaders in his administration of Media, Lydia and Babylonia, and subsequent kings followed this policy in newly conquered areas. People from conquered lands who had been in positions of power were often granted high status and were accepted into the king's court with the honorary title of 'royal friend'. Similar treatment was sometimes granted to exiles from states outside the empire who sought the protection and assistance of the Great King.

The Persian kings exploited their huge empire in two main ways. They taxed the subject peoples, demanding regular payments of tribute and they utilized their manpower in military expeditions to conquer new territories or to suppress revolts in those they already ruled. In several satrapies lower-ranking

OVERLEAF

Persepolis. The Achaemenids built a number of palaces, though only those at Persepolis, Pasargadae and Susa have been excavated. Darius the Great began construction of a grand series of palaces at Persepolis in the late 6th century, and the building continued under Xerxes. The palaces brought together artistic styles from throughout the empire, creating the 'Persepolis style'. The eastern stairs to Darius the Great's audience hall are covered in carvings of subjects from the different regions of Persia bringing tribute to the king. The tribute brought by the subjects reflects the cultural and natural resources from their regions, including camels from Arabia and Bactria, gold from India and horses from Scythia. As well as tribute, the Achaemenid kings exacted a tax in silver. (akg-images/Suzanne Held)

ACHAEMENID KINGS OF THE PERSIAN EMPIRE

Cyrus II, the Great	559–530	Sogdianus	423
Cambyses II	529–522	Darius II Nothus	423–404
Smerdis	522	Artaxerxes II Mnemon	404–358
Darius I, the Great	522–486	Artaxerxes III Ochus	358–338
Xerxes I	485–465	Artaxerxes IV Arses	338–336
Artaxerxes I	465–424	Darius III Codomanus	336–330
Xerxes II	423	Artaxerxes V Bessus	330–329

Persians and Medians were granted small estates that provided them with modest revenues. In return they were expected to maintain themselves as cavalrymen or charioteers, or to provide infantry soldiers for the king's armies. In years when such services were not demanded their estates were subject to taxes in silver or in kind, much like the rest of the satrapy.

Surviving records show that the Persian Empire created a complex bureaucracy to administer the satrapies and dispose of their revenues according to the king's instructions. Members of the royal court and many other persons of importance were granted food and provisions from the royal storehouses. A system of roads linked together the main centres, Sardis, Ecbatana, Babylon, Susa and Persepolis. These roads were primarily for the use of soldiers and royal couriers who were provided with way-stations, but the roads also facilitated the movement of trade and tribute across the empire.

In addition to the satraps, there were rulers of smaller administrative units known to the Greeks as hyparchs (*hyparchoi*), but the use of terminology is often inconsistent in Greek sources and the titles 'satrap' and 'hyparch' are sometimes used interchangeably. Both can be found commanding regionally recruited troops.

THE PERSIAN ARMY

Under the Achaemenids, the army of the peoples of the Iranian plateau developed significantly. Earlier in Media, the army, known in Old Persian as the *spada*, was first organized into distinct units at the end of the 7th century by the Median king, Cyaxares. After the Medes were superseded and brought into the Persian Empire, the Medes, along with the Persians formed the core of the spada. As the Empire expanded, subjugated peoples, such as the Hyrcanians and the Bactrians, were incorporated into the army, using their native weapons, skills and techniques. The carvings at Persepolis, and official Persian documents used by Herodotus, indicate that the closer a nation was to the Persians, the more it shared in the domination of the empire, contributing more troops and paying less tribute; hence the large numbers of Medes in the army and among the commanders. The Persians were also prepared to adapt their warfare: they were keen to make use of Greek mercenaries after their superiority as heavy infantry had been learned at first hand during the Greek and Persian Wars.

The Persian army was composed primarily of satrapal levies, each of the Achaemenid provinces providing troops. These troops were then divided into decimal units. Herodotus and Xenophon speak regularly of myriads and chiliarchies, units of 10,000 and 1,000, which the Persians themselves called *baivaraba* and *hazaraba* (sing. *baivarabam* and *hazarabam*). Each baivarabam had its *baivarpatish* (myriarch); and there was a *hazarapatish* (chiliarch) for every hazarabam, which in turn was subdivided into ten groups of 100 (*sataba*), and these into ten units of ten (*dathaba*). These were, in reality, only nominal strengths, and thus we can explain, at least in part, the wildly exaggerated numbers of Persians in the Greek sources, especially in Herodotus' account of the Persian Wars. Apart from the standing army, for major campaigns the Persians levied troops from all the subject peoples of the empire, gathering men from as far afield as Egypt and India, but the most reliable soldiers were always the Persians and the mercenaries from Iran and central Asia.

Some type of uniform seems to have been worn in the Achaemenid army long before it appeared in Greek armies. Cyrus the Great is documented as having handed out Median cloaks to his officers in the 6th century. Uniformity in dress seems to have applied to officers of the royal administration and units of the central army. Regimental commanders had their own standards, behind which the regiment would form up. These standards marked the commander so that he could be quickly located on the battlefield or in camp by messengers, and the standard was used to signal that the regiment should move.

Cavalry

Native Persian military strength lay in their cavalry. The horse stocks of Nisea provided the finest mounts in the ancient Near East. The conquest of Lydia in 547 had demonstrated to Cyrus the Great the need for a reliable corps of Persian cavalry, so he distributed conquered land among the Persian nobles so that they could raise horses and fight as cavalry. The Persian king also used Medes as cavalry and from the reign of Darius I onwards the Persians recruited mercenary infantry and cavalry from the Saka tribes of central Asia.

The 3,000-strong cavalry of the Persian standing army are mentioned in several sources. Under the command of the Master of Horse, they were

DARIUS III AND SPEAR-BEARERS

The appearance of Darius III, on the right, is based on the Alexander mosaic. He wears the royal robe in purple with a wide white median stripe. He wears a red belt and an akenakes dagger with golden sheath. He wears his hood upright, a distinction of dress reserved only for the king. Other Persians wore the hood turned down at the side or front. This kitaris headdress is bound with a blue diadem. On the left is a spear-bearer carrying the royal standard, as shown in the Alexander mosaic. He is wearing royal dress, the main component of which is the purple tunic with central white stripe. The sources indicate that royal dress could be awarded by the king to individuals, or in the case of the spear-bearers, to a whole group. Sea-purple dye was the most expensive dye known in antiquity, and even substitute shades were expensive. Its value led the king to hoard purple cloth and distribute it as a mark of his power. Alexander captured large stores of the cloth, but was so generous in his distribution that he had to write to the cities of Ionia directing them to send him more so that he could dress all his Companions in purple. Saffron was the most valuable luxury dye after purple. Harvested from the three pistils inside a crocus blossom, at least 20,000 blossoms have to be stripped and toasted to yield one kilogram of dry saffron. Thus after purple, yellow was the most common colour used to dress elite Achaemenid units.

The central figure is a man of some importance. The details of his dress are taken from the Alexander sarcophagus, and seem to indicate that

he may be the hazarapatish, the commanding officer of the spear-bearers. The blue stripe on his tunic may have been to differentiate him from the king. Presumably such an important officer would have had decoration at the collar, but the sarcophagus is too faded to enable restoration. He wears a golden torque, given to him by the king. It is not known who held the post of *hazarapatish* during Darius' reign, but as Plutarch described Mazaeus as the greatest Persian after Darius, it seems probable that he held the post, as well as that of satrap of Cilicia. The evidence suggests that all members of the spear-bearers carried the hoplite shield. (Simon Chew © Osprey Publishing Ltd)

supplied with horses from central studs. The Persian cavalry were mainly recruited from the nobility, and the elite cavalry units would have been drawn from the highest circles. It seems there were at least three regiments of elite cavalry. Men in these units might have been marked out by distinctive badges of status given to them by the king, such as golden jewellery, weapons or clothes. At least one of these regiments, if not all of them, was composed of men from the most esteemed group of nobles, the King's 'Kinsmen'. The 15,000 Kinsmen were not actual relatives, but were awarded this honorific status. They alone were allowed to exchange kisses with the king, a form of greeting only permissible between social equals, and dine with him at the King's Banquet, for which a thousand animals were slaughtered daily. Diodorus Siculus mentions that at Gaugamela, Darius himself commanded a squadron of 1,000 Kinsmen, each chosen for their courage and loyalty.

Persian cavalry were armed and equipped in a variety of ways. Shields had been carried since the mid-5th century, and from the late 5th century, horsemen wore cuirasses and their mounts were equipped with armoured saddles and breastplates. Reforms in their equipment in the early 4th century introduced arm-guards, moving the cavalry one step further towards the fully armoured *cataphract* seen in later Persian armies. They were armed in a similar manner to the infantry, but with two spears.

A gold model chariot from the Oxus Treasure, Achaemenid Persian, 5th–4th century. This is one of the most outstanding pieces in the treasure, which is the most important collection of gold and silver to have survived from the Achaemenid period. The model chariot is drawn by four horses. Inside are two men in Median dress. The front of the chariot is decorated with the Egyptian dwarf-god Bes, a popular protective deity. (The British Museum/HIP/TopFoto)

The 360s saw a number of satrapal revolts and intrigues. Due to the upheaval during this period the quality of Persian cavalry began to deteriorate. The Persian landholders in the western satrapies who provided the empire with its cavalry regiments had been reduced by constant war. Previously they had supplied men for service from their own households, and only garrison troops were paid; now cavalrymen were recruited from wherever possible, and all of them had to be paid. When Artaxerxes III came to the throne in 358 he decided that the satrapal armies could no longer guarantee the security of the western borders and ordered them to be disbanded.

Also fighting in the Persian army were units of camel-borne troops, chariots and scythed chariots, which appear in some of the battles against Alexander.

Infantry

The principal soldiers seen in all Persian armies were usually infantrymen who were Persian by birth and who carried large shields, often made of hide and osier willow. They fought with a variety of weapons including long spears, axes, swords and bows and arrows. Their armour was minimal, consisting at most of a padded cuirass of linen and perhaps a helmet, although most images show them wearing caps or hoods.

The most important unit of the army was the king's personal division, his guards and the elite of the standing army. It unfailingly maintained its full strength of 10,000 and hence was known as the 'Immortals'. This infantry unit formed the elite – men selected for their physical excellence and their valour – and appears to have included a contingent of 1,000 spear-bearers, known from the golden apples that constituted their spearbutts as *melophoroi* or 'apple-bearers', though the sources are not conclusive. These spear-bearers would therefore have been the first infantry regiment of the army.

The traditional fighting formation for infantry in the Near East in the first millennium BC was the archer-pair. This consisted of an archer protected by a large shield held by a partner. During the early empire, the majority of Achaemenid infantry were *sparabara*, bearers of the large rectangular *spara* shields. The ten men of the front line of the unit carried shields, while behind, protected by the shields, were arrayed the other nine ranks, each man armed with a bow and falchion. The front row would have short fighting spears to protect the rest of the unit if the enemy reached the line. Sometimes, however, the whole unit was armed with bows, and the shields were propped up as a protecting wall at the front. After the battles of Plataea and Mycale, the Persians realized they needed to give the sparabara a means of protecting themselves if the spara wall was broached. Some wore cuirasses, but what was needed was a

THE IMMORTALS

Composite regiments in the Persian army are mentioned by Xenophon in the *Cyropedia*, comprising two ranks of infantry at the front, two of javelinmen or takabara, two of archers, and then at the back two ranks of 'file-closers', whose arms are not noted. This formation was designed to combine heavy missile power with heavy infantry. It is debatable whether such a formation really existed, although Alexander did attempt to form a composite phalanx of Macedonian and Persian forces towards the end of his campaign. If the composite regiment did exist, the evidence seems to suggest that the ten regiments of the Immortals might have been organized in this way, with some individuals carrying hoplite shields, others carrying the taka and some equipped as archers. These infantrymen, wearing tunics distinguished by purple collars and cuffs and hems decorated with silver braiding, are restored from the Alexander sarcophagus, and are likely to represent several different regiments of the Immortals, separate from the spear-bearers and the yellow and blue regiments distinctly shown in the carvings. All these figures seem to wear the purple tunic distinction and yellow hoods, though the hoods are worn by regiments other than the Immortals. The central figure carrying an axe wears a cloak with leopard-skin trim, and a lining made of the fur of small animals. The infantryman spearing the leopard is equipped as a cuirassed foot-soldier or officer from the front rank of a composite regiment. The archer at the left may also come from a composite regiment, one of several distinguished by scarlet tunics. Scarlet dye was obtained from the kermes oak, a tree especially abundant in ancient Iran. (Simon Chew © Osprey Publishing Ltd)

shield to ward off the Greek spear-thrusts. So shields to be carried by the individual were introduced. Called *taka*, they were constructed of wood or leather, and had a segment cut out of the top to give the archer good vision.

Persia employed mercenaries from within and without the empire. Many regiments of mercenary infantry were raised locally, often by the satrap. However, there was not a vast number of available men to fight, for after each nation was taken into the Persian Empire, military training for their young men ceased. This meant that mercenaries were raised from areas that were still 'free'. As well as Greek mercenaries, the Persians made use of mercenaries from the Saka tribes to the north, and the peoples of northern India to the east. From within the empire they could also call upon some hill tribes. These peoples, such as the Kurds, Mysians, Pisidians, Hyrcanians and Bactrians, were almost constantly in revolt against the authority of the Persian king, but the Persians did not destroy them because they were such a important source of mercenaries, and necessary to ensure the survival of the empire. Most of these troops fought with spears and the taka, so were known as *takabara*, and frequently fought as troops of the line in hand-to-hand fighting.

From at least the middle of the 5th century, Persia made extensive use of Greek mercenaries, usually in the form of personal bodyguards for provincial chiefs and garrisons for the Greek cities of western Asia Minor. In the 4th century, increasing numbers of mercenaries were employed by the western satraps and figured prominently in their periodic revolts against the Great King, most notably the 10,000 who fought for Cyrus the Younger in 401. It is certain that many mercenaries were recruited from the local Greek populations of Asia Minor. Great numbers of mainland Greek mercenaries were recruited from the mountainous regions of the Peloponnese, though their commanders came from all areas of Greece. There is evidence that some of the mercenaries at the Granicus hailed from Athens, Thebes and even Thessaly. During the 4th century, the increase in federal states in Greece led to new permanent armies, and hiring them out to Persia as a force rather than individually in peacetime was used as a way to pay for their upkeep.

The invasion of Asia Minor by Agesilaus in the early 4th century and earlier encounters had shown the Persians that their infantry were no match for Greek hoplites. In their attempts to re-conquer Egypt they had employed Greek mercenaries, among them the Athenian general Iphicrates, who created the 'Iphicratean peltast', converting the non-hoplite Greek mercenaries into takabara but further strengthening their equipment. Iphicrates armed these men with newly lengthened spears, and taka shields. These long spears may have been part of the inspiration for the Macedonian *sarissa*. These men could

Achaemenid takabara
fighting Greek hoplite.
The scene on this Athenian
vase was probably inspired
by war in the 390s. The
hoplite's shield-device may
preserve that of one of the
allied contingents fighting
on the Spartan side. (akg-
images/Erich Lessing)

Simon Chew

fight in the front line of the army and stand up to hoplites. Limits on the number of available Greek mercenaries following the battle of Leuctra in 371 then led to the equipping and training of 120,000 Asiatic mercenaries in the king's employ as hoplites.

Around 354, the satrap Artabazus rose up in revolt, supported by first an Athenian army, then a Theban contingent. Artaxerxes eventually put down the revolt, and took over control of the Theban army. He then spent some years settling other revolts, before turning to the reconquest of Egypt. For this contingents of troops were hired from Thebes, Argos and the Greek cities of

COULD PERSIA HAVE DEFEATED ALEXANDER?

The stunning successes of Alexander have tended to obscure the vitality of Persian military operations during Alexander's invasion. There were significant attempts after Issus to seize the strategic initiative, and to replace the troops lost in battle. New infantry forces were raised in Babylonia, and an army was sent into Anatolia to make contact with the Persian fleet. It failed to reach the coast. The Persians were depending on the cavalry to turn the situation around, and to help them do this a large force of scythed chariots was created to open up gaps in the Macedonian line that the cavalry could then exploit. Gaugamela would be the test of Persia's last hope.

Asia Minor. Though *kardaka* were also present, the expendable Greek contingents were supposed to take the worst of the fighting. The reconquest was complete by 343.

The kardaka seem to have been non-Persian, non-Greek, troops of the royal household, or royal mercenaries. It is not clear how far back in time they had existed, but they were present at Issus. It is possible that although they were not ethnically Persian, they were accorded the status of a Persian bondsman in return for their military service, and given some of the benefits restricted to the Persians. Under Artaxerxes III the system of settling retired mercenaries on land in the empire was revived, and whole communities of retired kardaka were placed in strategic locations in the empire with the aim of maintaining the local peace. The full extent of the system is unclear, but there is evidence of settlements in Egypt, Iran and Lycia. It seems the allotment of land to a retired mercenary incurred a liability for service from him and his descendants. This was exploited by the Hellenistic rulers who followed Alexander, and the sources note regiments of kardaka in Hellenistic armies in the 3rd century. The kardaka system inspired changes in the Greek and Macedonian practice of military settlements. Discharged soldiers were now settled on allotments in return for military service from themselves and their descendants, allowing the East to be Hellenicized.

This reconstruction shows various types of infantry in the Persian army in 333. On the left is an archer, perhaps from an elite regiment since he has silver braiding on his tunic. In the centre appears a kardaka infantryman, based on information from the Alexander mosaic. He carries a painted bronze hoplite shield. On the right is a satrapal infantryman, based on a fresco in a tomb in Macedonia. He is probably a takabara in the service of one of the western satraps. He therefore may not have been an Iranian, but may have been recruited in Anatolia. His white hood may indicate his non-Persian status. He carries a round shield, and a sword in a scabbard. His sword is probably his secondary weapon, to be used after losing the spear. (Simon Chew © Osprey Publishing Ltd)

THE RISE OF MACEDON

M acedon, for the most part, had been exempt from the continual state of war in Greece because its geographical position and strategic significance were of little account in Graeco-Persian politics. Macedon was the product of the union of Upper and Lower Macedon, which was completed in the time of King Philip II and to which were added new cities containing new – that is, naturalized – citizens. The country was not highly urbanized and most of the population were herdsmen. The origins of the Macedonian state in antiquity are obscure, as they were to the classical Greeks who generally regarded the inhabitants of Macedon as semi-barbarous and residing on the periphery of the civilized world. According to tradition, the Argead line of kings was established in the 8th century but little is heard of them until Herodotus mentions them in his coverage of the Greek and Persian Wars. The exact nature of Macedonian kingship is also unclear, but accession to the throne was often subject to internal and foreign intrigue, including assassination, with no fewer than 13 monarchs ruling between Alexander I and Philip II, in a period of less than a century.

During the Greek and Persian Wars, Macedon had been a vassal kingdom of the Persian Empire, and its king, Alexander I Philhellene, had acted primarily in his own interests, despite his nickname, which means 'friend of the Greeks'. He had dissuaded a Greek expeditionary force from occupying the Vale of Tempe, which separated Macedon from Thessaly, because he did not want Xerxes' large army bottled up in Macedon where it would be a drain on the kingdom's resources. Later he advised the Athenians to accept the reality of Persian power and surrender to Xerxes, which, of course, they decided not to do.

Alexander's son, Perdiccas II, ruled during the Peloponnesian War and maintained himself and the kingdom by vacillating between support of Sparta and Athens, according to the threat that each posed and the changing fortunes of the war. By the end of the century, Perdiccas' son Archelaus II had begun to strengthen the kingdom: new roads were created and an effort was made to import Greek culture from the south. Indeed, the playwright Euripides died in Macedon, where he had written his gruesome tragedy *The Bacchae*. But

OPPOSITE
4th-century iron breastplate with gold ornamentation found in the tomb of Philip II of Macedon. (The Art Archive/Archaeological Museum Salonica/Gianni Dagli Orti)

4TH-CENTURY CHRONOLOGY OF MACEDON

368–365	Philip, son of Amyntas III, future king of Macedon, resides in Thebes as a hostage	346	Peace of Philocrates; Philip becomes master of northern Greece
360/359	Perdiccas III killed in battle; accession of Philip II, first as regent to Amyntas IV	338	Battle of Chaeronea; Philip becomes master of all Greece
359–336	Reign of Philip II of Macedon	337	Formation of the League of Corinth, headed by Philip II
356	Birth of Alexander the Great		
352	Philip II's victory over the Phocians at the 'Crocus Field'	336	Death of Philip II; accession of Alexander III, the Great

4TH-CENTURY ARGEAD KINGS OF MACEDON

Craterus	399	Amyntas III (restored)	392–370
Orestes and Aeropus II	399–396	Alexander II	370–368
Archelaus II	396–393	Ptolemy I	368–365
Amyntas III	393	Perdiccas III	365–360/359
Pausanias	393	Amyntas IV	359–356
Amyntas III	393	Philip II	359–336
Argaeus II	393–392	Alexander III, the Great	336–323

Archelaus did not live to fulfil his ambitions succumbing, as so many Macedonians did, to an assassin's dagger.

The death of Archelaus was followed by a succession of short-lived rulers until Amyntas III re-established a measure of stability. Nevertheless, the kingdom was constantly threatened by the Illyrians to the west and the imperialistic (or, at least, hegemonic) tendencies of the Athenians and Thebans. By the queen Eurydice, Amyntas had three sons, all destined to rule. Alexander II held the throne only briefly (370–368) before he was murdered. A brother-in-law, Ptolemy of Alorus, then served as regent for the under-aged Perdiccas III, but was assassinated in 365. Perdiccas was now master of his own house and throne, but the kingdom continued to be threatened by the Illyrians to the west, and in 360/359 these destroyed the Macedonian army, leaving Perdiccas and 4,000 men dead on the battlefield and only a child as heir to the throne.

Amyntas III's remaining son, Philip II, now came to the fore at the age of 23, probably initially appointed regent to his infant nephew, Amyntas IV. To extricate

Macedon from its current precarious position, and to secure his own future, Philip had to expand the power of the throne. For this to be possible, diplomacy and military innovation – the creation of a powerful army – were imperative. During the reigns of his brothers, Philip had spent some time as a hostage in Thebes, where he had witnessed the Theban infantry reforms and had given thought to applying the same lessons to the Macedonian army. This experience gave him the knowledge and skills to deal with the ongoing threat from Illyria. Indeed, he dealt with the crisis so effectively – combining military action with diplomacy, or even duplicity – that the claims of Amyntas IV were swept aside, and Philip became king in 359.

Philip's diplomacy and army reforms elevated the status of the previously derided Macedon. A contemporary historian, Theopompus of Chios, claimed that 'Europe had never before produced such a man as Philip', and his impressive and startling achievements should not be overlooked, even though they are inevitably overshadowed by those of his son.

In 382 the Spartans sent an allied army to help King Amyntas of Macedon win back his lands from the Olynthians. While Macedon was mostly famed for its cavalry, some time around the end of the 5th century or the early 4th century one of the Macedonian kings raised a force of hoplites. On the left is a Spartan on horseback. The Macedonian hoplite, in the centre, is equipped in a very similar manner to the Spartans and their allies. Behind him stands a Cretan mercenary archer, serving with the Spartans. (Angus McBride © Osprey Publishing)

PARMENION

Parmenion (c.400–330) fought in the Macedonian army under both Philip II and Alexander. He was the son of a nobleman and Philip's most trusted general, winning a great victory over the Illyrians in 356. In 346 he was sent on the embassy to Athens that led to the Peace of Philocrates. With Attalus and Amyntas he led the advance force to Asia Minor in 336.

When Parmenion was recalled to Macedon after Philip's murder he quickly associated himself with Alexander, helping him to secure the throne by acquiescing in the murder of Attalus. This service won him and his family great rewards. He served as Alexander's second-in-command at all of Alexander's major battles, where he controlled the Macedonian left, and his sons Philotas and Nicanor obtained major commands.

Parmenion continued as second-in-command until 330 when he was charged with securing the captured treasure of Persia in Ecbatana. That year he was sentenced to death after being implicated in Philotas' alleged plot against Alexander. There seems to be no proof that he was involved, but as he posed a possible threat to Alexander's ambitions, the conspiracy provided a convenient excuse for his murder.

PHILIP II'S ARMY

In reorganizing the army Philip took into consideration the advances of the Thebans. In particular, he is likely to have noted the tactical innovations of the two great Theban military commanders, Epaminondas and Pelopidas, including the Theban wedge. By lengthening the leftmost columns of the traditional hoplite battle infantry line and co-ordinating cavalry to attack the flanks of the enemy, Epaminondas was able to lead the Boeotians to victory over Sparta and her Peloponnesian allies in decisive battles at Leuctra in 371 and Mantinea in 362, effectively ending Spartan supremacy in Greece. These innovations highlighted the changing nature of warfare in the 4th century. No longer would the traditional clash of heavy armed classical hoplites alone prove decisive on the battlefield. Rethinking the use and nature of heavy infantry, the place and role of lightly armed auxiliaries and, most importantly, the integration of cavalry into the battlefield were crucial lessons to be learned.

The 'New Model' phalanx

Philip's military innovations had an immediate and enduring effect. Diodorus Siculus wrote that:

> Philip was not panic-stricken by the magnitude of the expected perils, but, bringing together the Macedonians in a series of assemblies and exhorting them with eloquent speeches to be men, he built up their

morale, and, having improved the organization of his forces and equipped the men suitably with weapons of war, he held constant manoeuvres of the men under arms and competitive drills. Indeed he devised the compact order and the equipment of the phalanx imitating the close fighting with overlapping shields of the warriors at Troy and was the first to organize the Macedonian phalanx. (16.3.1–2)

Obviously, if Philip could not put a native hoplite army of any size into the field after his brother's Illyrian disaster, he would either have to rely on mercenaries, which in Macedon's current political and economic state he could ill afford, or he would have to provide his men with a distinct advantage, in weaponry, tactics or both, over their enemies. Compact formations alone do not explain his success, and Philip would scarcely have had time adequately to train his demoralized men in new tactics before their first battles, except to apply as much as possible of what he had learned. Furthermore, to attribute Philip's overnight success simply to the adoption of Theban tactics disparages the difficulty of the action. The only plausible explanation is that Philip experimented, right from the start, with a new tactic and weapon.

Philip was familiar with the Greek phalanx and hoplite warfare. He decided to adapt the phalanx to make it appropriate for his Macedonian infantry. Unlike

View of the archaeological remains at Pella, the capital of ancient Macedon. Alexander was born here in 356. (Ann Ronan Picture Library/HIP/TopFoto)

many of the Greek states south of Mount Olympus and the river Peneus, Macedon did not lack manpower. Rather, it lacked major urban centres and a solid middle class from which to draw hoplites who could afford their own equipment. However, Macedonian soldiers were herdsmen whose duties could be handled by the old, the young or women. From such peasant stock, hardy and accustomed to the simple life, Philip could raise full-time 'professional' soldiers, but he had to arm them. He did so with a weapon new to the Macedonians, a longer, heavier fighting spear – the *sarissa* (pl. *sarissai*). He also issued them with some light body armour, borrowing the ideas of the Athenian general Iphicrates, who had been campaigning in the area shortly before. As the new weapon required both hands for adequate control and handling, a button-shaped shield, some 24in (60cm) in diameter, was hung from the neck by means of a neck-strap and manoeuvred with the forearm as required.

It is possible that Philip's introduction of the sarissa was influenced by the very long spear used by the Thracians in the 4th century. Philip had been wounded through the thigh by a Triballian long spear which lamed him and killed his horse. The Macedonian sarissa was made of a cornel-wood shaft between 1¼ and 1½in (3–4cm) in diameter, and 15–18ft (4.5–5.5m) long. It was of two-piece construction fitted together by a bronze coupling sleeve. This was an essential feature of the weapon as it added sturdiness, improved balance and decreased the bend. It also allowed the weapon to be dismantled and carried in two parts on the march, and it must have facilitated repair or replacement of weapon parts. Equipped with an iron leaf-shaped blade and bronze butt-spike – both 17–20in (40–50cm) long – and weighing 14–15lb (6–7kg), the sarissa was held with a two-handed grip about 6ft (1.8m) from the butt. This meant the weapon extended some 12ft (4m) in front of the Macedonian phalangite, giving him an advantage in reach over the Greek hoplite. In a phalanx the spear tips of the levelled sarissai of the first three to four ranks would project beyond the front rank while the remaining ranks would hold their sarissai upright or inclined to protect against missile attack. The hedgehog-like front provided an unusual degree of offensive might. Under Philip the usual depth may have been ten ranks, as a file was called a *dekas* (meaning 'unit', originally of ten men).

To be tactically successful, the Macedonian phalanx needed a rank and file that was tough, disciplined and well trained. These requirements certainly tie in with Philip's regime to toughen up his troops. In his *Stratagemata*, Polyaenus relates that Philip trained his men by forcing them to march 300 stades (over 30 miles) in a single day, wearing their helmets and greaves and carrying their shields, sarissai and their daily provisions (*Strat.* 4.2.10). Indeed, Philip sought to improve the mobility and efficiency of the army by limiting the infantry to one servant for every ten men – or presumably, one per dekas – and ordering the troops to carry rations of grain sufficient for 30 days. Other luxuries were frowned upon. Polyaenus notes the Tarentine officer (though presumably a cavalryman) who was stripped of his command for taking warm baths (*Strat.* 4.2.1).

Actual tactical manoeuvres were also practised, for neither Philip's orderly feigned 'retreat' at Chaeronea nor Alexander's dazzling display before the Illyrians at Pelium could have been executed without regular training. The sarissa was awkward to handle at the best of times, and the entanglement of these weapons could spell disaster. Hence even in open formation, movement in unison was a practised art. The use of tightly packed spearmen in the phalanx may have been a Greek development, but it reached its peak of efficiency and prowess in the Macedonian armies commanded by Philip and Alexander.

Quintus Curtius Rufus describes the Macedonian phalanx in his *History of Alexander* written in the 1st century AD:

> The Macedonian line is certainly coarse and inelegant, but it protects behind its shields and lances immovable wedges of tough, densely packed soldiers. The Macedonians call it a phalanx, an infantry column that holds its ground. They stand man to man, arms interlocked with arms. They wait eagerly for their commander's signal, and they are trained to follow the standards and not break ranks. (3.2.13)

Philip's first battle was against the Illyrians near Lake Lychnitis in 359/358. Diodorus Siculus, drawing upon the mid-4th-century author Theopompus, states that Philip led the right wing, 'which consisted of the flower of the Macedonians' (16.4.5). It is assumed Diodorus is referring here to the *pezhetairoi* ('foot companions', Philip's elite guard), Philip having 'ordered his cavalry (*hetairoi*) to ride past the barbarians and attack them on the flank, while he himself fell on the enemy in a frontal assault' (16.4.5).

Cavalry

Originally, the core of the Macedonian military was the cavalry, particularly the nobility that formed the king's guard and rode into battle with him. These men were the king's hetairoi – his 'companions', or friends. From an original force of about 600 Companion cavalry, Philip created a large force of heavily equipped cavalry. Noble families from all over the Greek world were settled on fiefs created out of lands won from the king's enemies, and by the end of his reign their number had been multiplied many times over. Philip gave them heavy armour – cuirasses and helmets of the Phrygian type – and he further developed the new tactical formations Jason of Pherai had invented to enable his cavalry to take a leading role in battle.

The building block of the cavalry was the *ile* (squadron) of 200 men, commanded by an *ilarch* and divided into four *tetrachiai* of 49 men, each under the command of a *tetrach*. The tactical formation adopted by the *tetrachia* was the 'wedge', introduced by Philip, influenced by the Thracians who had themselves learnt it from the Scythians. The wedge was formed with the tetrach at the point, and senior troops riding in the middle and at each end of the 13-man base line. The ilarch was probably accompanied by a trumpeter to relay signals to the four troop commanders, and an aide (*hyperetes*) to help him administer the squadron. The four wedges would be drawn up in a squadron battle line with sufficient intervals between them to ensure they had space to manoeuvre and did not collide in the charge. With cavalry able to perform such tactical manoeuvres, the infantry no longer needed its mobility. In an early battle against the Illyrian king Bardylis, cavalry was used in co-ordination with the infantry, indicating that Philip was well able to use combined arms in battle.

PHILIP IN THE NORTH

After his reorganization and retraining of the army, Philip turned his attention to the precarious upland border regions. Defeating Bardylis with an intriguing use of outflanking cavalry, Philip proceeded further to consolidate relations on his western borders through marriage to the daughter of the king of the Molossians, the most significant of the tribes in the highlands of Epirus. With this wife, Olympias, he fathered his second son, Alexander, in 356.

ANTIPATER

Antipater (c.399–319) was a trusted general of Philip II, representing the king at Athens in 346 and 338, and governing Macedon while Alexander fought in the north in 335. While Alexander was in Asia, Antipater was regent in Macedon and strategos of Europe, dealing with a revolt in Thrace, and then defeating Agis III of Sparta, who had instigated war in the Peloponnese. His relations with Alexander soured, and in 324 Craterus was sent to replace him, though

Alexander's death interrupted this arrangement. This also set in motion the Lamian War, in which a Greek coalition almost defeated Macedon. When news of Perdiccas' dynastic wrangling reached Macedon, Antipater declared war and invaded Asia Minor with Craterus. After Perdiccas' death Antipater assumed the regency and took Alexander's heirs back to Macedon. His death caused civil war because he left the regency to Polyperchon rather than his son Cassander.

With the situation in the north and west stabilized, Philip turned east where vigilance against the formidable tribes of Thrace was always required. In addition, the wealthy Greek city-states in and around Chalcidice drew his interest. Amphipolis, astride the Strymon river on the route to the Hellespont, was an Athenian colony settled in 437. Its hinterland was rich in timber and bordered Mount Pangaion, a prodigious source of gold and silver. In 357, Philip besieged the city, which fell within weeks, much to the consternation of the Athenians who had regarded it as their satellite. Other Greek city-states in Chalcidice and around the Thermaic Gulf fell to Philip in successive campaigns, either through intrigue or force of arms: Potidea (356) Pydna (356), Crenides (355), Methone (354) and ultimately Olynthus (348).

Up to this point Philip had contented himself with securing the Balkan frontiers and picking off those Greek city-states in the northern Aegean which Athens, or any other Greek city-state of the south, was unable or unwilling to support. Although his military exploits were no doubt impressive, there does not seem to have been any explicit imperial impulse to his actions. Certainly, the Macedonian state was increasing in wealth and power, but Philip was usually satisfied to make defensive alliances with potentially quarrelsome neighbours or

Gold embossed quiver depicting a fighting scene, which is said to have belonged to King Philip II. It comes from the royal tombs at Vergina and is housed at the Archaeological Museum of Salonika. (© 2006 Alinari/TopFoto)

57

simply buy them off with bribes. Of course, force and the threat of force were sufficient to achieve these limited aims, but Philip, as Diodorus Siculus notes, was a very shrewd manipulator of diplomatic processes, which for the Macedonian royal line often meant political alliances through marriage (16.95.1–4). This aspect of Philip's foreign policy should not be overlooked nor should the Macedonians' acceptance of polygamy in the service of political aims. One ancient author commented that 'Philip always married a new wife with each new war he undertook' (Satyrus, quoted in Athenaeus' *Deipnosophistae* 13.557c–e). Although that claim is exaggerated, marriage to women from Illyria, Elymiotis, Molossia, Thrace, and Pherae and Larissa in Thessaly helped Philip secure vital border regions without recourse to constant, resource-draining military adventures.

PHILIP IN THE SOUTH

In the mid-350s Athens was embroiled in the Social War, expending energy to reassert control over rebellious allies while Philip, under the guise of supporting one side in a conflict between city-states on the island of Euboea, seized a subtle opportunity to meddle in the affairs of southern mainland Greece. He was then fully able to insinuate himself as a player in mainland Greece during the (third) Sacred War of 356–346. This decade-long conflict further weakened an already war-weary Greece. In 356 a dispute arose over pressure the Phocians were exerting on the sacred priestesses at Delphi. Fearing that the more powerful Thebes would remove their influence at Delphi, the Phocians seized the sanctuary and extorted money from the Delphians to raise a large mercenary army. Later they plundered the sacred treasuries and melted down bronze and iron from the temple statues to support their war effort. Enraged at this sacrilege, Thebes enlisted her Boeotian allies, the Locrians and the Thessalians amongst others, against Phocis who in turn garnered the support of Athens, Sparta and some of Sparta's Peloponnesian allies. While some desultory and indecisive engagements occurred between the two sides over the next three years, Philip completed his stranglehold on the cities of the Thermaic Gulf by sacking Methone and capturing Pagasae.

However, Philip was able to exert a more pointed influence in these southern affairs when he was invited by the Thessalian League to bring the rebellious city of Pherae back into the fold. After an initial success against the Phocians who had come to support Pherae, Philip was seriously defeated in two battles by the full Phocian army led by Onomarchus. Undeterred by these setbacks, Philip rallied the Macedonian army and, with the support of the Thessalian cavalry, crushed the Phocian and allied army at the battle of the 'Crocus Field' in 352, massacring the 'temple-robbers' and crucifying their leader Onomarchus.

ALEXANDER'S CHILDHOOD

Alexander's early years are described only through anecdotes created to reflect what he became in later life. There are stories about his mother before his birth, and the portents that attended it, of how he tamed the vicious horse Bucephalus, and questioned Persian ambassadors about their roads and resources. Facts about his childhood, however, are few and far between. Alexander was born to Philip and his wife Olympias in 356, probably on or near 20 July. His mother Olympias seems to have had a great influence on the young Alexander. Olympias has been cast as many things by historians. She probably was violent and headstrong, but she was usually justified in her anger, as when Philip put her aside for a new wife who could potentially bear an heir to challenge the claims of her own precious son.

Plutarch records that Alexander was fair skinned, and best represented by the sculptor Lysippus. At Pella, Alexander had tutors, and by the age of ten was reciting, debating and playing the lyre before his father's guests. Poetry and music continued to be Alexander's passions in his adult life. He also enjoyed the very Macedonian pastime of hunting, and riding his horse Bucephalus. Bucephalus was given to him when he was 12 years old, and was his warhorse until his death from old age in India. As Alexander grew older, he indulged in the drinking and partying that went on at the court. His drinking is a constant theme in some of the histories, and is even given as the reason for his death.

Alexander grew up surrounded by the Royal Pages, many of whom became his loyal officers. As well as the more military skills they learnt at court, the pages were versed in literature, reading poetry and Herodotus; Ptolemy later wrote a history, and Hephaestion had two volumes of letters dedicated to him by philosophers. These young men were well-trained and learned, adventurous and ambitious.

Philip appointed the philosopher Aristotle, Plato's pupil, to teach Alexander and his friends in Mieza. For about two years, Aristotle taught Alexander, and wrote pamphlets for him on kingship and other subjects. It has been said that Alexander read the *Iliad* over and over, and that he determined to live up to Homeric ideals, like his hero Achilles. Alexander also almost certainly read Xenophon's *Anabasis*, which may have encouraged him to look east. (The Art Archive/Museo Nazionale Romano Rome/Alfredo Dagli Orti)

Buoyed by this success, Philip probed farther south into central Greece. Beginning to realise the danger, Athens blocked the pass at Thermopylae, whereupon Philip retired.

Nevertheless, Philip had achieved a number of goals. His service to Thessaly saw him appointed leader of the League. Furthermore, when Phocis ultimately surrendered in 346, its two votes on the Amphictyonic Council, which administered the sacred site of Delphi, were given to Philip who championed himself as protector of the sanctuary and avenger against its defilers. On the other hand, southern Greece, riven by this indecisive and costly warfare, was further weakened.

The battle of Chaeronea

In Athens, the orator Demosthenes fulminated against Philip in a series of speeches known as the *Philippics*. After his gains in the south at the end of the Sacred War, Philip decided not to exacerbate Athenian hostility towards him. In 346 he reached an uneasy peace with Athens, and returned once again to affairs in the north where he overcame Thracian opposition and extended his power to the Hellespont and the Propontis (Sea of Marmara). By this time it was becoming increasingly evident to the city-states and states of Greece that the most dangerous and volatile threat to their independence was from Macedon.

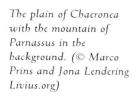

The plain of Chaeronea with the mountain of Parnassus in the background. (© Marco Prins and Jona Lendering Livius.org)

A 19th-century wood engraving of Aristotle and his pupil Alexander at the court of Philip II. Alexander was still a young man when he ascended the throne, but his education, both academic and military, seemed to have provided him with the necessary skills to pursue his ambitions. (akg-images)

In 348 the prosperous city of Olynthus pleaded for Athenian help when besieged by Philip. Only a pittance was forthcoming, and when the city duly fell a wrathful Philip razed it to the ground and sold off the population as slaves. Perinthus and Byzantium were besieged in 341 and when Philip seized Athenian grain ships in the Hellespont alarm bells were sounded in Athens. Grain shipments from the Black Sea were the life-blood of Athenian sustenance and these incursions could not be tolerated. Thebes, distanced from its fellow Boeotians by the machinations of Philip, also realized the potential dangers of Macedon perched on their very doorstep. They received overtures from the Persian Empire, which, wary of Philip's meddling near north-west Anatolia, reverted to its previous diplomatic strategy in Greece and sought to aid other Greeks against the latest emerging power.

By 338 events had come to a head. Although Philip had often tried to lessen Athenian and Greek unease over his activities, it was apparent that a confrontation with Thebes and Athens could no longer be avoided. Philip, now accompanied by his 18-year-old son, Alexander, led his army south into Phocis and seized the city of Elateia on the Boeotian border, which bypassed the strategic pass at Thermopylae. The route to Thebes and Athens now lay open. A frantic Athenian embassy led by Demosthenes successfully sought an alliance with Thebes against Macedon, and the full Athenian army joined the Thebans and loyal Boeotian allies at the town of Chaeronea.

In early August, Philip, at the head of the full Macedonian army of 30,000 infantry and roughly 2,000 cavalry, met them on the valley plain outside the little town. Philip had command of the right wing, while Alexander was positioned on the left with the other Macedonian generals. Alexander may have commanded the cavalry which were lined up against the Theban Sacred Band. As the most effective fighting force in the Greek world, the Sacred Band occupied the traditional prestigious position on the far right of the Greek battle line. According to Polyaenus, Philip withdrew his phalanx on the left to lure the Athenians into a charge (*Strat.*, 4.2.2). This opened a gap in the Greek line which Alexander then attacked with his cavalry, isolating the Sacred Band, enabling him to destroy it completely. Philip then attacked, eventually killing over 1,000 Athenians and capturing 2,000. This was a huge loss for an Athenian contingent of perhaps 6,000 hoplites. The Thebans and their allies also suffered heavy losses; the Sacred Band was never re-formed. It was a decisive Macedonian victory, a triumph of the new Macedonian phalanx over traditional hoplite tactics. In this battle, there are also hints of what was to come from Alexander. Still just a teenager, he commanded a perfectly timed, decisive cavalry attack into the disrupted enemy line. This use of a hammer-blow cavalry charge was a tactic that would win him his great battles in Persia. Alexander was already an able commander: he was prepared to ignore the traditional way of fighting battles when necessary, and not only to adopt new tactics, but also to be at the very sword-point of their implementation.

Once he had crushed Greek resistance at Chaeronea, Philip sought to establish his leadership over Greece and unite the whole of Greece with Macedon against Persia. He created the League of Corinth, which convened for the first time in spring 337. Delegates of all the states of Greece, except Sparta, elected Philip as the military leader of the league, setting the stage for a pan-Hellenic expedition against Persia.

PHILIP II'S PLANS FOR PERSIA

The idea of a pan-Hellenic campaign against Persia had been around for several decades, but it is not clear when Philip formulated his own plans to invade Persia, or indeed what his exact aims were. In 346, the rhetorician Isocrates produced *Philippus*, an open letter exhorting Philip to lead the campaign against Persia. However, it is unknown what effect, if any, this had on him. It has been suggested that Philip was formulating plans against Persia as early as 348, although this is doubtful. Indeed, in the decade from 348 to 338, Philip still had

THE ACHIEVEMENTS OF PHILIP II

The fame of his son means that Philip II's reputation has always suffered through comparison. Alexander, however, understood that his father had secured Macedon against the tribes from the north, and established control over the troublesome Greeks. To do so he was away campaigning with the army for years at a time, and he even lost an eye during the siege of Methone in 354. As he grew older, Alexander was at his father's side during his campaigns, and he fought at Chaeronea. Arrian records that when Alexander addressed the rebellious soldiers at Opis in 324, he related what he and his father had done for the Macedonians:

Philip found you a tribe of impoverished vagabonds, most of you dressed in skins, feeding a few sheep on the hills and fighting, feebly enough, to keep them from your neighbours – Thracians, Triballians and Illyrians. He gave you cloaks to wear instead of skins; he brought you down from the hills into the plains; he taught you to fight on equal terms with the enemy on your borders, till you knew that your safety lay not, as once, in your mountain strongholds, but in your own valour. He made you city-dwellers; he brought you law; he civilized you … Thessaly, so long your bugbear and your dread, he subjected to your rule, and by humbling the Phocians he made the narrow and difficult path into Greece a broad and easy road. The men of Athens and Thebes, who for years had kept watching for their moment to strike us down, he brought so low – and by this time I myself was working at my father's side – that they who once exacted from us either our money or our obedience, now, in their turn, looked to us as the means of their salvation. (7.9)

(G.T. Garvey © Ancient Art & Architecture Collection)

his hands full in Greece. It is more likely that he finally turned his attention to Persia after the battle of Chaeronea. According to Diodorus Siculus (16.89.2), shortly before the meeting which established the League of Corinth, Philip was making known throughout Greece his desire to attack Persia 'to punish them for the profanation of the temples' in the Greek and Persian Wars.

Philip's leniency in dealing with Athens after Chaeronea has been explained by suggesting that he desired its co-operation in an expedition against Persia. In particular he required the use of the Athenian fleet because the Macedonian navy was no match for a powerful Persian fleet operating in the Aegean. In any event he made little use of the fleet or, in fact, of his Greek allies as military assets during the campaign. Any concept of a pan-Hellenic campaign was clearly subordinated to Macedonian hegemony. The ancient historian Polybius maintained that Asia was attacked because Philip and Alexander believed it was weak – simply another ripe picking for their military machine and meat for their voracious appetite for expansion (3.6).

While clearly imperialistic, Philip's exact aims, in terms of territorial acquisition, are unclear. Perhaps he would have contented himself, initially at least, with the liberation of Asia Minor. This would certainly have been in keeping with Philip's practices in the past. From the time that he overcame internal opposition and secured his borders against barbarian incursions, Philip expanded slowly and cautiously over a period of almost 20 years. Unlike Alexander, whose practice it was to conquer first and consolidate later, Philip was content to acquire territory systematically, without overextending Macedonian power.

Whenever Philip's invasion plans were actually formulated, by 336 they were being implemented. In that year he sent an advance force of 10,000 soldiers under the command of two senior generals, Parmenion and Attalus, to 'liberate' the cities of western Asia Minor in preparation for the full-scale invasion. This force established Macedonian control from the Hellespont to Ephesus before it was rolled back in 335 by a 5,000-strong mercenary force under Memnon of Rhodes. Memnon was able to force the Macedonians out of Ephesus, Magnesia on the Sipylus and Lampsacus but was eventually rebuffed in his attempt to take Cyzicus. Despite the advance force's uneven success in this initial stage, a vital bridgehead in Asia had been secured which would be maintained until 334.

THE ASSASSINATION OF PHILIP II

Despite the security Philip had brought to Macedonia, his violent death soon threatened the new-found stability of the state. Macedonian kings, at least from the time of Persian influence in the region (after 513), were polygamous, and Philip married for the seventh time in October 337. Most of Philip's brides had been foreigners, but this time the bride was a teenager of aristocratic Macedonian background named Cleopatra. This marriage raised the possibility of a fully Macedonian heir, a fact which the bride's uncle Attalus brought up at the wedding party. Of the events Athenaeus said:

> Philip took seven wives in total. In the twenty years of his rule Philip married the Illyrian Audata, by whom he had a daughter, Cynnane, and he also married Phila, sister of Derdas and Machatas. Then, since he

wished to extend his realm to include the Thessalian nation, he had children by two Thessalian women, Nicesipolis of Pherae, who bore him Thessalonice, and Philinna of Larissa, by whom he produced Arrhidaeus. In addition, he took possession of the Molossian kingdom by marrying Olympias, by whom he had Alexander and Cleopatra, and when he took Thrace the Thracian king Cothelas came to him with his daughter Meda and many gifts. After marrying Meda, Philip also took her home to be a second wife along with Olympias. In addition to all these wives he also married Cleopatra, with whom he was in love; she was the daughter of Hippostratus and niece of Attalus. By bringing her home as another wife alongside Olympias he made a total shambles of his life. For straightaway, right at the wedding ceremony, Attalus made the remark 'Well, now we shall certainly see royalty born who are legitimate and not bastards'. Hearing this, Alexander hurled the cup he had in his hands at Attalus, who in turn hurled his goblet at Alexander. (13.557)

Alexander was understandably insulted by Attalus' remark and after the violent altercation that inevitably ensued, he and his mother went into exile in Epirus, Olympias' ancestral home. Diplomacy served eventually to bring about the son's return and a reconciliation, but Olympias remained in Epirus.

In 336 Philip married one of his daughters to Olympias' brother, Alexander, king of Epirus. At the celebrations of the wedding, Philip was stabbed to death by a bodyguard, Pausanias. The official explanation of the murder was that Pausanias had been furious that Philip had refused to redress a serious and personal grievance that Pausanias had against Attalus and so had decided to kill the king. The details of this sordid event are impossible to unravel satisfactorily and conspiracy theories, ancient and modern, abound. Whether Alexander or Olympias were involved and what their motives might have been cannot be known, though the reported actions of Olympias, and the benefits she gained from the death of her erstwhile husband, seem to make her a strong suspect.

Olympias, mother of Alexander. One of Philip's seven wives, she had a profound influence on her son's character and also created considerable political mischief in Macedon during Alexander's absence in Asia. From a series of medallions commissioned by Emperor Caracalla. (© World History Archive/TopFoto)

5

ALEXANDER'S ACCESSION

On acceding to the throne of Macedon, Alexander was quick to mete out punishment against those 'responsible' for his father's death, freeing himself at the same time of rivals to the throne. Antipater, who had in the past served as regent of Macedon in Philip's absence, supported Alexander's claim, and it was then an easy matter to round up and execute rivals. Attalus was found to have been corresponding with the Athenians – an unlikely scenario – and executed on the new king's orders by his colleague, Parmenion. A bloody purge masqueraded as filial piety, and those who could saved themselves by accommodation with the new king or by flight. Alexander acceded to more than just the throne of Macedon: he also inherited his father's Persian campaign. He was doubtless eager to depart, for we are told that as an adolescent he complained to his father that he was leaving little for him to conquer. Things did not, however, proceed as planned and there were other matters for Alexander to attend to before he could cross the Hellespont.

GREECE

The accession of Alexander incited rebellion amongst the subject states and the barbarian kingdoms that bordered on Macedon. The new king was forced to prove himself, especially in the south, where the Athenian orator Demosthenes, the implacable enemy of Philip II, was deriding Alexander as a child and a fool.

Resistance to the new king in Thessaly was crushed by speed and daring, as steps (known as 'Alexander's Ladder') cut into the side of Mount Ossa allowed the Macedonians to turn the Thessalians' position. The Thessalians responded with gestures of contrition and recognized Alexander as leader of the Thessalian League, a position previously held by his father. An initial uprising by Thebans, Athenians and Spartans was stifled by Alexander's timely arrival in Greece, where he summoned a meeting of the League of Corinth, the very existence of which was symbolic of Macedonian power. The meeting elected him leader and Philip's successor as general of the pan-Hellenic campaign.

Sparta, however, refused to join the league or make public recognition of Macedonian suzerainty, claiming that it could not follow another leader because

OPPOSITE
Thracian 4th-century gold ceremonial helmet found in Romania. (akg-images)

HARPALUS

Harpalus son of Machatas belonged to one of the royal houses of Upper Macedonia, that of Elimea. Afflicted by a physical ailment that left him unfit for military service, he nevertheless served Alexander in other ways. In the 330s he served as one of Alexander's hetairoi, in this case, probably one of his advisors; he was exiled by Philip for encouraging Alexander to offer himself as a prospective husband of the Carian princess Ada, whom Philip had intended to marry off to his son Philip Arrhidaeus. Harpalus was appointed treasurer early in the Persian campaign, but he became involved with an unscrupulous individual named Tauriscus, who persuaded him to flee from Alexander's camp, presumably with a sum of Alexander's money. Alexander, however, forgave him and recalled him, reinstating him as treasurer. Later in the campaign, when the king had gone to India and Harpalus remained in Babylon, the latter enjoyed a life of extravagance and debauchery, importing delicacies for his table and courtesans for his bed. When news arrived that Alexander was returning from the east, he fled to Athens, taking with him vast sums of money, and attempted to induce the Athenians to go to war. Rebuffed by the Athenians, he sailed away to Crete, where he was murdered by one of his followers, Pausanias.

it was the Spartan prerogative to lead. Spartan intransigence flared into open rebellion in 331, when Agis III attacked Macedonian troops in the Peloponnese, only to be defeated and killed at Megalopolis. For the time being, however, Alexander was content to ignore the Spartans, although they bore their military impotence with ill grace. Nevertheless, the Greek city-states were not yet ready to renounce all claims to independence and leadership. Alexander clearly thought that he had cowed them into submission with the mere show of force, and he now turned to deal with the border tribes of the Illyrians and Triballians before turning his attentions to Asia.

ALEXANDER IN THE NORTH

The Thracian tribes revolted on the accession of Alexander, plotting to invade Macedon in co-operation with the Illyrians, but Alexander forestalled them by quickly marching into Thrace. He defeated the mountain tribes and continued north, catching the Triballi while they were making camp. The Triballi were a tribe independent of the Odrysian

Empire (see page 71). They were a byword for savagery and their contact with the Scythians, Illyrians and Celts left influences upon the Triballi, and these influences may be why they are sometimes referred to as distinct from the Thracians. They often used Scythian equipment.

The Triballi took shelter in a wood by the river Lynginus. Alexander ordered his archers and slingers to move up and shoot into the woods. The Triballi surged forward to get to grips with the Macedonian archers, whereupon Alexander ordered Macedonian cavalry to attack the Triballi right wing, and Greek cavalry to attack the left. The rest of his cavalry attacked in the centre, followed by the main body of his infantry led by Alexander himself. The Triballi held their own while the fighting was at long range, but were ridden down by the cavalry and routed by the phalanx once they came into contact – some 300 Triballi were killed. King Syrmus, the Triballi, and other Thracians took refuge on an island in the Danube. Alexander manned warships with heavy infantry and archers, and attempted to force a landing. However, there were not enough ships and men; in most places the shore was too steep for a landing, and the current was too strong. Alexander accordingly withdrew the ships and attacked the Getai instead.

The Getai lived between the Haemus range of mountains and the Scythians, on both sides of the Danube. Herodotus called them 'the bravest and most noble of all the Thracians' (*Histories*, 4.93). Their god Zalmoxis taught them

OPPOSITE
Demosthenes.
The Athenian orator was a bitter opponent of Macedon and of Philip II in particular. At the time of Alexander's accession he mocked him as a 'child' and compared him with the simpleton, Margites. But Demosthenes soon discovered his mistake. (akg-images/Erich Lessing)

Thracians attacking the Thyni tribe in south-eastern Thrace in 400. (Angus McBride © Osprey Publishing Ltd)

THE THRACIANS

The Thracians were an Indo-European people who occupied the area between northern Greece, southern Russia and north-western Turkey. They shared the same language and culture, although the former had no written form. To a large extent they preserved the way of life of a tribal Homeric society. There may have been as many as a million Thracians, divided among up to 40 tribes. Ancient writers were hard put to decide which of the Thracian tribes was the most valiant: the plains tribes – Getai, Moesi and Odrysai; or the mountain tribes – Thyni, Odomanti, Dii, Bessi, Bisaltai and Satrai. Other Thracian tribes included the Triballi and, possibly, the Paeonians, although the latter are usually referred to separately. Herodotus described the Thracians as the most numerous people of all, after the Indians. They had the potential to field large numbers of troops, and the Greeks, and later the Romans, lived in fear of a dark Thracian cloud descending from the north.

Herodotus said that the Thracians would be the most powerful of all nations if they did not enjoy fighting each other so much. They lived almost entirely in villages: the city of Seuthopolis seems to be the only significant town in Thrace which was not built by the Greeks. Herodotus states that Thracians honoured warriors very highly and despised all other occupations (II, 167). Thracian warriors were ferocious opponents, and in high demand as mercenaries, though they were infamous for their love of plunder. There are also several recorded instances of Thracian mercenaries switching sides if offered bribes, or because they preferred to fight for the other side. Because of their savagery, they were often used to carry out executions or massacres.

The Thracians migrated to south-eastern Europe in the 7th millennium BC. After the 12th century they also settled in Asia Minor, especially in Bithynia and the Troad. Thracian tribes inhabited central Macedon until the founding of the kingdom of Macedon by the Temenids in the early 7th century, at which time they were forced to move eastwards. In the end, the Thracian tribes were restricted mainly to the north-eastern area of the Balkans. From the 7th century, many Greek colonies were founded on Thracian shores, leading to intense conflict and mutual influence between the Greeks and Thracians.

In the first decade of the 6th century, the Persians invaded Thrace. Thracians were forced to join the invasions of Scythia and Greece. However, Persian control was rather loose, and many Thracians resisted Persian occupation after Xerxes' invasion of Greece in 480. Only a few fought on the side of the Persians at Plataea in 479, and after the battle Thracians wounded the Persian commander and annihilated parts of the army as it retreated through Thrace. In about 460, the first Odrysian kingdom was founded in territory vacated by the Persians. The Odrysai was the most powerful Thracian tribe, the only one to briefly unite almost all the others.

During the Peloponnesian War, Thrace was an ally of Athens. They fought alongside both Macedonians and Athenians in some encounters. The Spartans tried to persuade the Odrysian king to change sides, but they failed and Spartan ambassadors on their way to Persia were murdered in Thrace. The Thracians continued to be important in the affairs of both the Spartans and Athenians throughout the Peloponnesian War.

Despite the rise of Macedon, the period 400–280 represented a sort of Thracian golden age, when the Triballi and Getai formed kingdoms in northern Thrace, and Thracian art flourished. Splendid gold and silver vessels, ornaments, pectorals, helmets, and horse-trappings were produced. Finds, such as this early 4th-century silver ornamental fitting from a grave in Bulgaria, still make a strong impression today, with their elaborate workmanship and imaginative designs.

When Philip II succeeded to the throne of Macedon in 359, he bribed the Thracians to stop their joint invasion of Macedon with the Illyrians. Shortly afterwards the Thracian king Kotys was assassinated, and the Thracian kingdom was divided between his three sons. In 357, Philip defeated

a coalition of Athenians, Thracians, Illyrians and Paeonians. His first Thracian campaign began in 347/346, waged first by Antipater, and then by himself. He conquered southern Thrace in 341, founding Philippopolis, Kabyle and other cities on top of older Thracian settlements. In 339 the Triballi defeated Philip when he tried to cross the Haemus range when returning from a campaign against the Scythians. After Philip's death, the Thracian tribes revolted again.

Over the years after their dealings with Alexander, the Thracians continued to face the Greeks, the Macedonians, and also the Celts, until they were finally conquered by Rome in AD 46. (akg-images/Erich Lessing)

that they were immortal; death, merely the gateway to an everlasting paradise, especially in battle, held no fears. Diodorus Siculus said that the Getai 'are barbarous and lead a bestial existence, live in a wintry land deficient in cultivated grain and fruit, normally sit on straw, eat from a wooden table, and drink from cups of horn or wood' (31.11–12).

The Getai held the riverbank against Alexander with 4,000 cavalry and 10,000 foot. Alexander demonstrated his characteristic decisiveness and gathered together many boats normally used by the local Thracians for plundering and raiding, and crossed at night with about 1,500 cavalry and 4,000 infantrymen. This daring crossing by so many men took the Getai totally by surprise; they were shocked to see the Danube crossed so easily, and unnerved by the sight of the phalanx advancing upon them in a solid mass. The first violent cavalry charge led them to turn and flee to their town, but the town had few defences, so they abandoned it. Taking as many women and children as their horses could carry, they continued their flight into the steppe. Alexander plundered the town, razed it to the ground and made camp. There he received envoys from various tribes in the area, including the Triballi, who soon afterwards sent troops to join his army. Thracian troops were later critical to Alexander's success: they formed about one-fifth of his army and took part in all his battles. While Alexander was far away, however, Thrace seethed with rebellion. In 331/330 this involved the participation of Memnon, Alexander's general, and the Odrysian ruler Seuthes III. Memnon was outmanoeuvred by Antipater, but came to such favourable terms with him that in 325 Memnon led 5,000 Thracian cavalry to join Alexander in Asia. In either 331 or 325, Zopyrion, governor of Thrace, and his 30,000-strong army perished in a campaign against the Getai and Scythians.

Tribal warfare similarly threatened Macedon from the Illyrian region adjacent to the Adriatic coast. As part of his strategy to intimidate and overawe the Illyrians, Alexander daringly drew his army up on some open ground and put his army through a variation of parade-ground drill, accompanied by the Macedonian war-cry. His bluff was successful, laying the groundwork for his eventual victory. However, while Alexander was fighting the Illyrian tribes, rebellion again broke out in Greece.

THEBES

Alexander's activities in the north gave rise to rumours – false, but deliberately spread – that the young king had been killed. In spring 335 the Thebans threw off the Macedonian yoke, besieging the garrison that Philip had planted on their acropolis after Chaeronea. The Thebans now proposed to use Persian funds to liberate Greece from the true oppressor, Macedon.

THE THRACIAN CAMPAIGN OF 336/335

Rugged terrain had always challenged the phalanx, but in his campaign against the Thracians, Alexander was able to maintain the cohesion of his forces in a mountain pass and to avoid the wagons of the Thracians that were being rolled down to disrupt his formations. By placing the less mobile pezhetairoi in the more level areas, where they could form alleys for the wagons to pass through, he kept the main portion of the phalanx intact and ready to meet the enemy if they should rush down the hill. The more difficult ground was occupied by the hypaspists, who were unencumbered by the sarissa and carried larger shields, which they placed over their bodies, linking them closely together to allow the wagons to pass over without doing serious harm. Arrian describes the incident but makes no distinction between the two types of troops, but clearly it would have been impossible for the pezhetairoi, with smaller and less concave shields, to find protection under them, to say nothing of the difficulty of grounding the sarissai in massed formation. In this way the Thracians were unable to disrupt the Macedonian phalanx and come to grips with it while it was in disarray. The hypaspists, once the danger had passed, continued uphill on the left side, led by Alexander and protected by the covering fire of the archers. The Thracians were dislodged from their position with ease. (Christa Hook © Osprey Publishing Ltd)

ANTIGONUS MONOPHTHALMOS

An officer of Philip II's generation, Antigonus Monophthalmos ('the One-Eyed') (c.382–301) was already approaching 60 when he accompanied Alexander to Asia. In the spring of 333 he was left behind as satrap of Phrygia, which had its administrative centre in Celaenae. There he remained for the duration of the war, attended by his wife Stratonice and his sons, one of whom, Demetrius, was to become known as Demetrius Poliorcetes ('the besieger'), due to his ingenuity in inventing new siege machines. After Alexander's death, Antigonus emerged as one of the leading Successors and, together with his son, made a bid for supreme power. He died on the battlefield of Ipsus in 301, and Demetrius, who experienced his share of victories and defeats, proved to possess more showmanship than generalship. Ultimately, Demetrius' son, Antigonus, named for his grandfather, established the Antigonid dynasty in Macedon.

Alexander's response was quick and brutal: within two weeks he was before the gates of Thebes. He hoped that the Thebans would come to terms, but they would not and he reacted accordingly. Athens and Demosthenes proved that they were more capable of inciting others to mischief than of supporting the causes they had so nobly espoused. Through their inaction, they saved themselves and stood by as Alexander dealt most harshly with Thebes, which now became an example to the other Greek city-states: Alexander would not tolerate rebellion in his absence, and he regarded those who preferred the barbarian cause to that of their fellow Greeks as Medisers and traitors to the common cause. Indeed, the city had a long history of Medism, and there was a tradition that the allied Greeks, at the time of Xerxes' invasion, had sworn the 'Oath of Plataea', which called for the destruction of the city.

Officially, the razing of Thebes could be presented as an act of vengeance. (Gryneum in Asia Minor later suffered a similar fate, with the same justification.) Terror might prove a more effective deterrent than any garrison. To avert the charge of senseless brutality, Alexander portrayed the decision to destroy the city of Thebes and enslave its population as the work of the Phocians and disaffected Boeotians. The example of Thebes was enough to produce a more conciliatory mood in the rest of Greece. Persuaded by the orator Demades, the Athenians sent an embassy to congratulate Alexander on his victories in the north and to beg forgiveness for their own recent indiscretions. The king demanded that they surrender the worst trouble-makers, ten prominent orators and generals including Demosthenes, Lycurgus and Hyperides, but in the event only one, Charidemus, was offered up, and he promptly fled to the court of Darius III.

Sculpture of Alexander dating from the 2nd century, found in Magnesia. (akg-images/Erich Lessing)

6

ALEXANDER'S ARMY

ORGANIZING THE ARMY

Alexander's army, like the Macedonian state, was run from the court that always travelled with the king. This comprised a hundred or so courtiers, known as 'Personal Companions', or sometimes simply 'Companions'. These Companions are distinct from the Companion cavalry. The sources also refer to the king's 'Friends', which may be either the highest grade of Personal Companion at court, or just another name for Personal Companions. In battle the Personal Companions fought alongside the king in the Royal Squadron of the Companion cavalry. In Hellenistic times, the king would give his courtiers purple cloaks as a sign of their rank, and there is evidence that the practice was already established in Alexander's reign. Alexander often wore elaborate dress in battle, but he normally dressed in the uniform of an officer of the Companion cavalry. He is dressed as such on the Alexander mosaic, but he wears the purple cloak with a yellow border of a Personal Companion instead of the regimental cloak.

The king ran the army from the royal tent, an impressive pavilion with a large chamber where the council of war met (perhaps separate from the main tent). The royal tent also included a vestibule beyond which none could enter without passing Chares, the royal usher; the armoury (perhaps also separate from the main tent); and beyond the vestibule, the king's apartments where he slept and bathed. The tent was erected by its own work-party, commanded by a Macedonian called Proxenus. The king was attended by his chamberlains, while the royal tent itself was guarded by a watch from the Bodyguards, and the area of the royal quarters was defended by a detachment of *hypaspists* (elite infantry). Also accompanying the king would be an augur, to provide omens before battle.

The army that Alexander took to Asia in spring 334 was far from homogeneous. The core was the army of Macedon, but added to this were contingents supplied to the expeditionary force by the vassal princedoms on Macedon's borders – Paeonians, Agrianians, Triballians, Odrysians and Illyrians. Alexander was also head of the Thessalian army and head of the League of Corinth, so the states of Greece supplied Alexander with contingents of infantry, cavalry and ships from their own armed forces. Finally, the numbers of the force were swelled by a large number of mercenaries. Most of these were Greek, though some of Alexander's units of Balkan troops may also have been mercenaries. Given the historical animosity between the different peoples in the army, and the fact that the different groups could not for the main part communicate due to language differences, it is a tribute to the leadership of the army that racial tensions were kept low enough for it to function.

At the highest level the army was commanded by its staff officers, the Royal Bodyguards, and by other generals. The army often divided into a number of divisions (*moirai*), especially during the later campaigns, and a general would be appointed to command each division. It was usual for these generals to retain direct command of an individual *taxis* too, so many of the infantry *taxeis* were commanded by generals rather than *taxiarchs*. Below the generals were the rest of the officers selected from Macedonian aristocratic families. Command of individual units was very much a family affair: many of the units seem to have been commanded by members of families prominent in the area where they had

A Companion cavalryman, a Royal Page and a Companion hunting a stag. (Angus McBride © Osprey Publishing Ltd)

been recruited. Command was centralized. The king himself would give the army its orders. These were given by trumpet signals, first by Alexander's trumpeter, and then taken up by the trumpeters attached to each unit.

The whole of Alexander's empire was run by a secretariat divided up into various sections, each run by a Royal Secretary, comparable in rank to the Royal Bodyguards. The Army Secretariat was under Eumenes of Cardia. The men who made up the secretariat, though they might be able and even Personal Companions of the king, were usually debarred by obscurity of birth or physical infirmity from holding a field command, and were thus despised by the serving officers.

The Army Secretariat was based in the tent of the Royal Secretary of the Army, which contained copies of all correspondence relevant to the army and all army documentation. The bases of army documentation were the muster-rolls and conduct sheets, which gave the current strengths of the various units, and according to which pay and equipment, reinforcements and on occasions rations were distributed and promotions made. Arms, armour, clothing, goblets and baggage-animals were issued in this way, on an occasional general issue basis rather than on a permanent one-for-one basis. It seems therefore that stores were held centrally in the baggage train. Stores were distributed in this way by *lochoi* (units of 256 men) in the infantry, and *ilai* (squadrons) or *hekatostuas* (century) in the cavalry. It was then the duty of the attendants to the units to allocate the stores further.

The Army Secretariat was divided into various sections, each under a Secretary assisted by a number of inspectors. There is evidence of a Secretary of Cavalry, and a Secretary of Mercenaries for Egypt, who had two inspectors under him. There is also evidence of inspectors being detached from the main army to administer the military forces left in a province.

THE INFANTRY

At the lowest level the tactical unit of the infantry was the *dekas* (file of ten men) which, as the name implies, had once consisted of ten men, but expanded to 16 well before Alexander's reign. Sixteen such files (16 x 16) formed a lochos (later known as a *syntagma*) of 256 men, under the command of a *lochagos*. Thus the strength of the taxis was probably six lochoi (1,536 men) and that of a chiliarchy was four lochoi (1,024 men). Half a chiliarchy would be a *pentakosiarchy* (512 men). The size of the lochos made the relaying of commands more difficult, for, according to Asclepiodotus, in a unit of 64 (8 x 8), the men could easily hear all the commands, but with the doubling of the file-size and the creation of squares of 256 men (16 x 16), it became necessary to add supernumeraries or *ektaktoi*. The general who served as the taxiarches was almost certainly stationed behind the taxis and on horseback, from which position he sent orders to the various ektaktoi whose job it was to distribute the orders. Each taxis of pezhetairoi (1,536 men) would thus have had 30 supernumeraries.

Normally with the phalanx, the files would be drawn up in close order (*pyknos*, *pyknosis*), 16 deep with each man occupying a yard square. Locked shields (*synaspismose*) was a formation usually only adopted when receiving rather than delivering a charge. It was achieved by inserting the back half of each file into the spaces between the front half of the file. The depth of the phalanx was now eight yards, with each man occupying a frontage of one cubit (half a yard). Both formations, however, were found to be too cramped for manoeuvring or advancing in an orderly manner, so prior to contact the phalanx would be drawn up in open order with a depth of two files with each double file occupying a frontage of two yards. This was probably called 'deep order' (*bathos*) in Alexander's army. In all these formations, obviously, the frontage occupied by the phalanx remained constant. During all these evolutions the spear would be pointed upwards to allow free movement. The lowering of the spear was only ordered before the charge, which was sometimes carried out at the run. The charge would be delivered to the accompaniment of the Macedonian battle-cry – 'Alalalalai' – offered to Enyalios, an epithet of Ares, the god of war.

When Alexander crossed the Hellespont into Asia in 334, he took with him 12,000 Macedonian phalangites: 9,000 pezhetairoi and 3,000 hypaspists, the pezhetairoi or pezetairoi ('foot companions'), the regional 'heavy infantry,' and the elite infantry guard, the hypaspistai or hypaspists (literally, 'shield-bearers'). Within the pezhetairoi there were troops designated as *asthetairoi*, which could be a term for elite battalions, for battalions recruited in Upper Macedon, or for those who fought in a position closest to the king. The asthetairoi may have been better equipped or trained to fight next to the hypaspists. Within the hypaspists there were those who were distinguished by the adjective 'royal' (*basilikoi*). In terms of equipment, the pezhetairoi and asthetairoi were identical, but it is virtually certain that the hypaspists were not armed in the same way as the pezhetairoi.

Pezhetairoi

There has been a great deal of debate concerning the formation of the pezhetairoi and the name itself. It seems that the troops known as pezhetairoi during Philip II's time were known as hypaspists by Alexander's time. The extension of the name pezhetairoi to the heavy infantry seems to have been accompanied by a name-change that saw the former pezhetairoi become the hypaspists.

THE PHALANGITE

This Macedonian phalangite wears full armour. A man thus equipped would have fought in the front ranks. Towards the centre and the rear there would have been many infantrymen who lacked the linothorax or who wore the less protective slouch-hat known as the kausia.

The soldier wears the Phrygian helmet, with cheek pieces, which allows better hearing and visibility than the old closed Corinthian-style helmets worn by earlier Greek hoplites. The soldier is bearded, despite the commonly accepted view that Alexander required his troops to shave their beards in the belief that facial hair gave the enemy something to clutch in close combat. If this story is true, it need not have applied to the phalangites, for whom close, individual combat was undesirable.

The warrior is protected by a light cuirass of glued layers of linen, a linothorax, worn over the short-sleeved exomis tunic, the bottom of which extends beyond the corselet itself. The various layers of linen that made up the corselet are illustrated at the upper right, with coarser linen on the inside and smoother layers on the outside. The warrior also wears greaves.

A leather baldric slung over the shoulder supports the shield. Details of the outside of the shield, with the embossed eight-rayed star of the Macedonian kingdom, can be seen at the bottom left. In battle, the soldier's forearm would have been drawn through the armband in the centre of the shield, but the hand would have been free to grasp the sarissa, which because of its length and weight required the use of both hands. The illustration shows a handgrip (antilabe). Although

there is no certainty about the existence of this handgrip, without it the shield would have been all but useless to a phalangite out of formation.

The end of the sarissa bears a butt spike like the one found at Aegae (Vergina). Shown on the right are the sarissa head and the butt spike, and also the coupling link or collar. This joined the two parts of the sarissa and allowed it to be dismantled on the march (as shown in the top left-hand corner); it also made repairs quicker and less expensive, and allowed replacement parts to be more easily transported. This warrior has slung at his side a kopis. The illustration shows the curved handle, which gave some protection to the knuckles and allowed for a more secure grip. (Christa Hook © Osprey Publishing Ltd)

The available evidence indicates that the Macedonian kings recruited their infantrymen in two ways and that the bulk of the heavy infantry, known during Alexander's campaigns as pezhetairoi, or 'foot companions', was regional levies, commanded by members of its own aristocracies. This organization reflected the age-old pattern of life in the mountain areas that had only recently been merged into the greater Macedonian state. These were men proud of their origins and loyal to their commanders. Not only were the commanders also from the same regions as their troops, but an individual taxis was sometimes commanded by members of the same family on different occasions. It may seem likely that Alexander would take taxeis from all areas of Macedon with him, but the names of all the known taxiarchai in the first three years of the campaign suggest Upper Macedonian origins and it would be extremely unlikely that half or two-thirds of the pezhetairoi were led by officers of their own region, whereas the remainder were not. At least half the total number of infantry remained in Macedon with the regent, Antipater, and it would make good sense to assume that those from the politically volatile areas, like the uplands of Upper Macedon, would be removed from the homeland and kept under Alexander's watchful eye.

All pezhetairoi were armed with the sarissa. The sarissa measured as much as 12 cubits (18ft/5.5m) in Alexander's time. By 300, the length had increased in some cases to 16 cubits (24ft/7m), but these are maximum lengths, and many sarissai may have been shorter. The historians do not mention a secondary weapon for the phalangites, though clearly they must have had a sword or blade. Later regulations list a *machaira* blade as a standard piece of equipment, but the terminology is not clear. The *xiphos* was apparently the shorter, double-edged sword, whereas the slashing weapon, the *kopis* (or 'cleaver'), was longer, curved and more suitable for cavalrymen. By contrast the machaira could be a shorter, curved knife – it is often translated as a 'dagger' – used for dispatching the defeated foe. Yet Xenophon uses machaira as the equivalent of kopis. If the Macedonian phalangite carried the kopis, it was most likely for use in open fighting where the formation had disintegrated, and possibly a post-Alexandrian addition to his equipment, resulting from the experience of fighting the Romans, whose weapon of choice was the sword.

Armour would have varied according to what was available and where the soldier stood in the phalanx. The pezhetairoi are not mentioned as wearing cuirasses or corselets, except for officers. However, some kind of breastplate was worn, at least in the front ranks; this was probably the *linothorax*, a cuirass made of glued layers of linen. The weight of the corselet was about 11–14lb (5–6.3kg), and thus considerably lighter than the leather, bronze and (especially) iron cuirasses worn by some infantry and cavalrymen. The skirt of the corselet, made up of 'wings' (*pteruges*), was loose and unstiffened for ease of movement. Phalangites wore conical or Phrygian helmets, however all helmets in use in the Greek world were probably represented in the Macedonian phalanx, as fully functional equipment was often stripped from the dead on the battlefield and used by the victors. Greaves appear to have been a standard feature, and later regulations prescribe a fine for those who did not wear them. This may have been a necessity because the butt spikes of the sarissai could easily harm the legs of the

PEZHETAIROI IN TRAINING

The butt spike of the sarissa was almost as potent a weapon as the sarissa head, and since the sarissa was held at a point that allowed 12–15ft to project in front, with several feet extending to the rear, it was essential that the soldier learnt to position himself in relation to his comrades in the formation in such a way as to provide maximum danger to the enemy and protection against the sarissa-ends of his own colleagues.

The first five of the 16 rows of the lochos were so closely packed together that, when their sarissai were levelled, even that of the fifth man projected in front of the file leader. To allow for such a dense formation, each man must have been stationed behind the next, with the extended sarissa gripped at nearly the same point where he was level with the butt spike of the man in front of him. Exit from the file, in the event of injury or loss of weapons, could thus only have been possible by moving to the left and backwards through whatever alley the formation allowed. Those in rows six and higher elevated their sarissai in stages until those standing from about the middle to the back held their weapons upright.

This arrangement was also advantageous in that it protected the phalangites from projectiles launched by the enemy's archers, slingers and javelinmen. Furthermore, the gradual elevation of the sarissai towards the middle involved a concomitant raising of the shields for added protection. (Christa Hook © Osprey Publishing Ltd)

phalangites in formation. Instead of the concave, larger shield of the hoplite, the Macedonian phalangite carried a smaller, less concave shield, which was eight palms in diameter (about 2ft/0.7m). It hung from a strap over the shoulder.

In Alexander's expeditionary army, the pezhetairoi numbered 9,000, in six taxeis of three lochoi each. The taxeis were normally named after their commanders. Four taxeis had the same commanders down to 330, those of Coenus son of Polemocrates, Perdiccas son of Orontes, Craterus son of Alexander, and Meleager son of Neoptolemus. The taxis of Amyntas son of Andromenes was temporarily commanded by his brother Simmias while Amyntas was back in Macedon levying reinforcements. The last taxis was commanded by Philip son of Amyntas, at Granicus, by Ptolemy son of Seleucus, at Issus, where he was killed, and afterwards by Polyperchon son of Simmias. The battalions would be drawn up on the battlefield in order of precedence for the day, although Coenus' taxis, which seems to have been of elite status, occupied the position of honour on the right wing at Issus and Gaugamela. Some of the taxeis, including Coenus', were termed asthetairoi.

Hypaspists

By contrast with the regional levies of pezhetairoi, the hypaspists were an elite force, chosen on an individual basis for their physical strength and valour. For this reason, a portion of them constituted the Guard (the *agema*) and in battle all 3,000 of them were stationed between the pezhetairoi and the cavalry, where the king himself directed affairs. Recruitment was based on social standing, and the hypaspists were divided into 'regular' and 'royal' hypaspists.

The hypaspists were almost certainly more mobile than the pezhetairoi. In the major battles they acted as a link between the heavy infantry and the cavalry. They were taken by the king on special missions that involved speed and endurance, often fighting in rugged areas. Named for their shields – and indeed the hypaspist veterans formed the so-called *argyraspids* or 'silver shields' – they were the infantry guard and, of all the infantry troops, they fought closest to the king. Small detachments of hypaspists acted as guards at official events and banquets, and also as a police force. There is a strong likelihood that, on occasion at least, they were armed more like traditional Greek hoplites and they are often referred to, loosely, as *doryphoroi* ('spear-bearers'). Those who commanded the regular hypaspists as chiliarchs or pentakosiarchs were selected on the basis of valour, although their overall commander, the *archihypaspistes* (literally, 'the leader of the hypaspists'), was a Macedonian noble appointed by the king. Between 334 and 330 this was Nicanor son of Parmenion; his successor may have been Neoptolemus, one of the Aeacidae.

The debate on whether the pezhetairoi and the hypaspists were normally armed in the same fashion is ongoing. Some historians argue that there was no significant difference in armament, others are coming around to the opposite view. The Alexander sarcophagus shows a Macedonian fighter, in the midst of the cavalry fray, carrying a slightly smaller hoplite shield about 34in (86cm) in diameter and wearing a *thorax* with elongated pteruges – perhaps a linothorax – and in the act of making an overhand thrust with what must have been a hoplite spear (*dory*), although the weapon is lost. Although this could be a depiction of a Greek mercenary, his proximity to Alexander suggests that he is a member of the hypaspists. Certain functions of the hypaspists may have required them to put aside the sarissa, or at least to use a considerably shorter one. Arrian's reference to hypaspists as 'the lightest troops and best armed' implies that they carried a lighter spear, which was just under 8ft (2.4m) in length. Hypaspists were used primarily on rough terrain, in siege warfare, and in close hand-to-hand fighting. In such situations the sarissa would have been at best cumbersome, and at worst useless. In the taking of city walls it would have been difficult for the hypaspists to scale ladders while carrying 18ft (5.5m) sarissai and protecting themselves only with the 2ft (0.6m) pelte. The term *hyperaspizantes* used of hypaspists who held up their shields to protect the king or a comrade also implies something larger than the 2ft (0.6m) shield of the pezhetairoi.

The main difference between the regular and royal hypaspists was that the latter were clearly of aristocratic background, and most if not all of them were formerly members of the Royal Pages. We do not know how numerous the royal hypaspists were or exactly how they fought in major battles. During the storming of city walls they are found in the immediate vicinity of the king, and if they stayed close to the king on the battlefield they may have operated as *hamippoi*, interspersed among the horsemen. The known commanders of royal hypaspists are Admetus (probably), Hephaestion (possibly), and Seleucus (certainly). Of these, Hephaestion was wounded at Gaugamela by a cavalryman's lance (*xyston*) in the thick of the action. As commander of this group, he may himself have been mounted.

Crossing the Hellespont in Alexander's army were 3,000 hypaspists, who may have been from the very start of the campaign assigned to 1,024-man units called chiliarchies, although it is possible that the chiliarchy structure was not imposed until 331 and that earlier references to chiliarchs and chiliarchies are anachronistic.

Argyraspids

Literally the 'silver shields', the argyraspids were named for the decoration of their armour. The unit had its origins in Alexander's regular hypaspists, and already in the accounts of Gaugamela, Diodorus Siculus and Curtius Rufus (following the same source) refer anachronistically to the hypaspists as argyraspids. Both units numbered 3,000 and their distinguishing characteristic was their shield. In fact, Diodorus says that 'the infantry unit of the argyraspids [was] distinguished by the brilliance of its arms and the bravery of its men' (17.57.2). It is likely that their shields were not simply decorated but of a larger size than those of the pezhetairoi. In the time of the Successors, the argyraspids spoke of themselves as a unit that had not known defeat in Alexander's lifetime and as men who were advanced in age, victorious veterans who had been dismissed in 324 but prevented by the turmoil that accompanied the king's death from reaching home and enjoying the fruits of a well-deserved retirement. In 318, they joined Eumenes in the war against Antigonus Monophthalmos, and although they fought with distinction at Paraetacene and Gabiene in the following year they surrendered their commander to the enemy in exchange for their wives and baggage, which had been captured in the second battle.

Greek infantry

Some 7,000 Greek allied infantry crossed the Hellespont with Alexander. The corps was composed of contingents sent by the member states of the League of Corinth. Each contingent was composed of selected men from the state's army and served under its own officers. The corps as a whole was commanded by a Macedonian general.

Following the shattering blow dealt them at Chaeronea, the armies of Greece underwent a series of reforms. In Athens, the results of these reforms, carried out under Lycurgus, can be seen on gravestones: body armour, abandoned since the Peloponnesian Wars, was re-introduced in the form of the muscle-cuirass and the Spartan *pilos* helmet (shaped like the conical *pilos* cap) is replaced by the Macedonian 'Phrygian' helmet. In Megara, the Phrygian helmet is not seen, but a similar muscle-cuirass is adopted.

The army also contained a large number of Greek mercenary infantry. Alexander led 7,000 allies and 5,000 mercenary infantry to Asia, and there was a steady flow of reinforcements throughout the campaign. The main role of the mercenary infantry was to provide garrison troops to keep newly conquered provinces in check. Troops for this purpose were frequently enrolled on the spot, usually from Greek mercenaries previously in Persian service. These mercenary bands were not altogether reliable: many had anti-Macedonian sympathies, and mutinies were not infrequent, particularly in the later years of Alexander's reign. At the time of Alexander's death, some 10,000 men in the upper satrapies were planning to abandon their posts and return to Greece, something they had previously attempted upon hearing the false news of the

A Roman bronze copy
of a statue of Alexander
the Great. It may
depict the original of a
sculptural group Alexander
commissioned his sculptor,
Lysippus, to make
in honour of the
25 Companions who fell
at Granicus. The rudder
which supports the rearing
horse may signify the
crossing of the Granicus.
(akg-images/Nimatallah)

king's death in 325. Mercenaries were also used to supplement the number of infantry in the field army, but these units seem to have been composed of altogether more reliable troops who had been with the army a long time or who had been recruited more recently from friendly states in Greece. The surviving accounts of Gaugamela are incomplete and differ significantly, but they seem to mention two separate units of mercenaries participating in the battle. The veteran (*archaioi*) mercenaries, who fought on the right wing, were probably the 5,000 who crossed the Hellespont with Alexander either in part or in full. The Achaean mercenaries, who fought on the left wing, were probably the 4,000 mercenaries recruited in the Peloponnese who had joined the army at Sidon the year before.

Greek mercenary infantry at this time were still equipped with bronze hoplite shield and helmet but no other body armour, carrying the normal infantry spear and sword, and dressed in red *exomis* tunics. Certainly Greek mercenary infantry in Persian service appear with this dress and equipment on both the Alexander sarcophagus and the Alexander mosaic. It is possible that those in Macedonian service wore cuirasses, but given their position on the wings at Gaugamela, where mobility would have been crucial, it is more probable that they did not.

Light infantry

There is little known about the light infantry (*psiloi*) of the army. They presumably fought in open order, perhaps in less depth than the phalanx, and their sub-units may have occupied greater frontages than those of the phalanx. The basic sub-unit seems to be the company of 500, but it is not clear whether these companies were called lochoi as they were in the phalanx.

The corps of archers (*toxotai*) as a whole was under the command of a strategos, and was divided into a number of companies of 500, each, it seems, under the command of a *toxarch*. The first strategos, Cleander, died in the Pisidian campaign and was replaced by Antiochus, who in turn died and was replaced by the Cretan Ombrion in Egypt in 331.

Alexander seems to have had a company of Cretan archers from the beginning of his reign. These Cretans could have been mercenaries, but it is more likely that they were an allied contingent supplied by those cities of Crete favourable to Macedon. They are not mentioned after the dismissal of the allies at Ecbatana in 330. Cretan archers were equipped with a small bronze pelte, which enabled them to fight at close quarters as well as provide missile fire. The Cretans served under their own officers – Eurybotas, who was killed at Thebes in 335, and thereafter Ombrion who was promoted to the command of the whole corps of archers at Memphis.

A second company of archers soon joined the expedition under the command of the *toxarch* Clearchus, who died during the siege of Halicarnassus. He seems to have been replaced by Antiochus, who is mentioned as a toxarch at Issus, although he may have doubled as strategos of the whole corps after the death of Cleander. The name of the toxarch appointed to command the second company after Antiochus' death in 331 is not known, nor is the nationality of the company, although they may have been Macedonian. A third company, under Briso, joined the expedition before Gaugamela, and these are definitely called Macedonians. The non-Cretans did not, it seems, carry the bronze pelte.

The Agrianian javelinmen, under the command of the Macedonian Attalus, were the crack light infantry unit of the army. They were probably supplied for the expedition by the client king of the Agrianians, Langarus, out of his household troops. Only one company was present at the crossing of the Hellespont, but a second company joined the army before Issus, bringing up their strength to 1,000.

Little is known of the other light infantry, who are given the general term 'Thracians' in the texts. They are the 7,000 Odrysians, Triballians and Illyrians who appear in Diodorus Siculus' description of the army which crossed the Hellespont. They could be mercenaries, but given Alexander's shortage of money in the earlier campaigns, they are more probably further contingents sent for the expedition by other client kings. Probably all the light infantry were javelinmen (*akontistai*), divided into a number of taxeis, although there may also have been some units of slingers. The Odrysians were commanded by Sitalkes, a prince of the Odrysian royal house, and other units may also have been under native commanders. Another unit of javelinmen was commanded by Balacrus.

THE CAVALRY

The ile (squadron) of 200 men in four tetrarchies continued to be the building block of the cavalry. A number of ilai, usually two, three or four, might be formed into a cavalry brigade, *hipparchy*, commanded by a *hipparch*. At first the number of squadrons per brigade was variable, but later on the system became more standardized.

Each cavalryman was allowed a groom, who might have been mounted, to look after his horse and equipment. The grooms were stationed behind the squadron in battle. The cavalrymen owned their own horses, though it was customary for a man drafted into the cavalry to be granted an initial sum to enable him to buy a mount of suitable quality. Horses lost in action were replaced from the pool of remounts, a system run by the Secretary for Cavalry. He had a difficult job as huge numbers of horses died in battle, and in an age before horseshoes, a horse could easily be ruined by a long march. At Gaugamela, the cavalry, 7,000 strong, lost 1,000 horses; nearly one in three of the Companion cavalry lost theirs. Commandeering was used to obtain remounts locally, but more usually it was the duty of provincial governors to procure horses and send them to the remount pool. Many cities or provinces paid tribute on the hoof. In the last resort, recourse had to be made to sequestration of surplus mounts within the army itself.

Cavalry equipment

Alexander replaced the Phrygian helmet with the Boeotian helmet. Cavalry helmets on the Alexander sarcophagus and mosaic seem to show insignia of rank. Horsehair 'tails', gold or silver wreaths and the silvering of the helmet

MACEDONIAN CAVALRY TACTICS

The cavalry formations that developed in the early 4th century allowed cavalry squadrons to redeploy rapidly and to reorient the axis of their attack, giving them flexibility. Alexander's battle tactics exploited this flexibility. He aimed to advance his army obliquely so as to cause dislocations in the Persian line as it attempted to outflank him on his right. The Persian cavalry column attempting to turn his right flank would be kept at bay by successive charges of his light cavalry, delivered squadron by squadron. As the Persian cavalry was forced to move further to the right, they would eventually lose contact with their main battle line. As soon as a dislocation was observed in the Persian battle line, Alexander personally led his heavy cavalry straight for it.

could all have indicated different ranks, although Alexander was known to give gold crowns to his troops for bravery, which could be an alternative, though less likely, explanation for the wreaths. Bracelets were also worn as badges of rank, as they were by the Persians.

The long cavalry spear (xyston), though made of strong cornel wood, often shattered in action, so was fitted with a second spear-head at the butt to allow the trooper to continue fighting. The xyston was used to stab at the faces of enemy riders and horses. The sword, a secondary weapon, was slung under the left arm. The aristocratic cavalrymen may have chosen to use their own highly decorated swords. Greek cavalry did not carry shields at this time, although it was normal for generals to be accompanied by their personal shield-bearers to enable them to fight on foot if necessary.

Some cavalrymen wore only a short-sleeved tunic, but most wore a long-sleeved outer tunic over the first. The heavy cavalry – Companion, Thessalian and allied – were issued with cuirasses. The cuirass was made of small metal plates, linked together, lined or covered with leather or linen, which made the cuirass resilient but flexible. In the early campaigns, Alexander himself rarely wore a cuirass, and this may have been widely copied by the young nobles in the cavalry, especially in the Companion cavalry. Cavalry boots seem to have been standard throughout the cavalry. It is possible that saddle cloths, made of a shaggy felt-like material, were dyed in the regimental colour and faced in the squadron colour, but this is speculative. Over the saddle cloth a pantherskin saddle cloth was sometimes seen, perhaps restricted just to officers. Persian saddle cloths were sometimes used. These probably do not represent booty, as highly decorated Persian saddle cloths were much favoured by the aristocracy and had long been a luxury import into the Greek world.

ALEXANDER AND A COMPANION CAVALRYMAN

Alexander is seen here dressed as a senior officer of the Companion cavalry. His uniform details are taken from the Alexander mosaic. On the mosaic the tunic is a light purplish-grey, but the mosaic was copied from a painting several hundred years old, and all the colours had faded. The cloak is damaged in the mosaic, but has been reconstructed with a yellow border. The green girdle on the cuirass and matching edging on the saddle cloth may have some significance as a squadron colour.

Normally the king would have worn a Boeotian helmet. The cavalryman is taken from the Alexander sarcophagus. He wears the long-sleeved purple tunic and yellow Macedonian cloak (chlamys) of a Companion cavalryman. Normally the Companion cavalry would have worn white cuirasses, similar but less ornate to that worn by Alexander. A Persian saddle cloth is used instead of the Greek saddle cloth. (Angus McBride © Osprey Publishing Ltd)

Companion cavalry

The Companion cavalry, the senior regiment of the army, was recruited from the noble youth of Macedon. Diodorus gives the regiment's strength at the start of the expedition as 1,800, but perhaps some squadrons were left in Macedon. The regiment comprised eight squadrons, the first of which was the Royal Squadron (*basilike ile*), which was the vanguard squadron of the regiment, and held the position of honour in the battle line. The Royal Squadron, in whose ranks the Personal Companions fought, was kept at double strength. The other seven squadrons, at the normal strength of 200 lances each, formed up on the left of the Royal Squadron according to the order of precedence for the day. The line squadrons are generally named for their commanders in the texts, but each may have been recruited from a distinct area, and with appropriately territorial official names.

Thessalian cavalry

The sources frequently state that the Thessalians were the best cavalry unit in the whole army. This is unsurprising as they were raised from the aristocracy of Thessaly, the finest horsemen in the Greek world. For political and social reasons, however, the Companion cavalry were the senior regiment. The Thessalians fought on the left wing under the general command of Parmenion, but since Thessaly belonged to the political orbit of Macedon and Alexander was the leader of the Thessalian League, these troops must be regarded as distinct from those of the 'allies'. The Thessalian cavalry equalled in strength the Macedonian Companions (1,800–2,000 men), so it may be assumed that the Thessalian regiment was also organized in eight ilai. Their vanguard squadron was the Pharsalian ile, which formed Parmenion's personal bodyguard on the left wing at Gaugamela. It was the Thessalian regiment's counterpart to the Royal Squadron, so it was probably also double-strength. The names of the other seven ilai are not given by the sources, but it is fairly certain that they were named after the other principal cities of Thessaly in which they had been raised. Two hundred Thessalian horse joined the army at Gordion, but they probably made up losses in the existing squadrons rather than creating a ninth.

The Thessalian regiment was disbanded at Ecbatana, when the allied contingents were sent back to Greece, but 130 volunteers remained with the army. These formed their own small unit, but after less than a year of mercenary service, it was disbanded.

The Allied Horse

The Greek states of the Corinthian League were obliged to make contributions of cavalry and infantry to the expeditionary force. Not all of these states were asked to contribute cavalry, however, and no city seems to have made an individual contribution of a full squadron; rather, each squadron seems to have been formed by brigading together the various contingents from a particular area. From their positions in the various battles it is likely that the Allied Horse were a unit of heavy cavalry. No details of their dress or equipment have survived.

Diodorus Siculus mentions the presence of 600 Greek horse under the command of Erigyius crossing to Asia with the army. These are probably the three squadrons mentioned as fighting under Erigyius son of Larichus at Gaugamela: the squadron of Peloponnesian and Achaean horse, the cavalry of Phthiotis and Malis, and the squadron of Locrian and Phocian horse. At the Granicus the allied cavalry were commanded by Philip son of Menelaus; this was presumably a temporary command. Reinforcements which reached the army at Gordion included a further 150 horsemen from Elis. At Issus, the Peloponnesian and other allied horse fought with Parmenion on the left wing, though their commander is not given. It is difficult to identify exactly the reinforcements reaching the army in Asia. The allied cavalry were detached to the satrap of Syria after Issus, and they probably received further reinforcements while stationed there. It may be that an Acarnanian and Aetolian squadron reached the army even before Issus. It is certain that a Boeotian squadron reached the army in Asia. As well as Erigyius' three squadrons at Issus, there was a second brigade of Allied Horse commanded by Coeranus, on the opposite, left wing. This brigade probably also numbered 600, and comprised three squadrons, probably one of Boeotians, and possibly another of Achaeans and Acarnanians. The Eleians could have fought either in the Peloponnesian and Achaean squadron on the right or in a third squadron on the left. The regiment of Allied Horse was disbanded at Ecbatana, but many men were enrolled into the Mercenary Horse.

Thracian cavalry

There were four squadrons of Thracian light cavalry belonging to Alexander's army, supplemented by further squadrons of auxiliary Thracian cavalry. The Thracians were considered a wild, uncivilized group of soldiers, much tempted by drink, plunder and women.

Prodromoi (scouts, sometimes also called *skopoi*) is a name usually applied to the Thracian squadrons of the main Macedonian army, but occasionally to the other auxiliary squadrons. The prodromoi were probably recruited from inside the border of Macedon, from the Thracian provinces annexed by Philip, and served under Macedonian officers. The light cavalry squadrons seem to have been under strength at the crossing of the Hellespont, as Diodorus says that the prodromoi and the Paeonian squadron only numbered 900. Presumably the prodromoi, the Paeonian squadron and Odrysian cavalry were fully brought up to strength by the reinforcement of 500 Thracian cavalry which reached the army at Memphis. A further reinforcement of 600 joined the army at Sittacene.

The primary role of the prodromoi, as the name indicates, was to scout ahead of the advancing army. For this purpose they were occasionally brigaded with units of light infantry or detachments of heavy cavalry. During the Balkan campaigns some units of cavalry used javelins; these were probably prodromoi, who seem to have been equipped with the xyston and javelins in the first years of Alexander's reign. After the crossing of the Hellespont, however, the terms prodromoi and *sarissophoroi* are used indiscriminately and javelins are never mentioned again, so it seems that Alexander re-equipped them with longer spears before the expedition crossed over. The prodromoi did use helmets, but probably no other armour. The helmets would have been changed from the painted Phrygian type to bronze Boeotian helmets. Tunics and cloaks were worn, and horses would have had pantherskin saddle cloths.

The Thracian cavalry squadrons of Alexander's army were supplemented by further auxiliary Thracian squadrons. The Paeonian squadron who crossed the Hellespont with the army seem to be a detachment of cavalry contributed by the client king of Paeonia. They were commanded by a prince of the Paeonian royal house called Ariston. The Odrysian cavalry were probably contributed in a similar way by the king of the Odrysians, but they were under the command of a Macedonian, Agathon son of Tyrimmas. The Odrysians joined the expedition in

Royal Pages hunting lions in a mosaic at the royal palace at Pella, dating from the 4th century. (© World History Archive/TopFoto)

time to take part in the battle of Granicus. They were probably two squadrons strong at Gaugamela. The Paeonian and Odrysian squadrons may have been equipped similarly to the regular squadrons of prodromoi, but could also have been markedly different as they were not part of the main Macedonian army.

Mercenary cavalry

Alexander was deficient in light cavalry in his early campaigns, and the mercenary cavalry were raised to offset this serious deficiency. We hear of a squadron of 200 mercenary cavalry as early as the siege of Halicarnassus, but these troops were left in Caria as part of the provincial army. At Gaugamela we hear of two brigades of mercenary horse, the Foreign Mercenary Cavalry under Andromachus, son of Hieron, and the Mercenary Cavalry under Menidas. It is usually assumed that the latter unit is to be identified with the 400 Greek mercenaries who joined the expedition at Memphis under the command of Menoitas son of Hegesander. The Foreign Mercenary Cavalry were presumably of the same strength – two squadrons – but we are not told whether they had been raised earlier or at the same time as Menidas' unit, possibly in Syria.

Alexander seems to have considered these new, and as yet untried, units expendable. At Gaugamela Andromachus' unit is stationed in front of the left wing, while Menidas rides point to the whole army on the right wing. Battle commenced when Alexander ordered Menidas to charge the Scythians and Bactrian brigades of armoured cavalry, the latter unit alone some 1,000 strong. The Mercenary Cavalry certainly earned their pay that day.

When the Greek allies were dismissed at Ecbatana, Alexander encouraged all who wished to continue to serve in the army to enrol as mercenaries, and apparently many did so. The mercenary cavalry was expanded with those of the Allied Horse who signed on, supplemented with newly recruited mercenaries sent east, and the new units were commanded by officers previously serving in the Allied Horse. The precise details are obscure, but it seems that both Menidas and Andromachus together with their troops were left behind under Parmenion in Media when Alexander pushed on to hunt down Darius. Soon after we hear that command of the Mercenary Cavalry had passed to Philip son of Menelaus, who had commanded the Allied Horse at Granicus. Andromachus retained command of the Foreign Mercenary Cavalry. Alexander took the Mercenary Cavalry under Erigyius with him, so in mid-330 there were at least three units of mercenary horse. A year later, during operations near Samarkand, Alexander heard that the garrison left behind in that city was being besieged by Spitamenes. He sent back a relief column, which included 800 mercenary horse, retaining one hipparchy under his command. The whole of the column, exhausted after a long forced march, was exterminated by an ambush of Scythian horse archers.

The description of the unequal fight between Menidas' cavalry and the Bactrians at Gaugamela makes it obvious that the mercenary horse were lightly equipped. They probably fought with spear and swords and wore only the Boeotian helmet, boots, tunic and cloak. No representation survives that can be associated with them, but their appearance was probably identical to that of the prodromoi, with only different colours to distinguish them.

7

ALEXANDER ENTERS PERSIA

THE MARCH TO THE HELLESPONT

With Greece and Thrace in order, Alexander could turn his army towards Persia. At Thebes in 335, Alexander's army comprised 30,000 infantry, but these must have included allied troops and mercenaries. For the protection of the homeland, and to deal with uprisings by the Greeks, the regent Antipater was left with 12,000 infantry, of whom some were hypaspists. Alexander made regular demands on Macedonian manpower throughout the campaign, but Antipater managed to amass a force of 40,000 infantry to deal with Agis III in 331; perhaps more than half of these were of Macedonian peasant stock. In 323, when the outbreak of the Lamian War left Macedon denuded of allies, Antipater marched south through Thessaly with 13,000 Macedonian infantry.

The numbers for Alexander's expeditionary army are given in the ancient sources, and vary between 30,000 and 43,000 infantry and 4,000 and 5,500 cavalry. Diodorus Siculus provides the most detailed force numbers for the expeditionary force. He states that the infantry was composed of 12,000 Macedonians, 7,000 allied infantry, 5,000 mercenaries, 7,000 infantry from the Odrysians, Triballians, and Illyrians, and 1,000 archers and Agrianians. This total of 32,000 infantry largely agrees with the estimates of other ancient historians. The highest estimate of 43,000 infantry, from contemporary source Anaximenes of Lampsacus, could well be explained by his including in this figure the 10,000-strong advance force sent in 336, already present in the region, in which case the figures essentially agree. Diodorus' numbers for the cavalry are not so straightforward. He says there were 1,800 Macedonians, 1,800 Thessalian, 600 allied, and 900 Thracian and Paeonian scouts. Strangely, he continues to say that the total figure for the cavalry was 4,500 when, in fact, the figures he provides total 5,100, which has provoked much debate among modern historians. His total of 5,100 agrees quite well with Arrian's 'more than' 5,000,

OPPOSITE
Greek vase showing priests sacrificing to the gods.
(akg-images/Erich Lessing)

which was based on a contemporary source, and Ptolemy, whom Plutarch reports gave a cavalry figure of 5,000. In addition, Anaximenes provided a figure of 5,500 cavalry. This is the highest cavalry figure given and probably again includes the cavalry already operating with the advance force. It is therefore safe to conclude that the cavalry that was ferried across the Hellespont numbered around 5,000.

Before joining the army, which was perhaps mustered at Therme near modern Thessaloniki, Alexander held games and made sacrifices to the Muses and Zeus. After this the army set out along the southern coast of Thrace, bypassing Lake Cercinitis, heading towards the town of Amphipolis, which straddled the river Strymon. From Amphipolis he passed Mount Pangaion, heading east towards the Greek city foundations of Abdera and Maronea on the coast of the north Aegean. Crossing the river Hebrus, the army traversed the Thracian region of the Paetice tribe. At the western point of the Chersonese, Alexander led the army across the 'black' river. Twenty days and over 300 miles after setting out from Macedon, the army reached Sestos in the Thracian Chersonese (Gallipoli peninsula) on the western shore of the Hellespont, across which lay Asia proper.

The land route to Asia, at least initially, obviated the need to rely on the Greek navy for support. In the event, the vaunted Persian navy made no attempt to oppose the crossing of the Hellespont in early 334.

THE CROSSING INTO ASIA

After Alexander reached Sestos, he left Parmenion to oversee the ferrying of the army to Abydos on Asian soil, less than a mile across this narrow stretch of the Hellespont. Leaving the logistics of this operation to his deputy, Alexander took the opportunity to go to Troy, a visit laden with deep symbolic significance. At Elaeus on the southern tip of the Chersonese, he sacrificed at the tomb of Protesilaus who was reputed to have been the first of the Greek soldiers to land in Asia during the Trojan War. Sailing across the strait towards the 'Achaean harbour', Alexander steered the ship himself and sacrificed a bull to Poseidon and the Nereids as well as pouring libations into the Hellespont in appeal for a safe crossing. Diodorus even says that, upon landing, Alexander flung his spear towards Asia and leapt onto the shore before his comrades to signify 'that he had received Asia from the gods as a spear-won prize'. Further appropriate sacrifices and dedications were made at Troy itself, including Alexander's own armour which he exchanged for some left in the temple of Athena Ilias from the time of the Trojan War. The tombs of Achilles and other Homeric heroes were visited, venerated and sacrificed at, and the spirit of Trojan Priam appeased with a sacrifice as well.

These heady religious observations and honours were certainly called for in order to elicit divine support for an arduous and long military campaign, but they also provided a significant propaganda opportunity for Alexander. Like Homer's heroes of the epic *Iliad*, Alexander was leading 'Greeks' against their traditional enemies in Asia itself. Perhaps more important than the propitiatory

The walls of 'Troy VI' excavated in the late 19th century. Alexander made a pilgrimage to Troy before rejoining the army outside Abydos. (Michael Thompson)

TRIREMES

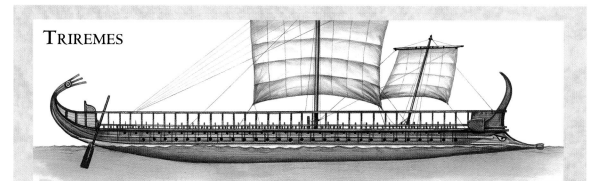

During the Classical period triremes were the most formidable and sophisticated warships in the Mediterranean. They were galleys designed to fight under oar power, although two square sails were provided for cruising. The principal weapon was a ram, designed to cause maximum waterline damage without penetrating the hull too far and making it difficult for the attacking vessel to back off.

The other method of fighting, besides ramming the opponent, was boarding. As no triremes survive, many aspects of their construction and operation are hotly disputed, especially the arrangement of the oars. Triremes were no longer than 120ft (37m) and their fundamental innovation was that rowers sat in three staggered banks, which enabled the oarsmen to row within the limited space. Oarsmen were sometimes slaves, but in Athens they were highly trained professionals, drawn from the poorest Athenian citizens. The trireme was at the forefront of contemporary technology, so it was not only expensive to build, but also had to be maintained and repaired, and the crew had to be paid. The top level of oarsmen were paid a higher rate because they had a greater responsibility for synchronized rowing, a crucial element in the success of the trireme.

A fully manned 'fast' trireme was propelled by 170 oarsmen rowing in three benches containing respectively 62, 54 and 54 men. The trireme also needed a dozen or so sailors to steer the ship, trim the sails and so on. These men were professional mariners. Both hoplites and archers might serve on a trireme as marines (epibatai). Triremes could be used as horse- or troop-transports as well as fighting galleys. Horse-transports were rowed only by the upper row of 60 oarsmen and might carry 30 horses. The troop-carrier (stratiotis) had a more variable number of oarsmen and hoplite passengers up to a total maximum of about 200. (Peter Bull © Osprey Publishing Ltd)

MEMNON OF RHODES

Memnon of Rhodes and his brother Mentor served the Persians as mercenary commanders in the Troad from at least the 350s. Mentor married Barsine, the sister of Artabazus, the satrap of Lower Phrygia, who in turn had married one of the Rhodians' sisters. When Artabazus failed in his rebellion against Artaxerxes III in 353/352, they were forced into exile at Pella in Macedon. Their capabilities as military commanders were still, however, highly valued and Mentor was pardoned by the Great King in 343, after which he subjugated the province of Egypt, which had been free from Persian control for 60 years. In return for this service, Memnon and Artabazus were also allowed to return. Upon Mentor's death in 340, Memnon was granted his lands and military authority, and even married his brother's widow.

Memnon was tasked with countering Parmenion's advance force in 336, and he was largely successful in forcing the Macedonian incursion back to the Troad and Hellespont region. However, in 335 he was unable to eject the advance force from Asia. At the war council at Zeleia, Memnon's scorched earth strategy was rejected. At Granicus, Memnon was active in the battle, but unlike the Greek mercenaries, he fled the field and escaped. Despite the defeat at Granicus, Memnon was put in charge of the defence of western Asia Minor and organized the defence of Halicarnassus in 334. He collected a large fleet and operated in the Aegean, seizing islands and cities and threatening Alexander's rear. At the siege of Mytilene in 333, Memnon fell ill and died. With the threat of this capable commander removed, Alexander was able to continue his campaign with his supplies safe.

acts themselves was the identification of Alexander's expedition as heir to Homer's tale. The new Achilles had, literally, landed.

Meanwhile, Parmenion was ferrying the bulk of the army across the Hellespont. That he was able to carry out this task with 160 triremes and a great many cargo vessels indicates that Alexander was able to muster a naval force of some size to cover the crossing against any possible Persian naval attack.

PERSIAN PLANS

The decision of the Persians not to contest Alexander's entry into Asia is perhaps not as surprising as it first appears. The newly installed king, Darius, had other priorities that immediately concerned him, such as the possibility of satrapal revolts, unrest in the northern province of Cadusia, and the need to quash rebellion in Egypt. In comparison to these Alexander may have seemed of little importance: Greek affairs were usually handled diplomatically, largely through bribery, and Greek military incursions could be dealt with by the western satraps and hired Greek mercenaries. The Persians may also have decided that with a Macedonian bridgehead already established in the Troad

A Foot Companion and an officer of the Foot Companions finishing off a Greek mercenary in Persian service. (Angus McBride © Osprey Publishing Ltd)

by Parmenion's advance force, the fleet could not successfully stop the crossing and that it would be better to meet Alexander in a decisive battle in Asia Minor. From the Persian point of view, the stability of the monarchy and the military situation in western Asia Minor had greatly improved from the early 330s when the situation was quite chaotic. Alexander was not a reason

KING DARIUS III

Darius III (c.380–330) was the last king of the Achaemenid Empire of Persia. When Alexander crossed to Asia, Darius III had only recently become king as a result of the convulsions at the Achaemenid court. The ruthless Artaxerxes III Ochus had elevated a eunuch called Bagoas to positions of great power at the court and in the army. In 338, Bagoas murdered first Artaxerxes and then his sons. The throne then went to a certain Artashata, a distant relative of the royal dynasty whom Greek writers called Codomanus, and who took the dynastic name Darius (III). Unlike the sons of Artaxerxes, Darius was a mature individual, already in his early forties, and an experienced warrior – he had defeated a Cadusian champion in single combat. Wise to the machinations of Bagoas he forced him to drink his own poison. When he turned his attention to the Macedonian invaders, he had only just returned from suppressing a fresh uprising in Egypt. After defeat at Issus and Gaugamela, Darius fled to Ecbatana to raise a new army. He was deposed by his satrap Bessus, and assassinated at his order in 330. Alexander gave Darius a magnificent funeral, and eventually married his daughter in 324.

for unnecessary panic. Darius was aware of the invasion and preparations had begun to counter the incursion even if he was not yet able, or did not yet deem it necessary, to lead the opposition in person. The immediate task of engaging the Macedonians was left to the Persian satraps of western Asia Minor who were best placed to deal with Alexander's expedition.

ON THE MARCH

In Alexander's army, the infantry dekas was the basic unit that stayed together on the march and shared living quarters. Each dekas of the infantry was allowed one attendant to look after its heavy baggage, which was carried by a baggage animal, usually a mule or donkey. Later in the campaigns, in Egypt and afterwards, the army increasingly used camels, which could carry more and were more suitable for campaigning in Asia. The attendants were ektaktoi, supernumeraries, because they did not fight in the ranks. The bulkiest items carried were the tents. It is not clear how many men shared a single tent, although descriptions of camps indicate that a dekas might have slept in eight tents, two men per tent, arranged in two lines of four facing a single campfire. The tents were carried in waterproof leather tent covers which acted as fly-sheets when the tents were erected. During river crossings the tent covers were sewn together and stuffed with chaff to make rafts. Usually the animals would be ferried on these rafts while the men crossed supported by inflated water-skins. On the march, water-skins, along with the

MACEDONIAN EQUIPMENT

1. Phrygian helmet with plumes on the sides and crest.

2. Thracian helmet with cheek pieces and a narrow crest.

3. The iron 'Vergina' helmet. Similar to the Phrygian helmet, but instead of tapering gradually to a rounded crest, the Vergina crest sits straight and narrow atop the helmet.

4. Bronze thorax, hinged on one side. When the armour was fitted around the warrior the hinges were fixed with pins, and laces secured the breastplate. The breastplate weighed as much as 25–30lb.

5. Bronze hemithorakion or half-thorax.

6. Iron cuirass.

7. Two swords, the shorter and straighter xiphos, and the kopis, the curved slashing sword with a protective handle.

8. Linothorax, with two rows of flexible wings (pteruges) for manoeuvring.

(Angus McBride © Osprey Publishing Ltd)

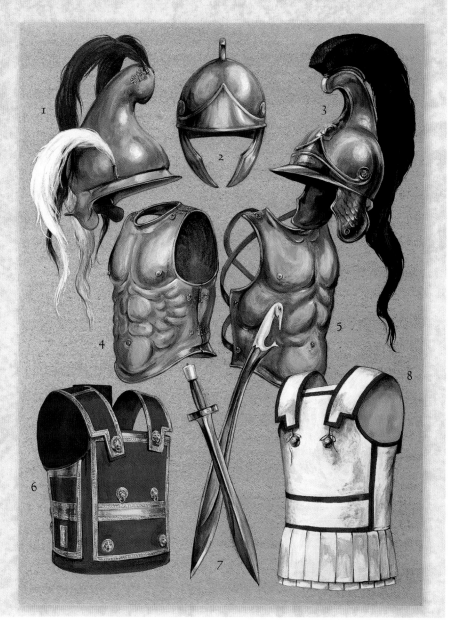

iron tent-pegs and guy ropes, were usually carried by the baggage animal. The dekas also carried a hand-mill, and presumably other implements and construction tools.

The cavalry usually marched on foot to spare the horses, as troopers have done throughout history, and the horses were left unbridled unless action was imminent; this was because the very severe bit used could ruin a horse's mouth if left in too long.

The infantry marched with their own weapons and armour, though replacing the helmet with the kausia slouch-hat. A personal pack was also carried. This included a bedroll, a drinking cup and other domestic items. The men also carried their food, which would have been ready cooked if rapid movement were required. Cooking was slow and difficult before flint and steel came into use in medieval times, so it was standard Greek military practice to carry fire in some form or other inside earthenware pots. Other personal possessions were carried in the baggage wagons, as was their booty. The sick travelled in wagons, possibly in special ambulances. The baggage train consisted of these wagons and others containing artillery and siege engines in kit form, accompanied by the families of the soldiers and the sutlers who followed the army, marching at the back of the army protected by a rearguard. As rations were not generally issued, it was the responsibility of each soldier to purchase his own rations from the traders who followed the army. Many of the debts incurred by the common Macedonians were the result of interactions with these traders, who offered the attractions of prostitution and gambling. Commandeering was used as a last resort. If the army was about to cross barren areas where the normal system would not function, rations were collected and carried centrally in the baggage train.

The official baggage train of the army increased steadily as the army wound its way across Asia, and the accumulated booty included slaves and concubines, and ultimately large numbers of illegitimate children. At Susa, at the end of the campaign, Alexander legitimized the unions of some 10,000 of his veterans. The camp-followers suffered the most on the difficult marches, and formed a high percentage of those who perished in the Gedrosian Desert in 325. In such situations the baggage animals doubled as emergency rations, though their slaughter necessitated the abandoning of baggage, not all of it non-essential.

For the soldier on the march there were also benefits to campaigning in the Persian Empire. Its infrastructure, especially the system of roads, made movement and communication relatively easy. The Macedonian army did seem to be able to maintain its lines of communication and received a steady

PUNISHMENT

The discipline imposed upon the Macedonian phalangite was certainly harsher than that employed by 'democratic' armies, where citizen soldiers had legal recourse against perceived abuses by their elected officers. In Macedon, the ultimate authority rested with the king. He regulated the conduct of his officers and punished them, and the rules of conduct were the same, if not more severe, for the rank and file. The sources say little about punishment for minor offences, though it appears that flogging was a standard form of corporal punishment. Dress-code violations may have invoked a fine. In Greek armies, soldiers guilty of insubordination were required to stand at attention in full armour for an extended period, and this punishment was also used by the Macedonians. Others may simply have been moved to disciplinary units, ataktoi, where the demands made of them were greater and their behaviour was closely monitored.

Other regulations clearly existed for the protection of property, including the women who had become attached to the army. Although rape was a standard feature of the looting and destruction of an enemy city or camp, the women who had been carried off as booty or those of the camp-followers who had become, in effect, the common-law wives of soldiers, were treated as personal property. Plutarch reports that when two men were being tried for seducing other men's wives, Alexander said that if found guilty they should be put to death.

Serious offences were punishable by death by stoning or javelins, or in a more dramatic way in the case of mutineers. The ringleaders of the mutiny at Opis in 324 seem to have been hurled into the Tigris still in their chains. The men who mutinied against their officers at the time of Alexander's death were treated to an even more cruel form of punishment: some 300 were trampled to death by elephants.

flow of reinforcements and supplies. Individuals were therefore able to send and receive letters, though the time for such a letter to be delivered must have been considerable.

The troops were treated to periods of rest and relaxation, and the army was on occasion joined by troupes of actors and artists. Athletic and artistic competitions are recorded. The nobles probably indulged in the hunting of exotic animals (as shown on the Alexander sarcophagus) just as they had hunted at home in Macedon.

OPPOSITE

On the left is a light cavalryman of the prodromoi of the early 330s. In the centre is an infantryman in camp dress. Around his arm is wrapped the ephaptis, the military 'wrap-around' cloak, which could be wrapped around the arm to form a makeshift shield. On the right is a Foot Companion in hunting dress; he is an officer or a senior soldier. (Angus McBride © Osprey Publishing Ltd)

Cy commence le .vme. qui contient .xxiii. chapitres . Ou pre
mier il fait mencion dune remoustrance que fist Alexandre a
ses gens . Des bestes insitees . Et dauaines citez a luy ren
dues Premier chapitre .

Lexandre ioieux
de tant memora
ble victore / par
laquele il pen
soit auoir ouuer
ture aux fins de tout orient
Il fist sacrefier au solleil / &
adfin que ses gens darmee

entreprenissent le sourplus
de prompt courage il les
loa deuant lassemblee / en
leur moustrant que toute la
puissance des Indiens estoit
renuersee par celle bataille
Le sourplus nestoit que rich
proie / et que les plus richees

8

THE BATTLE OF THE RIVER GRANICUS

THE ROUTE TO THE RIVER GRANICUS

Rather than set off south towards the Greek cities on the coast of western Asia Minor where the advance force had largely campaigned over the last two seasons, Alexander headed east around Mount Ida towards Dascylium, the capital of the Persian satrapy of Hellespontine Phrygia. Either he had intelligence, or he (rightly) suspected that the satraps of the region would be collecting forces to oppose him in this location. The ancient sources also indicate that he now had provisions for only 30 days and that his treasury amounted to only 70 talents, while he owed 200 talents (Plutarch, *Alex.*, 15.1). If he could engage and destroy whatever field army the local satraps brought against him, he would both gain the resources of the region and secure his supply and communications line to Macedon.

Before setting off, Alexander decided to leave behind the 7,000 Greek allied infantry and 5,000 mercenaries who had been brought over with the invasion force. Perhaps he suspected the loyalties of his Greek allies after the revolt of Thebes a year earlier. He probably assumed that since he was sure to face Greek mercenaries as the most significant part of the Persian infantry he would encounter, his own should be left behind. He would not test the loyalties of mercenaries brought over from Greece in this initial engagement. Moreover, this large force of allied and mercenary infantry would be a certain drain on his already dwindling supplies. He may also have thought they could provide useful consolidation and garrison duties in and around the Hellespont and Troad, with the intention that they should rejoin the Macedonian army when it returned.

In addition to these considerations, Alexander was to move swiftly, covering the roughly 60 miles from Arisbe to the Granicus in three days. For this sort of movement, he would require only his Macedonian infantry, the six 'brigades' (taxeis) of the sarissa-armed phalanx, and the hypaspists. These were all tough, veteran and experienced campaigners. Although numbering only 12,000,

THE ROUTE FROM TROY TO THE GRANICUS

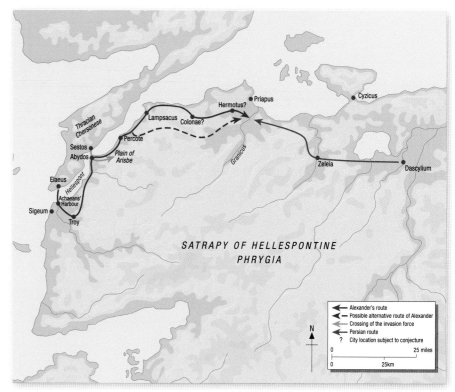

Alexander could be confident that they would be more than a match for the infantry of the opposition, likely to be at best Greek hoplite mercenaries. On the other hand, Alexander knew that Persian military strength, in number and quality, lay in their cavalry, and he therefore opted to take all of the cavalry available to him. The principal strike force of his army, the 1,800-strong Companion cavalry, and the 1,800 Thessalian cavalry were joined by the heavy cavalry of his Greek allies, which, numbering 600, was less of a potential concern regarding any questions of loyalty. The 900 light cavalry of prodromoi, Thracians and Paeonians were also part of the force. They were too useful to be left behind.

Leaving Arisbe, Alexander reached Percote and the following day came to the city of Lampsacus. At the end of the day's march the army encamped near the river Practicus, which may be identified with the river Paesus which empties into the Propontis (Sea of Marmara) at the northern end of the Hellespont. The following day the army struck camp for Colonae and must have arrived at the town of Hermotus around midday. The exact route from Lampsacus to the

Granicus is difficult to identify. Unfortunately, Colonae and Hermotus, the only two place names mentioned regarding Alexander's route between Lampsacus and the river Granicus, have not been positively identified. Unless otherwise required, ancient armies generally followed coastal routes, and as Alexander made the journey in three or slightly more days it is likely that he avoided the mountainous region of the northern Ida uplands.

At some point after reaching Hermotus, Alexander dispatched a force under the command of one of the Companion cavalry, Panegorus, son of Lycagoras, to seize the coastal town of Priapus, which occupies a stretch of land roughly two miles north of where the Granicus empties into the Propontis. At Hermotus, Alexander was now just west of the river Granicus and from the hills would have been able to survey the plain surrounding the river in the distance.

Scouts were now sent forward to reconnoitre the area. Alexander placed the scouts under the overall direction of Amyntas, son of Arrhabaeus, who led a squadron of Companion cavalry recruited from Apollonia in Chalcidice. Amyntas' squadron commander was Socrates son of Sathon and both of these men were to see important action in the opening stage of the battle. In addition to the scouts, four squadrons of the prodromoi were sent in front of the army.

PERSIAN MOVEMENTS

In early May the local satraps gathered in the region of Dascylium. Arsites, the satrap of Hellespontine Phrygia, the territory through which Alexander was now marching, was joined by satraps from the other Anatolian provinces. Arsames from Cilicia, the province north of Cyprus in the south-east of the peninsula, Atizyes, satrap of 'Greater' Phrygia in the interior of Anatolia, Mithrobuzanes, the satrap of southern Cappadocia, and Spithridates, the satrap of Lydia and Ionia, and his brother Rhoesaces, gathered their forces in the fertile plain around Dascylium, roughly 50 miles east of the Granicus. These were joined by other Persian nobles, some of whom were relations of Darius, and the Greek mercenary commander Memnon of Rhodes, who had earlier received estates in the Troad from Darius.

Alexander's movement east would have been a point of concern, but perhaps not unduly so. It is important to remember that in early 334 he was still very much an unknown quantity. From intelligence, the Persians would have been aware of his exploits, particularly since assuming the throne, but they had not had any direct contact with the young Macedonian king. Darius III felt no compulsion to rush to meet him. Over 1,000 miles away in the heart of his empire, he must have felt confident in the ability of his local commanders and their forces to stop the Macedonian incursion.

A low rise of hills about 100m in height lies roughly two-and-a-half miles east of the river. Much further away runs another range of much higher hills. (Michael Thompson)

The forces that were marshalled by the satraps would have been raised locally. Around 5,000 Greek mercenaries were gathered to provide the infantry, which was how the Persian satraps of Asia Minor regularly raised infantry. Modern historians have often placed Persian or native 'Asian' infantry at the battle and this may be an attempt to account for the incredibly high infantry figure given by Diodorus of 100,000. However there is no need to account for what it certainly an erroneously high number of 'Persian' infantry by postulating native infantry in addition to the Greek mercenaries. It is simpler and more coherent to assume that only a relatively small force of Greek mercenaries was present.

Cavalry was traditionally the strongest arm of any Persian military force, and it is likely that more than 10,000 were assembled by the satraps. Diodorus Siculus, the only source for the Persian order of battle, indicates that Arsames brought his own cavalry from Cilicia and that Memnon also commanded his own cavalry, presumably raised from his estates in the Troad. Arsites, in the battle order, commands cavalry from Paphlagonia, the region on the southern coast of the Black Sea. Cavalry from Media, Bactria and Hyrcania are also listed as present, which may appear anomalous as these provinces are from the central and eastern parts of the Persian Empire. However, there is no need to believe that these were brought to the region specifically to face Alexander. Rather, they would have been raised locally from colonists of these regions who had long ago settled in Asia Minor in return for their services to the Great King in this area.

The fertile plain around Dascylium meant this western Persian field army was well provisioned. In addition, the town lay on an important crossroads in the region. The road south led to the chief city of Lydia, Sardis, and access to the large cities on the western Anatolian seaboard further south such as Ephesus and Miletus. In fact, Sardis was the western terminus of the famous Persian Royal

Road, which led eastwards to the capital Susa. North of Dascylium lay the important coastal city of Cyzicus, which remained autonomous and supportive of the Macedonians. As the interior of the Troad region is dominated by the Ida mountain range, roads eastwards from the Hellespont took a north-easterly direction and descended into the plain of Adrasteia through which the river Granicus flows. As Alexander was approaching from this direction, the Persian army and its commanders set out from Dascylium to the town of Zeleia (modern Sariköy) approximately 20 miles east of the Granicus.

The war council at Zeleia

The Persian force apparently reached Zeleia by late May and it was here that Alexander's crossing into Asia was probably reported to the commanders. In the histories of Arrian and Diodorus Siculus, there is a report preserved of a war council that was held between the Persian satraps and Memnon very shortly before, perhaps even on the eve of, the battle. Memnon initially suggested that the best course of action was not to engage Alexander immediately because the Macedonians were 'far superior' in infantry and had their own commander leading them, while Darius was not present to lead his army. Rather, Memnon counselled, the Persians should withdraw, destroying the fodder and provisions in the area, burning the growing crops, and even destroying the towns and cities of the region. This scorched-earth policy would deprive Alexander of the supplies he would require, and it is perhaps tempting to wonder whether Memnon had intelligence that Alexander's army was already reduced to a month's supply of provisions, a claim made in Plutarch (*Alex.*, 15.1). Diodorus mentions that Memnon also advocated sending land and naval forces across to mainland Europe instead of immediate engagement in Asia, in effect opening up a diversionary second front. It is doubtful that this grandiose plan was actually mooted before the battle of the Granicus, although it may have been more seriously considered throughout the latter half of 334 and in 333 before Memnon, the one man who might lead such an expedition, died of illness.

Memnon's proposal would have required a considerable sacrifice on the part of those satraps whose territories he was effectively arguing should be surrendered without a fight in the interests of the greater strategic objective. Arsites, the satrap of Hellespontine Phrygia whose province would be the first to suffer under Memnon's policy, flatly refused. The obligation of a satrap was to protect the lands which had been conferred upon him by the Great King and simply abandoning his satrapy to the enemy could surely be interpreted as a violation of his duties as a Persian noble. Moreover, as Diodorus states, Memnon's advice probably struck at the dignity and code of honour held by the Persian nobles.

The other satraps agreed with Arsites and Memnon's counsel was rejected. Memnon's suggestion was apparently so outrageous that they even began to distrust his motives. It may have been that the satraps were jealous of Memnon's position and it has been suggested that Arsites, as the satrap of Hellespontine Phrygia, had particular reason to mistrust Memnon who held territories within Arsites' own satrapy. Despite Memnon's earlier services to the Persian throne, why should the local satraps defer to a Greek mercenary at the expense of their own authority? On the other hand, it may be that those who wrote the report of the council used by the extant authors desired to make a Greek, Memnon, appear wiser than his Persian counterparts.

Although it has been suggested that Darius had made early preparations for the Macedonian invasion, the fact that there was a war council at Zeleia implies that the local satraps had not received explicit instructions from the Great King. The nature of this war council raises the interesting question of the Persian command structure at the battle of the Granicus. It has been argued that part of the reason for the Persian failure there was that the Persians conducted a battle by committee. However, it may have been the case that Arsites held a position closer to supreme commander. It was his territory where a first engagement with Alexander would take place; he also took the lead in rejecting, on behalf of the satraps, Memnon's advice; and perhaps most tellingly, he survived the battle but later committed suicide, which implies a responsibility and, indeed, culpability greater than those of the other Persian nobility who survived.

PRELIMINARIES TO THE BATTLE

Approaching the river, Alexander marched his army in a 'double' (*diplon*) phalanx formation, with two phalanxes of infantry flanked by cavalry on either side and screened by light infantry and scouts in the front. When the scouts reported that the Persians were occupying the far bank of the river, Alexander was quickly able to arrange the army in battle formation. With the phalanx in the centre drawn up to a depth of eight men, the Macedonian line extended approximately 2.5 miles (4km) from the confluence of the river where Alexander and the Companion cavalry were stationed on the right wing northwards towards the cavalry under Parmenion on the left wing.

A rough Persian order of battle is given by Diodorus Siculus. Surprisingly, Memnon was not in command of the Greek mercenaries who were positioned behind the full line of Persian cavalry. The contingents are variously reported at strengths of 1,000 or 2,000 and the total cavalry force probably numbered more than 10,000, or roughly twice the number of Alexander's cavalry. The number of Greek mercenaries was around 5,000, significantly fewer than the 12,000-

strong Macedonian phalanx. The decision by the Persians to position their cavalry at or near the river and place the infantry behind has been criticized as a serious tactical error, but the practice was not unknown to the Persians; Xenophon reports its use in the *Anabasis*. Similarly, at the Granicus, given their inferiority in infantry, it would have made little sense for the Persians to have placed their Greek mercenaries directly opposite the Macedonian phalanx because the mercenaries would not have been able to match the length of the Macedonian line without being spread hopelessly thin.

After the two armies had been arrayed, Arrian reports a conversation where Parmenion advises that the battle be delayed until the following morning. This advice is strongly rejected by Alexander, but the ultimate source of this story must also have been known to Diodorus Siculus because he writes as if Alexander accepted Parmenion's advice, encamped that night, crossed the river at dawn and deployed his forces before the Persians could stop him. The irreconcilable accounts of Diodorus and Arrian in this regard have caused difficulties for later historians reconstructing the course of events. Plutarch was of the opinion that Alexander attacked immediately, impetuously disregarding the reservations of his officers, a view which is in accord with Arrian's depiction of events. It is highly unlikely that Alexander would have delayed his attack once he had brought the Persians to battle positions. In addition, it is even more unlikely that the Persians, having sought what protection and advantage the river Granicus could afford, would allow themselves to be caught unawares whilst Alexander's entire army crossed the river and deployed for battle the following morning. It seems therefore that Diodorus' account is confused on this point, and should be disregarded.

With both armies nervously lined up on opposite banks of the riverbed, Alexander made himself conspicuous by his appearance and entourage. His helmet with its two large white plumes would have clearly marked him out to the Persians on the far bank and certainly to Memnon, Arsames and Arsites directly opposite. The other satraps may have noticed this as well as in the course of events many of them appear in battle near Alexander. In fact, the disposition of Memnon and Arsites in particular may indicate that the immediate Persian tactical objective was to kill Alexander himself. Attacking the head of an army was a typical Persian tactic, and in this case particularly apt. At the battle of Cunaxa in 401, Cyrus ordered his Greek mercenary commander, Clearchus, to attack the Persian Great King directly, hoping that overpowering him would give them victory. Perhaps by placing the cavalry in front of their mercenary infantry, contrary to received wisdom and normal practice, they intended to reach Alexander himself as soon as was possible, in the belief that killing the young Macedonian king would end the war at its inception.

THE CAVALRY ENGAGEMENT AT THE GRANICUS

Macedonian and allies

Left wing

1 Thessalian cavalry (Parmenion)
2 Allied Greek cavalry (Calas)
3 Thracian Odrysian cavalry (Agathon)

Centre

4 Foot companion taxis (Meleager)
5 Foot companion taxis (Philip)
6 Foot companion taxis (Amyntas)
7 Foot companion taxis (Craterus)
8 Foot companion taxis (Coenus)
9 Foot companion taxis (Perdiccas)
10 Hypaspists (Nicanor)

Right wing (Alexander)

11 Prodromoi (no known commander)
12 Paeonian cavalry (no known commander)
13a Socrates' ile of Companion cavalry (Socrates)
13 Companion cavalry (Philotas)
14 Agrianian javelinmen (Amyntas as overall commander of the 'advance force' of prodromoi, Paeonian cavalry, Socrates' ile and probably the Agrianians)
15 Cretan archers (no known commander)

Persian and Greek mercenaries

Persian cavalry

A Cavalry of unspecified nationality (Memnon and Arsames)
B Paphlagonian cavalry (Arsites)
C Hyrcanian cavalry (Spithridates)
D Cavalry of unspecified nationality (Mithridates and Rhoesaces)
E Bactrian cavalry (no known commander)
F Cavalry of unspecified nationality (Rhoemithres)
G Median cavalry (no known commander)
H Greek mercenaries (Omares)

Events

1. Alexander's army arrives in march formation, with the baggage train in the rear.
2. Initial attack into the river led by Socrates' ile, the prodromoi, Paeonian cavalry, and a 'unit' of infantry.
3. Alexander and the Companion cavalry engage Persian cavalry in the river. Ascending the far bank, the Macedonians and Alexander begin to engage Persian cavalry on the plain beyond the far bank.
4. Mithridates and other satraps attempt to lead a counter-attack to stem the tide of Macedonian cavalry. Mithridates is killed.
5. The phalanx begins to move across the river.
6. Parmenion and the left-wing cavalry attack across the river.

THE INITIAL ATTACK

Once deployed and ready for battle, the two armies observed each other in silence for some time. It was perhaps during this lull that the satraps leading other cavalry contingents gravitated towards Alexander's position at the southern end of the river near its confluence with a branching tributary. The Persians were waiting for the Macedonians to enter the river, where the attack would be slowed and the possibility of counter-attacks could break up any forward momentum.

Alexander ordered Amyntas son of Arrhabaeus to lead a vanguard force into the river. The prodromoi, the Paeonian cavalry and the contingent of Agrianian javelinmen descended into the riverbed along with an ile of the Companion cavalry led by Socrates. The Persian reaction was swift and severe as they began to rain down javelins from their bank while some of the cavalry also descended into the riverbed to obstruct the access points out of the river. Clearly, the Persians were intent on attacking the Macedonians while the latter were navigating the river. The ancient sources note that in the course of the action the footing became difficult and slippery for the attackers, which further hindered the attack.

The advance force began to take serious casualties with Socrates' 200-strong ile of the Companion cavalry losing 25 men in the fighting. Although fighting bravely and staunchly, the advance force was now engaged with some of the strongest Persian cavalry led by Memnon and his sons. In addition, they were becoming seriously outnumbered as further Persian cavalry began to reinforce the counter-attack. Some portions of the advance force were being forced back in retreat to the Macedonian lines when the trumpets sounded and the Macedonian war cry was raised throughout the Macedonian right wing.

Alexander's advance force had not succeeded in gaining the far bank, but the action had drawn some, and increasingly more, of the Persian cavalry off the bank on the far side, engaged Memnon in the initial fighting, and disrupted the orderliness of the Persian defence as units and their commanders pushed towards the initial area of contact. More than simply a feint, the advance force had, in modern terms, begun to 'shape the battlefield' in Alexander's favour.

THE MAIN CAVALRY ENGAGEMENT

Alexander now committed himself and the full weight of the Companion cavalry, the most potent force in his army, against the Persian left wing. Having descended into the riverbed, Alexander led the formation obliquely to the right of the units in Amyntas' advance force that were engaged in heavy combat in and around the river channel, some of whom were in disarrayed retreat or were being pushed back. He used the confluence of the Granicus with a tributary of the river just to the south of his deployment as protection against his own right wing being outflanked. Not only was the attack initially oblique in direction, but according to Arrian the formation was echeloned in order to reach the far bank in a line and not be caught in columns. This fanning out of the Companion cavalry allowed them to approach the far bank as a more or less solid line, since those squadrons on the left would have slowed as they approached the mêlée involving the advance force and the Persian cavalry. If the bulk of Persian cavalry in the vicinity was moving directly towards the initial point of attack, the Companion cavalry, last to extend rightwards, may have met less opposition during the crossing of the riverbed and channel as they drove for their access points out of the river. Alexander, leading the charge of the Companion cavalry, made first contact with the enemy right of the point where the initial attack had been blunted. Here the Persian cavalry were now massed and Arrian comments that the 'leaders themselves were posted' here as well.

The cavalry of both sides were now fully committed in and around the river with the Macedonians struggling up the far bank. The two sides had now become so enmeshed that, 'though they fought on horseback, it seemed more like an infantry than a cavalry battle' (Arrian, 1.15.4). Amidst the confusion of the intense close combat the discipline and strength of the Macedonian Companion cavalry began to tell. Although the short sword and even shoulder-barging must have been used to good effect in the heated mêlée, Arrian ascribed the turning point to the Macedonians' efficient use of the cornel-wood cavalry xyston, which was used to strike at the face of both horse and rider. Thrusting at the face was the most effective use of a xyston against a horse as it caused the animal to rear up and greatly increased the chances of it unseating its rider. If the xyston was used to strike the horse's chest or body the force required for a fatal blow was likely to cause the xyston to fracture and break, and a horse not killed in this manner was likely to lash out at the goading.

In amongst these individual battles, the Persian satraps made for Alexander himself. All three ancient sources relate that Alexander was involved in a fierce struggle that very nearly cost him his life (see opposite). That Alexander's life was very nearly lost at the Granicus, at the very outset of his career, is perhaps the most intriguing aspect of this battle.

While Alexander and the Companion cavalry were struggling to overcome the Persians on the Macedonian right wing, the phalanx in the centre was also moving forwards across the river. As it would not have been possible for the Persian cavalry stationed on the far bank to stop the Macedonian phalanx, they would have resorted to harassing the slowly moving force by missile fire as long

ALEXANDER'S LIFE IS SAVED BY CLEITUS

In the midst of the intense fighting in the river Granicus, the ancient sources relate that Alexander was set upon by the satraps Mithridates, Rhoesaces and Spithridates. The accounts of the historians are not entirely consistent, but the main elements reconstructed in this scene are largely based on Arrian's version of events. After striking down the Persian satrap Mithridates, Alexander was struck on the helmet by another satrap, Rhoesaces, whom he was able to kill with his lance. However, Rhoesaces' blow cracked Alexander's helmet and Alexander was left dazed. Another satrap, Spithridates, raised his curved kopis sword to finish off the Macedonian king. At the last moment, Spithridates' arm was cut off by Cleitus, commander of the Royal Squadron of the Companion cavalry.

Diodorus Siculus and Plutarch offer accounts which differ in the details of who attacked who, with what, and in what order. Although it is impossible to reconcile these accounts, they do agree on three common points.

First, the Persian satraps made a concerted attack on Alexander as a main objective. Second, they very nearly succeeded in this because all the accounts agree that Alexander was struck on the head and that it was likely that his conspicuous helmet had saved his life from the initial blow. Third, his life was ultimately preserved by Cleitus, who was able to eliminate the attacker.

There is no reason to believe that this event was a literary creation to heroicize the king because, although the hand-to-hand combat is spectacularly dramatic, it is Cleitus who appears most heroic. It is more plausible, particularly as the accounts agree in their fundamentals, that Arrian, Plutarch and Diodorus took this story from an author (or authors) who composed a history much nearer to, or even during, Alexander's own lifetime. If this is so, then that source (or sources) is unlikely to have either invented or ignored what was clearly a pivotal moment in the battle. (Richard Hook © Osprey Publishing Ltd)

as practicable and then turned away. One can only speculate as to whether the Greek mercenaries were intended to move forwards in order to engage the Macedonian phalanx as it emerged from the riverbed. Arrian states that they did not move because they were 'stunned', presumably at the course of events. Meeting the Macedonians as they attempted to emerge up the riverbank would have given the hoplites some advantage over the sarissa-wielding phalangites, but if the cavalry on the wings collapsed, as indeed was happening, they would have been dangerously liable to a swift encirclement from the Macedonian and allied cavalry on either wing. Nevertheless, this was to be their ultimate fate despite being positioned back beyond the river line.

The ancient sources say very little of the left wing of the Macedonian line. The Thessalian and other cavalry of the left wing under Parmenion would later play a holding role in Alexander's battles against the Persians at Issus and Gaugamela, and may have performed a similar function at the Granicus but there is nothing conclusive in the sources. At some point during the battle, the Persian cavalry on their right fled, probably following the cavalry who had fled from the centre, and Parmenion's cavalry on the left wing were able to cross the river and join in the encirclement of the ill-fated Greek mercenaries whom the Persians had left behind.

On the right wing, Alexander and the Companion cavalry were gradually overcoming the Persian cavalry. They were ably assisted by the lightly armed Agrianian javelinmen who were intermingled with the cavalry of both sides. Furthermore, a number of the commanding satraps had now been slain in the attempt to kill Alexander and this must have affected both the morale and unit cohesion of the Persian cavalry. The Persian counter-attack against Amyntas' initial advance force had been continually reinforced by the Persians when they noted Alexander's entrance into the fray. Mithridates' cavalry, arriving in wedge formation, is an instance of this, although he himself was killed by Alexander. This somewhat desperate attack is the only tactical movement on the Persian side mentioned in the ancient sources and may betray the inability of their command structure to cope with the failure of their original battle plan or to react sufficiently to conditions on the ground. The Persians now found themselves disorganized and in disarray, unable to compete with the Macedonian cavalry lance, Macedonian unit cohesion, strength, determination and, ultimately, the Macedonian king, Alexander.

Although no precise time references are provided in the ancient sources, the two sides had perhaps been engaged for less than an hour when the pressure finally told on the Persians. The thrust of Alexander's charge to the immediate right of the point attacked by the advance force seems to have been where the Persian defence initially buckled and cracked. The Persian line to the right of this point then became disordered and very quickly gave way all along the line to the centre, where those cavalry who had tentatively opposed the phalanx were now fleeing. Those cavalry who had committed to fighting in the river were dead or dying, while those on the banks were failing in their struggle to contain the push of the Companion cavalry up and onto the plain beyond. At this point a general collapse rippled out to both the far left and right wings of the Persian cavalry and, turning away from the river, they joined their comrades in fleeing the field.

THE ENCIRCLEMENT OF THE GREEK MERCENARIES

Instead of pursuing the Persian cavalry, the Macedonians turned their attention to the Greek mercenaries. By now the Macedonian phalanx had crossed the river and was moving across the half a mile which separated them from the mercenaries on the gently sloping plain to the east. On the left, Parmenion with the Thessalian and Allied horse began to encircle the right side of the 5,000 mercenaries while, on the right, Alexander and the Companion cavalry were doing the same to the left side.

Abandoned by the Persian cavalry, the heavily armed Greek hoplites were in no position to escape the Macedonian cavalry. In this desperate position they asked Alexander for quarter. Despite the apparent hopelessness of their situation, the mercenaries probably thought this petition stood a good chance of success. Although clearly outnumbered, they remained a formidable fighting force that it would be costly for Alexander to reduce. They perhaps thought that Alexander would be happy to spare his men this unnecessary combat and would simply take them into his army. Plutarch says that Alexander 'influenced more by anger than by reason' refused the mercenaries' appeal for terms and straightaway led the final attack. Perhaps influenced by a desire to make a point to Greek mercenaries in Persian pay or simply carried away by the fury of the action and his own near-fatal experience in the river, he was not in any mood to accept terms. This is certainly how Plutarch portrays the event. However, Alexander's actions may also have been calculated to send a clear message that those Greeks who accepted Persian gold were traitors and would not be spared.

The Macedonians now attacked the Greek mercenaries en masse. Encircled on three sides by the cavalry, they were engaged from the front by the phalanx. Few details of this phase of the battle are provided in the ancient sources, but they may have formed square to counter the encirclement. Outnumbered, the experienced and disciplined mercenaries fought fiercely. The combat was heavy going for the Macedonians and, according to Plutarch, it was in this phase of the battle that they suffered the greatest number of casualties. It was said that Alexander even

OVERLEAF
One of the best-known artefacts connected to Alexander, the Alexander sarcophagus, was discovered near Sidon, Lebanon in the 19th century. It was once thought to be the sarcophagus of King Abdalonymus of Sidon, appointed by Alexander after the battle of Issus in 333, but now some scholars think it belonged to Mazaeus, a Persian noble and governor of Babylon. The once-vivid paint that originally adorned the figures was already greatly faded when the sarcophagus was excavated and faded rapidly thereafter, making it difficult to establish the original shades. It seems that originally ornaments, weapons and horse harnesses were attached in gold, silver and bronze, but they have been removed by grave-robbers. It is thought that the faces show Macedonians and Persians in combat at Issus, and hunting; a battle scene identified as Abdalonymus at the battle of Gazze in 312; and the murder of Perdiccas in 320. The sarcophagus is an important source for the reconstruction of the appearance of the troops who fought at Alexander's battles. (akg-images/Erich Lessing)

THE INFANTRY ENGAGEMENT AT THE GRANICUS

Macedonian and allies

Left wing

1 Thessalian cavalry (Parmenion)
2 Allied Greek cavalry (Calas)
3 Thracian Odrysian cavalry (Agathon)

Centre

4 Foot companion taxis (Meleager)
5 Foot companion taxis (Philip)
6 Foot companion taxis (Amyntas)
7 Foot companion taxis (Craterus)
8 Foot companion taxis (Coenus)
9 Foot companion taxis (Perdiccas)
10 Hypaspists (Nicanor)

Right wing (Alexander)

11 Prodromoi (no known commander)
12 Paeonian cavalry (no known commander)
13 Companion cavalry (Philotas)
14 Agrianian javelinmen (Amyntas)
15 Cretan archers (no known commander)

Persian and Greek mercenaries

A Cavalry of unspecified nationality (Memnon and Arsames)
B Paphlagonian cavalry (Arsites)
C Hyrcanian cavalry (Spithridates)
D Cavalry of unspecified nationality (Mithridates and Rhoesaces)
E Bactrian cavalry (no known commander)
F Cavalry of unspecified nationality (Rhoemithres)
G Median cavalry (no known commander)
H Greek mercenaries (Omares)

Events

1. The Persian cavalry on the left wing flee.
2. The Persian cavalry in the centre flee from the advancing Macedonian phalanx.
3. The Persian cavalry on the right wing flee from Parmenion's advancing cavalry.
4. Alexander decides to encircle the Greek mercenaries who have not yet taken part in the battle.
5. Parmenion and the left-wing cavalry complete the encirclement.
6. The mercenaries ask Alexander for quarter, which is refused.
   The Macedonian phalanx attacks from the front. The mercenaries are further attacked from the side and rear by the Macedonian cavalry and are destroyed.

had his horse killed underneath him after it was struck through the ribs by a sword. Nevertheless, the final outcome was never in doubt. The mercenaries were destroyed. About 2,000 were ultimately captured and these were led away in chains, intended for slave labour back in Macedon. Whether this bloody denouement sated Alexander's anger on the day is not recorded, but the perhaps unnecessary attack was costly for the king. In fact, he mitigated this hard-line approach to Greek mercenaries in future encounters, often taking those who surrendered into his service. However, that policy shift could not undo the memory of his action at the Granicus and in general Greek mercenaries in Persian pay felt they had better fight to the death rather than risk asking for terms.

CASUALTIES

Persian cavalry losses at the battle were moderated by the fact that their flight from the battlefield was not pursued by Alexander's cavalry. If the total Persian cavalry figure at the battle was slightly more than 10,000, the sources indicate that the Persian cavalry suffered losses of 10–20 per cent. This is not an unusually high ratio for the losing side in ancient warfare. However, the percentage of commanders killed was much higher and Diodorus Siculus implies that this was a significant cause of the Persian collapse. From the sources it seems that virtually two-thirds of the named Persian commanders at the battle perished.

It was the Greek mercenaries who bore the brunt of the casualties on the losing side. Arrian says that about 2,000 of the mercenaries were eventually captured which would mean that 2,000 to 3,000 of the Greek mercenaries were killed or seriously wounded in the final phase of the battle. This very high ratio of 50 to 60 per cent is explained by their encirclement but it is shocking to contemplate the butchery required to reach such percentages, even based on a minimum force figure of 5,000.

On the Macedonian side the casualties were far fewer. The sources indicate that roughly 25 Companion cavalry were lost from Socrates' ile in the initial attack and, according to Arrian, 60 other cavalry were lost as well. Plutarch says that 25 cavalry perished, while Justin claims 120 cavalry perished. Even lower figures are provided for the Macedonian infantry. Both Plutarch and Justin claim that only nine Macedonian infantry fell in the battle, while Arrian says that about 30 died. These figures seem low, and may be due to the common problem of history as written by the victors: the minimizing of their own losses and the highlighting of those of the enemy. It is also important to note that these figures from the sources relate only to the dead and not the wounded, which would have made the total number of casualties considerably higher. It has been argued that there are good reasons to believe that these figures are generally accurate, and it should be recalled that the infantry phalanx did not actually engage the enemy until they met the surrounded Greek mercenaries on the plain beyond the river. However, with the fierce and confusing cavalry fighting in the river higher cavalry casualties might be expected.

Alexander made a point of visiting the wounded after the battle, and the following day he buried the dead with much ceremony, not only the Macedonian fallen, but also the Persian commanders and Greek mercenaries. The greatest tribute was reserved for the 25 fallen Companions: Alexander commissioned his personal court sculptor, Lysippus, to erect bronze statues in their honour at Dium in Macedon, where they remained until removed to Rome in 146. For the parents

DESTRUCTION OF THE GREEK MERCENARIES

After the Persian cavalry had been routed at the river line and fled the battlefield, the 5,000 Greek mercenaries in their hire were left holding a very slight rise east of the river. They had hitherto taken no part in the battle. Refused quarter by Alexander, the front of the mercenary position was attacked by the Macedonian phalanx as the cavalry completed their encirclement. Marshalled to a depth of eight ranks, the Macedonians must have presented a formidable front of sarissai points to their enemy. The Macedonian sarissa significantly outreached the traditional hoplite spear in length, a devastating advantage for the Macedonian infantry. The long sarissa enabled them to engage the first ranks of the mercenary phalanx before being immediately threatened with contact themselves and very few of the Greek hoplites would have been able to penetrate the wall of sarissai points before falling victim to them.

However, the heavily armed Greek hoplite was formidable in defence and marshalled at even eight ranks was difficult to dislodge. If a hoplite could manage to pierce the Macedonian line he could cause damage through overarm or underarm thrusts of his spear. The fighting in this final phase of the battle was tough going and the Macedonian infantry probably took most, if not all, of their casualties here. Ultimately, the mercenary resistance was in vain as they were gradually but remorselessly destroyed. In this scene, the diversity of uniform and shield devices indicates the multifarious origins of the mercenaries, many of whom may have hailed from Athens, Thebes, Thessaly, or the Peloponnese, as well as the Greek cities of western Asia Minor. In any event, those fortunate enough to survive were unlikely ever to see their homelands again. (Richard Hook © Osprey Publishing Ltd)

and children of the dead left behind in Macedon, Alexander remitted taxes and relieved them of certain services due to the state. In addition, he sent 300 captured Persian panoplies to Athens to be hung up on the Acropolis as a votive offering to Athena. With these gestures, Alexander proclaimed the importance of his victory at the river Granicus throughout Greece, Macedon, and Asia Minor.

At the Granicus Alexander showed not only the superiority of his army's skills and training, but his ability as a commander. He employed the tactics he had seen his father use, an angled cavalry charge to one wing, then turning into the centre, followed up by the infantry in the centre. However, having appraised the field, he preceded this by sending an advance force to disrupt the enemy line, before leading his cavalry charge crashing into the disarrayed Persian cavalry. His infantry in the centre then steadily advanced until the cavalry fled, and the Greek mercenaries were left to the king's wrath. Following the Granicus, Alexander was clearly no longer an unknown quantity. This is borne out by the reaction of cities in Asia Minor to his advance. Some opened their gates to him, some decided to hold out, but none disregarded his presence. Alexander was a threat, or a welcome liberator, and he was clearly not finished yet.

THE MARCH SOUTH TO THE COAST

After the battle, Alexander appeared, as he had intended, as the liberator of Greek cities in Asia. A move in this direction was an obvious next step for him. Whether he already saw it as a first step in a grand strategy of world conquest cannot be known. Liberation on Alexander's terms was now evidently more acceptable to the provincial Persian government than to some of the Greek city-states that were the object of his benevolent intentions.

Alexander made Calas satrap of the now conquered Hellespontine Phrygia. The city of Zeleia from where the satraps had set out to the river Granicus was pardoned because Alexander decided that it had been compelled to succour the Persians. Parmenion was sent farther east to secure the provincial capital of Dascylium, which he found abandoned by the Persian military. Alexander and the army headed south to the city of Sardis and, about ten miles outside of the city, he was met by Mithrenes, the garrison commander, who surrendered to him the very defensible citadel and the significant treasury without a fight. However, when Alexander turned his attention to the Greek cities of the east Aegean coast that had been administered from Sardis, he met with a varying reception. Four days later, travelling south-west towards the coast, Alexander reached Ephesus where the Persian garrison and their mercenaries had abandoned the city prior to his arrival. He established democracy there, subject to his own suzerainty, and when the pre-existing pro-Persian oligarchy was massacred, Alexander swiftly intervened to halt mob rule. The cities of Lydia went over to Alexander without a quarrel, but farther south in Caria he was to meet resistance.

Miletus

Memnon, having survived the Granicus, was now active on the Aegean seaboard, conducting the kind of naval warfare that he had advocated before the battle, supplying and supporting the Greek coastal cities against the Macedonians. The other part of his plan, to lay waste to the hinterland to deprive Alexander of supplies, was not possible for him to carry out, so the Macedonian remained well supplied on land. Miletus, south of Ephesus, might have surrendered easily enough to Alexander had the Persian fleet, containing substantial Phoenician and Cyprian contingents, not been close at hand to support resistance. The decision of Hegesistratus, the commander of the garrison, to resist forced Alexander to commence his first siege of the campaign. Fortunately, the Greek fleet of 160 ships reached the area three days before the arrival of the Persian fleet from the south and anchored off the island of Lade opposite the city. The Thracian and 4,000 other mercenary troops were stationed on the island. However, once the Milesian commander realized that a Persian fleet were on their way, he refused to surrender. When the Persian fleet of 400 ships berthed opposite Alexander under the promontory of Mycale on the mainland, he decided not to risk a sea fight against such numerical odds. The Milesians now pleaded their neutrality, but Alexander was not listening any more, and he brought up his siege engines. He had already been allowed to occupy the outer city unopposed before his brief parley with the Milesian representatives. Alexander's ships now slipped across from Lade and blocked the entrance of the city harbour, anchored in line abreast to cut off the defenders from any hope of seaborne relief. Alexander battered his way into the city with his siege engines. Many Milesian citizens came out and surrendered, delivering themselves into Alexander's hands, but a few fought alongside the hired garrison. As the besiegers closed in, some of the garrison tried to save themselves by swimming, and 300 mercenaries reached a high rocky island not far out at sea; after capturing the city, Alexander assaulted this island with scaling ladders mounted on boats. He admired the desperate courage of the mercenaries, however, and took them into his service. This signalled a more lenient policy towards Greek mercenaries.

Persian ships were small with no space for provisions, so needed daily contact with supply bases. Alexander used this fact to deal with the Persian fleet waiting outside Miletus. He sent several units to drive the ships off when they came in for water and food along the coast from Miletus. They returned to Miletus, but still unable to get water they sailed away south. Alexander now decided to disband the bulk of his navy due to its cost, and instead capture the cities and ports on the coast from which the Persian navy might operate and re-supply. By denying access to safe harbours and supplies, Alexander could negate the power of the Persian fleet. Dismissing the fleet was a hazardous option in the short term, but Alexander was shrewd in his calculations and saw his strategy through to the end.

Halicarnassus

The most important city and supply base in the vicinity was Halicarnassus. Probably the strongest fortified city in Asia Minor, it was set in a natural amphitheatre, and well fortified with a number of strong citadels. The defences had been recently augmented with a 13.5m (44ft) wide and 7m (23ft) deep defensive ditch. Memnon of Rhodes, now given full command of the west by

DITCH-FILLING TORTOISES AT HALICARNASSUS

At Halicarnassus, Alexander needed to fill the newly cut ditch in order to bring up heavy machinery. To do this he used ditch-filling tortoises. According to Athenaeus, the ditch-filling tortoise could be rolled sideways as well as backwards and forwards, probably by briefly raising each corner in turn and changing the orientation of the axle. The large frame would have allowed a dozen or more men to congregate around each wheel assembly

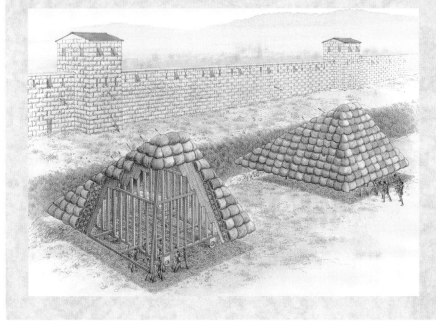

and take its weight. With the machine in position, there would have been ample space in the interior for men to work unhindered, evening out depressions in the ground. The gap between the rafters and the ground would have been sufficient to allow baskets of earth and rubble to be brought in at the rear, from where they could be dragged forwards for the task of ditch filling. (Brian Delf © Osprey Publishing Ltd)

Darius, had gathered the Greek mercenaries of the nearby cities to defend the fortress, and without the possibility of a naval blockade by Alexander, the city could be indefinitely supplied by sea. As the Persian fleet protected the seaward side, Alexander had to attack from the north-east or west, where the outer walls descended to fairly level ground. The sources minimize the difficulties of the siege; however, it lasted two months, and the city was eventually attacked and defended by every means known to the siegecraft of the ancient world. There was a delay for Alexander at the beginning as he waited for his siege machinery to be transported to Halicarnassus. After an unsuccessful attempt to take a sea port 12 miles away, Alexander put his men to filling the ditch in front of the walls, using ditch-filling tortoises. Once this was done the siege towers could roll across and into position. Catapults were used to keep the defenders back, while a section of wall was flattened. The defenders made defiant sallies at night, then built an interior containing wall around the breach. A night attack against the new wall, perhaps fuelled by drink, was quashed by the defenders, and for the one and only time in Alexander's career, he was forced to ask for a truce to recover his dead. Alexander continued to inflict heavy casualties and damage, and despite effective counter-attacks and the construction of inner walls to defend breaches created by the siege engines, Memnon and his commanders

The Myndus gate at Halicarnassus where Alexander first approached the major fortifications of the city. (Jona Lendering, Livius.org)

realized they could no longer hold the city. They therefore burned the outer fortifications and the city itself and withdrew to the inner citadels. The next day Alexander hurried into the city and allegedly razed it to the ground. This is probably an exaggeration, but he would have needed to clear space for his machines in order to besiege the remaining stronghold and to garrison the city. Realizing that the Persians would not be easily defeated, Alexander left a holding force of 3,000 troops under Ptolemy to continue the siege, and handed back government of the city to the ruling family of Mausolus, as represented by Mausolus' sister Ada. The citadel held out for another whole year, acting as a supply base for Persian ships. Alexander's perseverance at Halicarnassus cannot be doubted, but his success was mixed. Though he eventually took the city, it was not by assault but because the outnumbered Persian garrison made the strategic decision to forfeit the town and protect the supply base, a decision validated by the fact that the stronghold continued to function as a base for the Persian fleet for many more months.

After dealing with Halicarnassus, Alexander sent home on leave some of his soldiers who had been newly married before their departure, and also sent one of his officers on a recruiting drive to the Greek Peloponnese. That winter he led his men into Lycia to the east. Travelling through the mountainous region of Lycia he reached the coast at Phaselis. The army headed into Pamphylia via a specially engineered pass over Mount Climax while Alexander and a smaller group passed along the coast. After bivouacking in Aspendus, he campaigned against the rugged mountain towns of Pisidia before reaching Caelenae on the road to Gordion in the satrapy of Greater Phrygia. Reaching the city a few weeks later, Alexander probably met up with Parmenion and the Greek allies who had previously been sent to campaign against remnants of Persian forces on the Anatolian plateau. He was also rejoined by the Macedonians returned from leave and new levies from Macedon and the Greek mainland, 3,000 infantry and 300 horse, all Macedonian, with 200 Thessalian horse and 150 Peloponnesian mercenaries under their own commander. (See map on p.136.)

In Gordion, Alexander was shown the intricate knot that bound the yoke and shaft of the legendary king Gordias' ox-cart. The local inhabitants held that whoever should untie the knot would become king of Asia, a challenge Alexander could not resist. According to Plutarch, Alexander became frustrated at his inability to loosen the knot and resorted to hacking it free with his sword. However, another account attributed to Aristobulus says that Alexander merely pulled out the pin joining the yoke and shaft to reveal the loose ends which he then unravelled. In any event, his blushes were spared and the oracular prophecy appeared to be fulfilled.

9

THE BATTLE OF ISSUS

THE ROUTE TO ISSUS

During his stay at Gordion in the summer of 333, Alexander must have received the unwelcome news that Memnon, formerly holed up in Halicarnassus, was now freely operating against the islands of the western Aegean. These actions endangered his supply and communications line to Macedon and threatened to undo the work of the previous year's campaigning. However, in one of the most fortuitous events of Alexander's career, this potentially serious menace was removed when Memnon died of an illness during the siege of Mytilene. Furthermore, it appears that Darius then had a change of heart about carrying on operations behind Alexander's march and ordered his fleet, and the mercenaries operating with them, to return east with the intention of joining the army he was already collecting from all areas of the empire.

Alexander now marched his army south through Ancyra towards the Cilician Gates, which passed through the Taurus mountain range and into the fertile Aleian plain at the north-east corner of the Mediterranean. Alexander led a lightly armed highly mobile detachment against the Persian force under Arsames which was holding the Cilician Gates. Arsames was supported by an inadequate force and so did not offer battle, instead dropping back to burn Tarsus to prevent it falling into enemy hands, but Alexander was too quick, racing to the city in one day and capturing it before it could be burned.

While Alexander was taken ill after swimming in the freezing waters of the river Cydnus near Tarsus, Darius led his vast native army from Babylon to Sochi near the Amanus range east of the river Issus, where it encamped at the beginning of autumn 333. Ancient historians estimated its size at between 312,000 and 600,000, swelled by 30,000 Greek mercenaries. The figure of 600,000 is most probably extrapolated from the total possible troops available from the empire, perhaps because units of varying size from most provinces were present. The true figure is likely to be closer to the lower figure, and even if the grand total was 600,000, they would not have necessarily all have been present on the battlefield.

OPPOSITE
This 16th-century painting by Albrecht Altdorfer is a romantic depiction of the battle of Issus. (akg-images)

ALEXANDER'S ROUTE FROM GRANICUS TO ISSUS

After recovering from his illness, Alexander set out to find Darius. When Darius learned that Alexander was still advancing, his first thought was to remain in his present position. In the Syrian plain Persian numbers could be used to their best advantage. However, as the situation developed, opportunity for a master-stroke seemed to present itself, and Darius seized his chance.

Simon Chew

Persian national cavalry at Issus, based on figures from the Alexander sarcophagus. (Simon Chew © Osprey Publishing Ltd)

Alexander, having camped with his army at Mallus in Cilicia, passed through the coastal defile towards Syria and advanced on the small port of Issus, which had already been occupied by a detachment under Parmenion. A temporary base was established where the Macedonian sick and wounded were left. Alexander then marched southwards along the narrow low-lying coastal strip that separated the mountains from the sea, making for the Pillar of Jonah – the so-called Syrian or Assyrian Gates – south of modern Iskenderun, which gave access to Syria. Possibly he marched at night, as he had done in his swift advance on the Cilician Gates. But this time he led the main body of his army rather than a mobile striking force. Darius may have been deceived by the similarity to the Macedonian strategy in Cilicia. He decided to take a circuitous route in order to separate Alexander from his local base at Issus and isolate him from the main body of his army. This operation was made easier by a sudden violent storm, which halted Alexander at Myriandrus, on the coast near the Syrian Gates. Darius took advantage of a valley route just east of the Amanus mountain range and led his army north again, thus avoiding Alexander's army and bypassing the coastal strip. His manoeuvre, however, had the disadvantage that it brought the Persian army into the narrow lowland area between the sea and mountain, leaving the much wider Syrian plain where he could have deployed it more effectively.

ISSUS: ALEXANDER'S ADVANCE

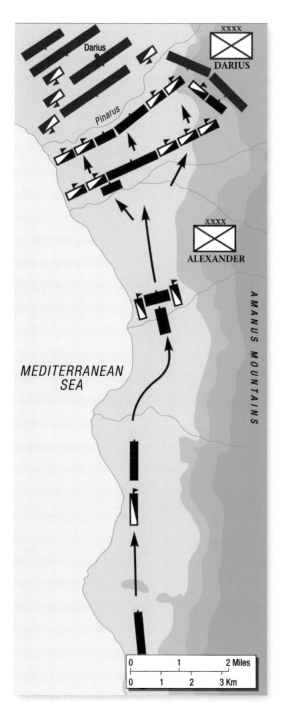

Alexander was certainly surprised at the move and sent a trireme up the Gulf of Issus to confirm the report that had reached him. In fact this new development came as a pleasant surprise: nothing could have pleased Alexander more than the prospect of fighting on a narrow battlefield. Darius on the other hand must soon have been disappointed. When he descended from the mountains near Issus, he found there no more than a hospital base. The Persians massacred many of the Macedonian sick and wounded and ensured a non-combatant role for others by cutting off their right hands. This was perhaps only to be expected – Darius could not leave any possible threat to his rear.

Meanwhile, Alexander with his entire army had wheeled about and was retracing his steps north. Darius perhaps still considered that he was trying to escape and accordingly advanced the Persian army south of Issus to block his way. When the two forces met, they were separated by the river Pinarus, a narrow torrent in which comparatively little water now flowed. Alexander faced north and Darius south.

In this position Darius sat astride the Macedonian lines of communication; however, by the same token, there was nothing to prevent Alexander from marching into Syria except the danger to his rear. But if the protagonists were to meet, it was advantageous for Alexander to fight in the restricted terrain of Cilicia, where the mountains and sea reduced the mobility of the enemy's troops and diluted his numerical superiority. Superficially, the situation was not very different from that at the Granicus. But the fact that the Granicus had been swollen with spring floods and that the Pinarus in late autumn now ran low meant that this battlefield was of another kind. Nevertheless, Alexander at once prepared to implement standard Macedonian tactics, with their effective co-ordination of infantry centre and cavalry wing. As he marched slowly and deliberately northward, the slender margin of coastal lowland widened slightly and he was able to deploy his army in stages, advancing at last in line of battle. He positioned himself with the Companion cavalry on the right wing, hard against the hills that restricted movement.

THE BATTLE

Darius had been persuaded that Alexander would not of his own accord seek a pitched battle, so he must now have been taken aback. He sent a force of 30,000 horsemen and 20,000 light infantry south of the Pinarus in order to buy time for the deployment of his own troops. He took up a defensive position, using the banks of the Pinarus as protection; where the riverbanks gave insufficient defence, he erected palisades.

Darius commanded 30,000 heavily armed Greek mercenaries, and these, with 60,000 Persian mercenary troops, now constituted the centre of his vanguard, in which position they would confront the Macedonian phalanx. Darius certainly had with him a much greater number of Asiatic foot-soldiers than his satraps had commanded at the Granicus. These he posted in large bodies in support of his forward troops, stringing them out in line as far as the narrow battlefield would permit – the sea was not far distant on his right, and the hills were on his left. In the centre of this array, Darius himself rode in his chariot. The central position was normal to Persian kings in battle, and from it they were able to dispatch orders in one direction or another to any part of their large armies. At Issus, the contours of the foothills were such that the Persian line actually curved forward, posing an encircling threat to Alexander's right wing. In the centre, the Asiatic infantry units, drawn up according to the various localities from which they had been recruited, were so densely mustered that they could not easily be brought into action.

In Alexander's advancing army, all troops left of the central phalanx were under the command of Parmenion. On the right, archers and lightly armed Agrianians were sent to dislodge the outflanking enemy on the foothills. This was done very easily, and Darius' infantry were quickly dispersed, seeking refuge higher up the mountains where they posed no threat; nevertheless, 300 of Alexander's horsemen were detailed to watch them.

At the last moment, Alexander withdrew two cavalry squadrons of his Companions from a comparatively central position and sent them to reinforce his right wing. This readjustment was no doubt much needed, for he had already moved the Thessalian cavalry from its original right-wing position to his left, where the Persians were massing. Indeed, Darius, as soon as he had been able to retract his cavalry screen from across the river, had concentrated these horsemen on his right against Parmenion. The plain here, close to the sea, no doubt seemed to favour cavalry combat. Both Alexander's late readjustments were made unobtrusively. The Thessalians rode around the rear of the advancing army, and

OVERLEAF

The Alexander mosaic is a Roman mosaic dating from about 200, from the House of the Faun in Pompeii. It is a copy of an earlier painting, possibly a contemporary apotheosis-painting of Alexander in battle against the Persians by Apelles. It is usually taken to show the battle of Issus, although some scholars now think it may show Gaugamela. Alexander is shown sweeping into battle at the left on his horse Bucephalus, focussed on Darius. Darius is shown in a chariot, desperately commanding his charioteer to flee the battle. His hand is stretched out, either as a mute gesture to Alexander, or possibly after throwing a javelin. His charioteer whips the horses as he tries to obey. (akg-images)

the Companion cavalry, warned that the enemy must not observe them, apparently found cover among the spurs that extended seaward from the inland foothills.

Alexander continued his slow advance, making sure that the whole army preserved a level front, until he was within missile range of the Persian lines. He then suddenly launched his attack on the right, personally leading his Companions across the riverbed and driving back the enemy opposite him. (That Alexander, in imitation of Cyrus at Cunaxa, charged directly at the Persian centre, where Darius himself was positioned, may be more than mere fiction. It seems to have been common in this period that leaders felt they had to seek each other out. If the story is true, this must have occurred in the second phase of the battle.) As happened often in ancient battles, the right wing's success carried it forward and out of touch with the centre. The steep and unequal banks of the river, not to mention Darius' stockades, here made it particularly difficult for the phalangites to keep abreast of each other, let alone with Alexander and his cavalry.

Into the gap that had opened between Alexander's cavalry and the Macedonian phalanx, Darius' Greek mercenaries now penetrated. This meant they could soon be in a position to force the phalangites back into the river and threaten from the rear the Macedonian cavalry that had routed the Persian left. It may be that the gap in the Macedonian line had opened at this point partly as a result of Alexander's last-minute decision to reinforce his right-wing cavalry at

Oxathres at Issus?

The sources say that the elite Persian cavalry were drawn up around the king at Issus. During the battle, Oxathres, the brother of Darius, put his cavalry between Alexander and Darius' chariot. Oxathres fought valiantly, but eventually his regiment was broken and Darius was forced to abandon his chariot and flee. It has been suggested that the figure in front of Darius on the mosaic is Oxathres. If this is correct, then Oxathres must wear the uniform of the commander of the elite cavalry regiment of the whole Persian Empire. He wears a tunic of either saffron, or cloth of gold edged in purple, and a cloak with a purple border. His horse is presumably a Nisean. (Simon Chew © Osprey Publishing Ltd)

Issus: The turn of the tide

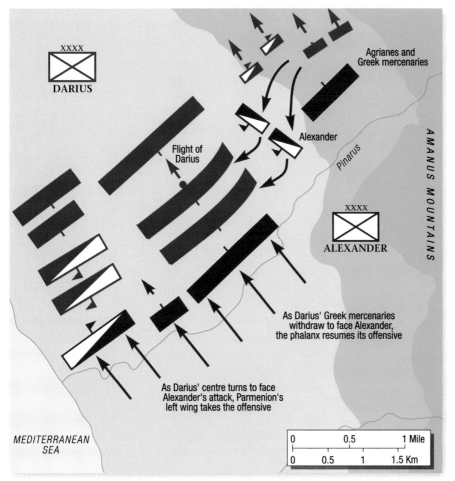

DARIUS

Agrianes and
Greek mercenaries

Alexander

Flight of
Darius

Pinarus

AMANUS MOUNTAINS

ALEXANDER

As Darius' Greek mercenaries
withdraw to face Alexander,
the phalanx resumes its offensive

As Darius' centre turns to face
Alexander's attack, Parmenion's
left wing takes the offensive

MEDITERRANEAN
SEA

| 0 | 0.5 | 1 Mile |
| 0 | 0.5 | 1 | 1.5 Km |

the expense of his centre. The phalangites took heavy casualties, including Ptolemy son of Seleucus, but they fought on. They turned back the dangerous counter-attack and managed to contain the salient that had developed on their right until Alexander was able to come to their aid.

Having put the Persian left to flight, Alexander now wheeled to his own left, slamming into the Greek mercenaries and destroying their formation, forcing them to retreat from the river or cutting them down where they stood. The Macedonian phalanx was then able to advance once more, destroying those infantry who had survived the impact of Alexander's cavalry.

Darius' army came closer to success on its right, against the Macedonian left wing where Parmenion was in command. Here, on the beach and the adjacent lowland plain, an overwhelming superiority in cavalry numbers could most obviously be turned to advantage. Whether the Persian right-wing cavalry on this occasion took its orders directly from Darius is not clear, but in any case its officers in this sector were impatient of their purely defensive role, and the Persian horsemen soon surged across the river to attack the Thessalian cavalry ranged against them. Desperate fighting took place, but when the Persian right wing saw that the centre and left of the army had collapsed, and that they were in danger of encirclement, they took to flight. Perversely their bid for safety caused them to suffer more grievously as the Thessalians pursued their confused retreat.

The rout of Darius' army in this sector soon became catastrophic. Many of the fugitives were heavily armed and equipped horsemen. Either they were encumbered in their flight or, discarding their weapons, were helpless when overtaken. As they converged in mountain defiles amid increasing panic, horses often fell with their riders, and many men were trampled to death by those who pressed on from behind. Parmenion's pursuing cavalry did not relax its pressure, and the fleeing Persian infantry, who had been posted behind their own cavalry, now suffered equally with the horsemen.

Darius did not wait long enough to see the defeat of his right wing. The moment that his left had crumpled before Alexander's onslaught, he had taken to flight in his chariot, which carried him swiftly enough as long as the ground was level. But when he found himself amid the rocky gorges that lay eastward and northward, he abandoned his chariot together with weapons and items of clothing, and mounted a horse to make good his escape. It is reported that the horses that drew his chariot had been wounded and become unmanageable and that the horse he ultimately mounted had been led behind his chariot for just such an emergency. In any case, nightfall saved the Persian king from Alexander's pursuit, and all that rewarded the Macedonian king was the capture of Darius' abandoned chariot and equipment.

THE OUTCOME OF THE BATTLE

Ancient sources tell us of 100,000 dead or captured Persian infantry at Issus, and of 10,000 cavalry casualties. This seems an inordinately high number, and must be taken as another example of inflated enemy losses by Alexander's historians. However, casualties were high for the Persian army. It would seem likely that more were killed in the rout that followed the battle than in the actual course of the fighting, not uncommon in ancient warfare. Several high-ranking Persians, more resolute than Darius himself, were killed in the battle. Some of them were survivors from the Granicus. By contrast, Alexander's losses were slight. But we have only Macedonian propaganda to go by, and stories like the

THE AFTERMATH OF BATTLE

Despite unequivocal successes against Persia, victory in battle always came at a cost, especially for the infantrymen, whose casualties were almost always far greater that those of the cavalry. The infantry casualties for Alexander's battles were most likely deflated for purposes of propaganda. For example, it was reported that about 300 infantrymen were killed at Issus, although the hard fighting against the Greek mercenaries in the centre makes this number risible. An anonymous historical papyrus found at Oxyrhynchus in Egypt gives a more reasonable figure of 1,000 infantry and 200 cavalry killed. It is unknown how many of these were pezhetairoi or hypaspists, and it is impossible to estimate how many of the wounded either died later, were invalided home or left behind as garrison troops. The recovery of the dead and wounded from the battlefield was a gruesome scene to confront a warrior. Here, two men carry a corpse to a wagon. Others support and console a wounded comrade, while some men pick through the debris, salvaging usable weapons or despoiling the dead. (Christa Hook © Osprey Publishing Ltd)

sensational tale of Alexander struggling with Darius in person must be treated with caution.

Again at Issus, Alexander used the shock hammer blow of the cavalry to crack open the enemy. Although his movement of the troops from the centre allowed a gap to develop, putting pressure on the phalanx, his angled charge from the right wing into the left wing of Darius' army, then turning into the centre and following up the advantage, was perfectly executed. The difficulties experienced by Parmenion on the left wing against superior numbers could have told if the story had been different elsewhere on the battlefield, but even had the Persian right not fled, the rest of the Macedonian army could have dealt with them after the left and centre had been dealt with. Alexander's choice of battlefield had helped him to negate Darius' superior numbers, but it was his decisive leadership that took the battle.

The Macedonian army quickly occupied the Persian camp, where they found and imprisoned the mother, wife and children of Darius himself. Alexander treated the royal ladies with great chivalry, reassuring them that Darius was not dead, and telling them that he had no personal grievance against him, but fought merely in pursuit of a legitimate political claim – the control of Asia.

Money had also been left behind. Arrian refers casually to 'no more than 3,000 talents', but he was making comparison with the much greater spoils found at Damascus. There was, at Issus, certainly enough to pay and supply Darius' huge field army through the expected campaign.

Although wounded in the leg by a sword-thrust, Alexander attended to the

This section of the Alexander sarcophagus shows Alexander fighting at Issus. He is mounted and wearing a lionskin on his head. It has been proposed that a second mounted Macedonian near the centre is Hephaestion, and a third is often identified as Perdiccas. (akg-images/Erich Lessing)

honourable burial of the dead and visited all his wounded men, offering consolation and congratulation as it was due, and conferring rewards on those who had merited them in the battle.

After the defeat at Issus, Damascus fell into the hands of Parmenion. The amount of treasure and the importance of the individuals captured there reveals that the city was not merely a convenient place to deposit the treasures and non-combatants, but that Darius had intended to move his base of operations forward. He clearly did not expect to be routed in a single engagement and forced to seek refuge in the centre of the empire.

Meanwhile Darius continued his flight eastward. He had been joined by other fugitives to the number of about 4,000, and his main intention was to put the river Euphrates between himself and Alexander as soon as possible. Some 8,000 Greek troops, who had previously deserted from Alexander to Darius, escaped westward. Reaching the Phoenician coast at Tripolis near Mount Lebanon, they found the ships that had originally brought them from Lesbos. Burning the surplus ships to prevent pursuit, some sailed to Egypt via Cyprus and others probably took service with King Agis of Sparta.

Considering the decisive nature of Alexander's victory and the scale of the forces involved, the actual duration of the fighting must have been remarkably short. The battle was fought on a November day, yet there seems to have been daylight enough for a long and eventful pursuit of the defeated army. In the morning, Alexander had advanced deliberately and slowly towards the Persian positions, and there had been time for both sides to observe each other and re-order their battle lines accordingly. The time taken by the battle itself cannot have been more than a few hours.

For Alexander the victory – particularly in the aftermath of Memnon's death – provided the opportunity of pushing ahead with the conquest and leaving his newly appointed satraps to deal with the continued resistance in Asia Minor. Antigonus Monophthalmos, a certain Ptolemy (perhaps even a kinsman of Antigonus) and Balacrus dealt effectively with what Persian forces remained behind.

AFTER ISSUS

On the death of Memnon, the Persian admirals Pharnabazus and Autophradates had taken over command of Darius' Aegean fleet and continued to base themselves at Chios. They also continued to implement Memnon's strategy, which had been to erode Macedonian power in the Greek mainland and islands while Alexander was occupied with a strategy of eastward conquest. Meanwhile in Greece, King Agis of Sparta was thinking along the same lines as the Persians and hoped to combine his efforts with theirs. He sailed with a single trireme to meet Pharnabazus on the island of Siphnos in the Cyclades, his objective being to obtain a subsidy of ships and money from the Persians in support of a war against Antipater in Greece.

The news of Issus reached Agis and the Persian commanders precisely as they were conferring in Siphnos. Pharnabazus hastened back to Chios. Indeed, there was a danger that all along the east Aegean seaboard pro-Macedonian elements might take heart at Alexander's victory and throw off Persian control. In the circumstances, Agis certainly did not receive the contribution he had hoped for: Autophradates gave him just ten ships and 30 talents of silver. These he sent to his brother Agesilaus, with instructions that the rowers should be paid in full and the flotilla dispatched to Crete, there to establish an anti-Macedonian presence. This operation was successfully carried out. Some months later Agis was joined by some of the Greek mercenaries who had opposed Alexander at Issus. However, he received no support from Athens. In the Peloponnese several cities rallied to Sparta's call, but Messene, Argos and Megalopolis – all Sparta's traditional enemies – were in no mind to oppose the Macedonians. Agis' problem was thus one of numbers, and when he was at last confronted before the walls of a hostile Megalopolis by Antipater's Macedonian relief force, he was overwhelmed by an army twice as large as his own. He himself died heroically, fighting on his knees after a leg wound made it impossible for him to stand.

At about the same time, there was some revival of the Persian war effort in the interior of Asia Minor. Darius' officers in Paphlagonia and Cappadocia managed to raise local levies from these provinces, and they were joined by fugitives from Issus, many of whom had made their way northward. These forces now threatened Antigonus, the commander to whom Alexander had entrusted Phrygia. Antigonus was all the more vulnerable because he had drafted troops to support Alexander's own operations farther east and the Phrygian garrison forces were now depleted. However, when the clash came, Antigonus vanquished the newly constituted Persian army in three separate engagements. Again, there was proof that Alexander had left the right man to fight the battles he left in his wake, and he himself was never obliged to deviate from his original plan as he led his forces south through Syria and Palestine.

At Damascus, Alexander captured a number of noble Persian ladies, from the families of Darius' officers, who had been quartered there before the battle of Issus. He treated them with scrupulous detachment, with only one exception: Barsine, the widow of Memnon, herself a daughter of a Persian nobleman, became his mistress, and she later bore him a son, whom he called Heracles in honour of his claimed ancestor.

Having reached the other side of the Euphrates, Darius resorted to diplomacy, sending letters to Alexander offering money and territory in exchange for his

A wounded Foot Companion is supported by a servant, as a senior soldier of the Foot Companions covers their withdrawal from the battle. (Angus McBride © Osprey Publishing Ltd)

kinfolk. But the exchanges between the two kings demonstrated merely the Persian king's refusal to recognize the gravity of the danger to the empire. Furthermore, Darius persisted in treating Alexander as an upstart, an inferior who could, he thought, be bought off with the cession of Asia Minor and 10,000 talents. But Alexander held the trump cards and was not prepared to fold when diplomacy offered less than he had obtained by conquest. Negotiations continued for almost two years, with an escalation of the terms – Darius was eventually to offer Asia west of the Euphrates, 30,000 talents and the hand of his daughter in marriage – but Persian concessions failed to keep pace with Macedonian conquests. Darius no longer had the authority to dispose of Alexander's 'spear-won land'.

PHOENICIA AND EGYPT

In Phoenicia, the news of Issus led to defection on a large scale. Representatives of the coastal cities brought Alexander crowns of gold to symbolize their surrender: Aradus, Marathus and Byblus submitted in short order. And, although the cities themselves received good treatment from the conqueror, there were some rulers, like Straton of Sidon, who despite their surrender were deposed. It appears that the Sidonians, who now welcomed Alexander as a 'liberator' – for Artaxerxes III had put down an insurrection in the city with the utmost brutality – were not inclined to retain in power a man with a lengthy record of collaboration with the Persians. According to the tradition, Alexander allowed his best friend Hephaestion to select a new king: he found a member of the royal house, Abdalonymus, reduced by poverty to working as a gardener, and upon him he bestowed the crown.

Possession of Phoenicia was critical for the survival of the Persian fleet. Alexander had abandoned attempts at defeating the Persian navy at sea and had disbanded the Macedonian fleet. Not only was the Persian fleet numerically superior, having recruited even pirate crews, but the Macedonian ships and sailors were of inferior quality; and, to make matters worse, the Greek naval powers could not be fully trusted. It was better to deprive the Persian navy of its bases and thereby reduce its power, without running the risk of a naval disaster that might turn the tide of the war and would almost certainly tarnish Alexander's reputation as an invincible foe. As it was, in attempts to guard and threaten various points in the Aegean simultaneously, the Persians split their forces too much. Units of the Persian navy that tried to recover command of the Hellespont were defeated by Alexander's fleet under the Macedonian officers Hegelochus and Amphoterus. Miletus was retaken by the Macedonians, and Pharnabazus himself was captured at Chios. The pirate crews that the Persians had enlisted were arrested and executed.

Alexander's naval strategy worked. As the inhabitants and governments of each region surrendered to him, their naval contingents abandoned the Persian cause. The Phoenicians found themselves in an awkward position, since large numbers of their citizens, including many of their local dynasts, served with the

SIEGE WARFARE

The history of siege warfare is characterized by alternating periods when defensive or offensive techniques dominate. In the Classical period defence had almost total supremacy. Cities were ringed by colossal fortifications which were all but impregnable. Towns did surrender in terror at the approach of their enemy, but more often, the townsfolk barred the gates and hoped that their fortifications would discourage the aggressor.

Under these circumstances, there were five courses of action available to the besieger. He could attempt to go over the fortifications, using ladders or embankments. He could break through the defences using battering rams, or make the walls collapse by digging beneath them. Thirdly, tunnels could be dug underneath the walls. This was dangerous, but if executed properly would give the attackers the advantage of surprise. If the attacker failed in these methods, or lacked the means to attempt them, he might threaten the townsfolk with starvation by blockading their supply routes. This was a far less dangerous strategy, but depending on the resources of the town and totality of the blockade, it could drag on indefinitely. The last option was to gain access by treachery or trickery. The standard form of trickery involved the conspicuous departure of the besieging forces in apparent abandonment of the operation. The relieved townsfolk would then be caught off guard by a concealed strike force left behind. This force would ideally infiltrate the town just as the besieging force returned.

The principal siege weapon was the battering ram, able to breach a wall or gate if a weak point could be found, but the party operating the ram was always exposed to attack, and risked prohibitive casualties. An army might try to capture a city by escalade, but such attempts could be extremely costly if the defender was well prepared. Realistically, an invading army had little chance of taking the enemy city by storm. To take a city by investment the invader had to sit outside its walls for months, if not years, until the food ran out. The enemy city had to be circumvallated by encircling it with a ditch and rampart; then the rampart had to be constantly manned to prevent food entering the city. A somewhat quicker method was to construct a siege-mound. The first siege-mound known within the Aegean area was one constructed by the Lydian king Alyattes against Smyrna around 600. The Persians made effective use of siege-mounds to reduce many fortified cities to their rule. However, both Lydia and Persia were rich and populous empires that could afford the resources necessary to construct siege-mounds, and field the considerable army necessary for a suitable length of time, which remained beyond the capacity of most Greek states.

The usual goal of an offensive campaign was to force the defender into battle in the open as quickly as possible. The key problem was to discourage him from retiring behind the safety of his city walls with his livestock. The so-called 'strategy of devastation' was developed to force the defender out of his city. When an invader reached the plain of the enemy state – its prime agricultural asset – he sought to do as much damage as possible. For maximum effect, cities were usually invaded immediately before the harvest season, when the crops were still in the fields. The invader did his best to spoil the crops, or to gather them in for his own use. He would also damage fruit and olive trees. If the defender did not accept terms, he would be forced outside his city walls to fight for his crops. If he chose to fight, the action would unfold as a hoplite battle, and took place on the level plains near the city. If he chose not to fight then the invader would invade again the next year, and subsequent years, in the hope that the cumulative damage caused to the agricultural infrastructure would either force the defender out to fight, or force him to eat his seed corn, which would ultimately result in starvation. Of course, if political rivalry existed within the town, one or other faction might be persuaded to grant the besieger access, thus saving time and avoiding unnecessary losses.

The Greeks realized the full potential of mechanized siege warfare with the advent of Philip II. Maintaining a siege train was expensive, and possessing one was only necessary if there was intention to besiege many cities, which before Macedonian imperialism was unusual. Also, it may be that Philip's full-time professional army was willing to assault walls that would have daunted the citizen militias of the previous century. More importantly, the professional character of the Macedonian army allowed for the incorporation of specialized craftsmen and engineers, without whom Alexander would have had no siege train.

In his *Third Philippic*, Demosthenes, the great Athenian orator, railed against the Macedonian style of warfare: fighting was no longer a fair and open contest reserved for a summer's day; on the contrary, Philip might arrive outside a town at any time of year, set up his machinery, and lay siege.

Philip was particularly associated in the ancient consciousness with the development of siege machinery. It has been suggested that in around 350, he established permanent workshops for mechanical engineering, but that inadequacies were shown up during the campaign of 340, and a new chief engineer, Polyidus the Thessalian, was appointed for the siege of Byzantium, where he was linked with the building of a giant siege tower.

Ancient writers preserve a long (but by no means exhaustive) list of Philip's conquests by siege: Amphipolis in 357, Pydna and Potidea in 356, Methone in 354, Pherae and Pagasae in 352, Stageira in 349, Olynthus in 348, Halus in 347, Pandosia, Bucheta and Elataea in 342, not to mention the 32 Thracian towns that he razed to the ground. Methone was certainly taken by assault, for it was here that Philip was struck in the eye by an arrow. Demosthenes alleged treachery at both Amphipolis and Pydna. The king certainly had a reputation for bribery: the towns of Mecyberna and Torone were also recorded as being taken by treachery, and there were probably more. However, Philip did not always enjoy success. In 340, his siege of Perinthus ended in miserable failure, despite the deployment of a full siege train, including 80-cubit (37m) siege towers, battering rams, mining operations, and the use of arrow-firing catapults. However, with Persian and Byzantine aid bolstering the Perinthian defence, Philip was soon bogged down in an impossible siege. Furthermore, his simultaneous strike on Byzantium, gambling that it had been left undefended, simply stirred up enmity among the neighbouring Greek communities, and Philip had to abandon both sieges.

Persian fleet. These rulers especially found it preferable to surrender to Alexander in the hope of retaining their power rather than remain loyal to Darius. By contrast, the inland Syrians were more inclined to stay with Darius, and we find them joining their former satrap, Mazaeus, in the army that faced Alexander again in 331 at Gaugamela.

TYRE

Whereas the northern Phoenician cities had capitulated on the news of Alexander's approach, Tyre resisted the king's request to make sacrifices to Heracles (Melqart) within their city. This was, of course, a transparent ploy to gain control of the place. But the Tyrians could afford to be defiant, or at least so they thought, for about half a mile (0.8km) of sea separated them from the Macedonian army, and the city fathers responded that Alexander was welcome to sacrifice to Heracles at 'Old Tyre', which was situated on the mainland. Furthermore, there was the expectation – vain, as it turned out – of aid from their north African colony, Carthage. Neither grand strategy nor Alexander's reputation, however, could allow the young king to bypass the city. The whole purpose of Alexander's present campaign was to leave no possible Persian base in his rear before marching eastward to resume hostilities with Darius. He could make no exceptions, especially in the case of a powerful naval centre like Tyre. The defences of the city appeared impregnable, but Alexander already seems to have regarded himself as invincible and was certainly so considered by the men who followed him.

Alexander realized that taking an island city would be no easy matter, and that a lengthy siege would buy valuable time for his enemy. Hence, he sent heralds into the city in the hope of persuading the Tyrians to surrender. But the diplomatic approaches were rebuffed, and the heralds executed and thrown into the sea.

Alexander therefore decided to build a mole from the mainland to the island across the narrow water that separated them. The building of Alexander's causeway at first proceeded briskly. The water near the mainland was shallow and the bottom muddy, and building material in the form of rock and timber was easily obtainable. Stakes were soon driven into the mud, which also made good binding material for the stone blocks above. But further out the sea became suddenly deep, and close to the island it reached a depth of three fathoms (18ft/5.5m). The builders' task here became both difficult and dangerous: not only had they to contend with the deep water but they were now within missile range of the city walls. Furthermore, the Tyrians were able to row their galleys in from the sea and harass them, making work almost impossible.

To these tactics Alexander replied by building two towers on the mole, covering their wooden structures with hides to give protection against missiles

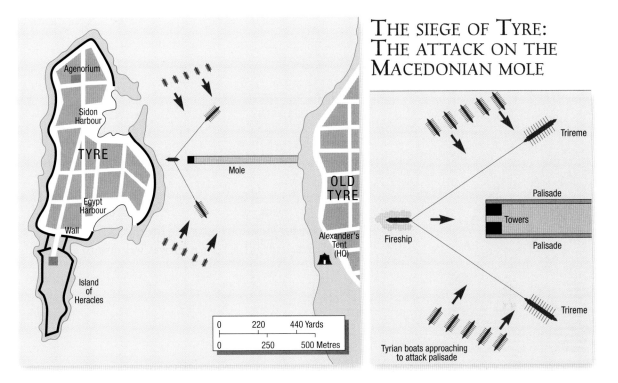

THE SIEGE OF TYRE: THE ATTACK ON THE MACEDONIAN MOLE

and render the wood less vulnerable to incendiary attack. He mounted artillery catapults in the tower and was thus able to retaliate against the raids of enemy ships by counterblasts of heavy missiles. The Tyrians then realized that they must at all cost destroy the towers, and they resorted to the use of a fire-ship. They made ready a large vessel, which had been a horse transport, filling it with wood shavings, chips, pitch, sulphur and every combustible material that they could lay hands on. Double yard-arms were fixed to the masts, and on these were hung cauldrons of an oily substance that could be relied upon to feed the flames. The fire-ship was also ballasted at the stern end in such a way as to tilt the prow upward over the edge of the mole and close to the foot of the towers. It was then towed in by triremes, and the crew that had manned the old hulk easily swam away when she was alight.

The result was what had been hoped – the towers were soon ablaze. Other Tyrian galleys cruised close to the mole, and put down a barrage of missiles, which prevented Alexander's fire-fighters approaching the towers. A sally was also launched from the city in small boats. Temporary landings were made on the mole, and its defensive palisades were torn down. Artillery catapults that had escaped the havoc wrought by the fire-ship were additionally set on fire by the daring raiders.

When the fire-ship had been grounded on the mole according to plan and the towers set alight, the triremes that had grounded it lay close to the mole and attacked Alexander's fire-fighters with missiles. As soon as the towers were on fire other Tyrians sallied out in boats and destroyed the palisades on the mole.

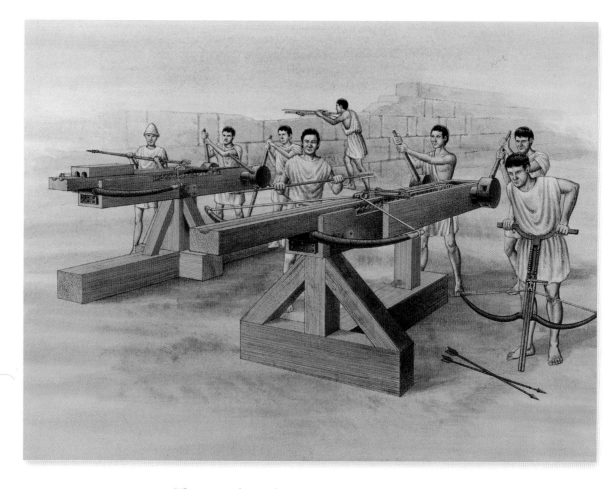

This was obviously a great set-back for Alexander, but as a strategist he possessed an indefatigable patience, which contrasted strongly with the fierce impetuosity of his tactics in battle. He now gave orders that work should begin again on the mole, although the ancient sources diverge on this matter, and it is not certain whether Alexander began a new one, approaching the city from a different angle, or merely widened the existing one. It seems more likely that he had the original mole widened to accommodate more towers. While the work was being carried out, he took with him a contingent of hypaspists and Agrianian light troops and marched back to the friendly Phoenicians of Sidon, where he had left his own triremes. He needed a fleet, for without superiority at sea, Tyre could not be taken.

The naval commanders of Aradus and Byblus now joined Alexander, as did ten triremes from Rhodes, 13 ships from the cities of the Lycian and Cilician coasts, and a 50-oared galley from Macedon itself. The massive desertion of the

Phoenicians, with 80 ships, had its repercussions in Cyprus, whose kings were also anxious to be on the winning side. A combined Cyprian fleet of 120 ships soon sailed to Sidon and swelled Alexander's already growing fleet as it lay there in readiness. This naval 'windfall' may be considered a great stroke of good fortune, though of course the actions of the cities were motivated by Alexander's resounding victory at Issus. He was in any case happy to overlook his new allies' earlier hostility towards him.

Naval operations

While the construction of his artillery engines was being completed, Alexander made a foray into Arabian territory inland, and after a ten-day demonstration of strength, in which he used a few cavalry squadrons with hypaspists and Agrianians, he received the submission of the people in this area. He perhaps regarded the raid as a military training exercise, but in any case it fitted well with his general strategy of leaving no active enemy in his rear.

On his return from this expedition, he found that Cleander, the son of Polemocrates, whom he had sent to Greece to recruit mercenaries, had returned with a body of 4,000 Peloponnesian troops. He was thus well prepared for a new confrontation with the Tyrians, and in terms of naval strength he now had the upper hand. The Tyrians did not realize until he was ready for battle that his fleet had been dramatically increased by the Phoenician and Cyprian contingents.

Leading his fleet from a warship on their right wing, he had hoped at first to tempt the Tyrians to a naval engagement in open sea. He had posted marines on the decks of his galleys and he was prepared either for boarding or ramming tactics. However, when they recognized the superiority of the numbers ranged against them the Tyrians prudently avoided this and concentrated merely on holding the entrance of their harbours in the face of the oncoming enemy; any fighting would then be in narrow waters, where Alexander's numbers could not be deployed to advantage.

The two harbours of the island faced north and south respectively, one towards Sidon, the other towards Egypt. Seeing their entrances heavily defended, Alexander did not at once try to force an entry. The mouth of the north harbour, as he approached, was blocked by triremes moored bow-on to him. But his Phoenician galleys sank three of the enemy ships that were anchored in a slightly exposed position, ramming them bow-on. The crews escaped easily enough, swimming back to the friendly territory of the island.

After this brief encounter, Alexander berthed his ships along the mainland shore and encamped on the adjacent land at a point where the mole gave some protection from the weather. His own headquarters were southwards, looking

Several variations of the gastraphetes were probably already known by the early years of the 4th century. The gastraphetes was an earlier mechanical weapon than the catapult. It was powered by a large composite bow, which consisted of a wooden core sandwiched between a layer of horn and a layer of sinew. When the bow was bent, prior to firing the shot, the sinew on the outer side of the bow stretched, while the horn along the belly was compressed. On release, each element snapped back to its original state, powerfully propelling the arrow forwards. Besides the original hand-held gastraphetes, the machines shown are the 'mountain' version, presumably for use over rugged terrain, and the twin-bore version, both created by Zopyrus of Tarentum. (Brian Delf © Osprey Publishing Ltd)

1. *120 Cyprian ships under Andromachus.*

2. *80 Phoenician ships plus 23 from Rhodes, Lycia, Soli and Mallus, and one Macedonian penteconter (50-oared ship).*

3. *Tyrian ships.*

THE SIEGE OF TYRE: ALEXANDER'S BLOCKADE

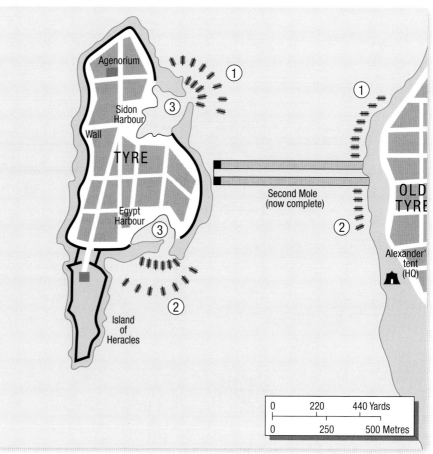

towards the island's southern harbour. He ordered the Cyprian fleet to blockade the north side of the island and the Phoenicians the south.

He had meanwhile recruited a large number of engineers both from Cyprus and the Phoenician coast. The construction of siege engines had proceeded swiftly, and these were installed on the extremity of the mole as well as on the besieging ships, both transports and slow triremes, which Alexander had caused to be anchored all around the city preparatory to bombarding the high walls. These walls are reported as being 150ft (46m) high on the side facing the mole. Even assuming that this refers to the height of the towers rather than the curtain wall, the figure seems exaggerated; the Mausoleum at Halicarnassus, one of the seven wonders of the ancient world, was only 134ft (41m) high. The masonry opposite the mole was massive, consisting of large mortared stone blocks. On top of these, the

ALEXANDER'S SIEGE OF TYRE

Alexander allegedly mobilized tens of thousands of men to construct the causeway, 2 plethra (62m) wide and 4 stades (740m) long. Building materials came from the demolition of the old town on the mainland, and timber was brought from the mountains of Lebanon; entire trees and rocks were added to build up the structure. Wicker screens protected the workmen, and two siege towers were erected so that missile troops could provide covering fire. The Tyrians responded with a fire-ship, a large transport vessel filled with combustible material and guided under sail against the causeway; cauldrons slung from the yard-arms were rigged to set the boat ablaze when it reached its goal. In the event, considerable damage was done, including the destruction of the siege towers, but Alexander's engineers set to work again and the causeway was finally completed.

Nothing now remains of the town fortifications, but Arrian's claim that the walls were 150ft (46m) high is unlikely. Both Diodorus Siculus and Curtius indicate that the walls were well furnished with arrow-firing catapults, and the city engineers had contrived all sorts of devices to counter the Macedonians. There were screens of stretched hides to protect the defenders, and a screen, padded with seaweed, was later lowered over the battlements to absorb the impact of flying stones. Also illustrated is an example of the 'iron hand' or harpax, used to grab individual men or machines. (Adam Hook © Osprey Publishing Ltd)

THE SIEGE OF TYRE: THE TYRIAN SALLY

Midday: Alexander's ships at anchor and almost unmanned.

1. *Tyrian galleys screened by ships in the harbour mouth.*
2. *Three Cyprian ships sunk.*
3. *Other Cyprian ships driven ashore for breaking up.*
4. *Approach of Alexander. The Tyrian ships raced for safety but were mostly rammed by Alexander's flotilla (five triremes and a few quinqueremes) before they could reach the harbour.*

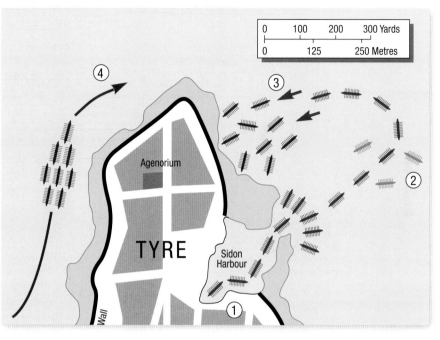

Tyrians now built wooden towers in order that they might increase their height advantage, and they showered down missiles of every kind, including fire-darts, on the besieging ships. As a further device, the Tyrians piled rocks in the sea under their walls, and this kept Alexander's vessels at a distance. As far as possible, Alexander hauled away the rocks, but this work had to be carried on from ships anchored nearby. The Tyrians accordingly armour-plated some of their triremes and ran in against the anchored siege vessels, cutting their moorings. Alexander retaliated by armouring some of his light, 30-oared ships, and obstructing the enemy triremes. The Tyrians then sent down divers to cut the mooring cables, so Alexander replaced these ropes with chains. On the landward side, his men also managed to throw out ropes from the mole and noose some of the rocks that had been dumped on the seabed. These rocks were then winched out and slung into deep water where they created no danger. The approach to the wall was thus at last clear, and Alexander's ships were able to lie under it.

The Tyrians, now increasingly conscious of their danger, realised that they had to challenge the blockading navy in some action at sea, and they decided to attack the Cyprian contingent, choosing the hour of the midday heat when the vigilance of the besiegers was relaxed, and Alexander himself had retired to his tent to rest. The Tyrians manned three quinqueremes, three quadriremes and seven triremes with picked crews and the best-armed fighting complements they could muster. The sails of the Tyrian ships in the harbour were used to screen their preparations, and the men went aboard unobserved by enemy watchers at sea or on land. The Tyrian flotilla now glided out of the north harbour in line ahead and at an angle where it was still unperceived by the enemy. On board, dead silence was maintained – even the boatswains did not call the stroke to the rowers. Only when they came within sight of the Cyprians did they permit themselves the ordinary words of command and break out into battle-cries. They then achieved a formidable surprise attack. At the first onslaught, they rammed and sank the quinqueremes of the Cyprian king Pnytagoras, as well as those of Androcles and Pasicrates – from the Cypriot cities of Amathus and Curion respectively. Other Cyprian ships were forced ashore and broken up. Indeed, the attack had been made when most of the anchored Cyprian fleet was unmanned.

However, the Tyrians were not entirely fortunate. It so happened that on this day Alexander had not taken his usual siesta, but returned almost immediately to the ships. Quickly aware of the enemy sally, he reacted at once and ordered men aboard. The first ships that were manned were commanded to block the south harbour mouth and to ensure that no further sortie was made from that quarter. He then put out with a few quinqueremes and five triremes and sailed around the city to challenge those of the enemy who had already broken out.

The Tyrian watchers on the battlements, observing Alexander's moves, tried to warn their comrades on the sea and nearby shore, but the seamen were deafened by the din of their own wrecking operations. When they understood what was happening it was too late – only a few of their ships made it back to harbour in time. The majority were rammed and disabled. A quinquereme and a quadrireme were captured by Alexander's men. Human casualties, however, were not many, for the Tyrian crews, as often happened in ancient sea fights, saved themselves by swimming.

The breaching of the wall

The walls of Tyre were now closely surrounded, and even the defenders' sally had been a costly and limited success. However, the walls themselves were still a formidable obstacle. In the north, the Greek contingent towed up siege engines, but the solidity of the walls defied their efforts. In the south, a part of the wall was slightly shaken, and a small breach was made, into which gangways were tentatively thrown. But the Macedonian assault party that tried to use the gangways was easily repulsed by the Tyrians.

However, after a three-day interval, with calmer weather prevailing, more siege engines were towed up to the same spot, and the breach was enlarged. Two ships

THE SIEGE OF TYRE: THE FINAL ASSAULT

1. *Mole completed. Siege engines made no impression on such strong defences.*
2. *Siege engines mounted on ships.*
3. *Harbour mouths defended by Tyrian ships and blockaded by Alexander's fleet.*
4. *Diversionary tactics. Ships were beached under the walls for beaching operations, or lay close and launched missiles.*
5. *Probing attacks.*
6. *Eventual breach.*

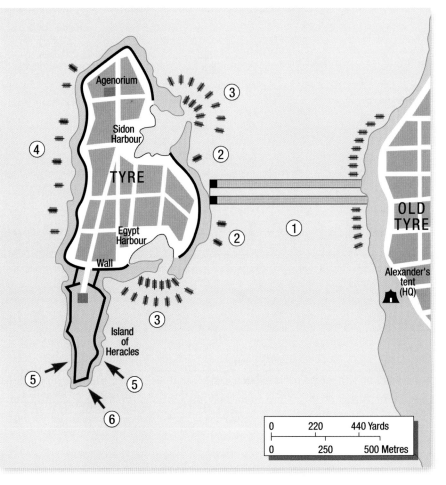

carrying gangways then approached, under the command of Admetus and Coenus respectively, and the way was open for a fresh assault. This was led by Alexander's best troops. The hypaspists were commanded by Admetus, who distinguished himself by valour in the ensuing action. The pezhetairoi were led by Coenus, who in the future was to prove one of Alexander's most trusted commanders. At the same time, widespread diversions and feints were made all around the perimeter of the city, as the besieging ships everywhere moved close under the walls. Attempts were already being made to penetrate the two harbours. The sector of the wall where Alexander himself was taking part in the assault was the first to be captured, Admetus being the first man upon the ramparts. Some of the towers that crowned the battlements were now occupied, and this gave the Macedonians control of the linking curtain walls. Soon Alexander's men were fighting their way down into the city itself. Even when the Tyrians had been driven from the walls, they defended the Agenorium at the north end of the city – a citadel named after Tyre's legendary King Agenor. Many of the defenders died fighting where they stood. Others were dispersed by Alexander and his hypaspists. The city was now entered from the harbours as well as from the walls. Alexander's Phoenician fleet broke the boom in the south and destroyed the shipping it had sheltered. In the north there was no boom and the Cyprians met little resistance when they sailed in. As Coenus' troops entered, the city was a scene of bloody massacre. The Macedonians were embittered by the length of the siege, and also by an incident in which the Tyrians had killed prisoners upon the wall before the eyes of the besiegers. The Tyrian dead numbered 8,000. Of Alexander's forces, up to 400 Macedonians are reported as having lost their lives in the siege; of these, 20 were hypaspists who fell with Admetus in the final assault. At the time of Tyre's capture, there were in the city many Carthaginian pilgrims visiting their mother city to pay honour to Melqart, the Phoenician Heracles – in whose temple they now took refuge. Alexander spared them, but other foreigners, along with the Tyrian survivors, were sold into slavery, in all about 30,000 people.

Alexander sacrificed to Heracles in fulfilment of his original avowed intent. The god's complacency over the treatment of a city where he had received supreme honour seems to have been easily assumed. The entire siege had lasted from January to July 332. Alexander had brought about the fall of an island city by the use of new siege machinery, ingenuity and perseverance. At times it must have seemed like an impossible task, yet in the end, the combination of ships, siege machinery, artillery and a determined leader was too much for the Tyrians.

GAZA

Alexander now marched for Egypt in pursuit of his immediate strategic objective, which was to secure the whole of the eastern Mediterranean coastline. No city dared resist him, with the single exception of Gaza. This stronghold was defended as fanatically as Tyre had been. Its Phoenician ruler recruited into his service large numbers of Arab mercenaries and laid in considerable provisions. The operations at Gaza are more difficult to analyze than those at Tyre, because the details are few and the two surviving descriptions, by Arrian and Quintus Curtius, are not entirely in agreement. Unlike Tyre, Gaza was not an island although the town was protected by its location on a high occupation mound or tell. This was clearly a formidable obstacle. Alexander's engineers protested that the city was too high to be taken when he ordered the machines shipped from

Tyre to be reassembled. But Gaza was a threat to Alexander's supply and communication routes, so he came up with the solution: a huge mound. Arrian claims that the embankment was 2 stades wide (370m) and 55ft high (17m). Catapults and siege towers were to be dragged to the top, and the defenders were to be battered from above. Curtius adds that the sandy ground subsided, damaging the undercarriages of the siege towers. At the same time, tunnels were dug under the walls, to cause them to subside; Curtius implies that the tunnels were the main thrust of the assault. Gaza was finally taken after two months. Attacked from above and below, the walls collapsed and the Macedonians poured in. Most of Gaza's male population died fighting, putting up a heroic resistance. Alexander himself sustained two wounds in the battle. After the city had been taken, the women and children were enslaved, and the governor, Batis, was punished, perhaps by being dragged behind Alexander's chariot around the city.

The taking of Gaza was one of Alexander's most remarkable achievements. He motivated his weary army to see through an audacious and difficult plan, creating a huge mound of sand in the late summer heat. He had reduced two well-defended cities, one of them an island, within ten months, an almost unique act in the ancient world.

EGYPT

With the example of Tyre and Gaza before them, the Egyptians were in no mind to oppose Alexander. Egypt was unlike the other provinces of the Persian Empire. It had been conquered in 525 by the Persian king Cambyses. The successful resistance of the Greeks to Persian invasion in 490 and 480 had shown that the Persians were not invincible, and Egypt had been restless and rebellious throughout much of the 5th century, regaining independence in 404. It had only been reconquered by Persia a few years before Alexander's arrival. Sabaces, the Persian governor of Egypt, had in fact been killed at Issus, and his successor accepted Alexander without demur. Thus ended the last period of Persian occupation and the brief reign of the Thirty-First Dynasty.

The Egyptians welcomed the Macedonians as liberators, and Alexander in turn flattered Egyptian national sentiment, doing conspicuous honour to their gods. Alexander took over the official treasury from Mazaces, the new governor, and garrisoned Pelusium at the eastern extremity of the Nile delta. He made a round tour over the desert via Heliopolis and Memphis, the ancient Egyptian capital and religious shrine, returning down the Nile to its mouth north of Mareotis.

From Egypt he marched across the desert to visit the oracle of Ammon at the Libyan oasis of Siwah. He may have been prompted by piety, curiosity or a

ALEXANDER THE GOD

Throughout his reign, Alexander drew comparisons and connections between himself and gods and heroes. As well as his lifelong attachment to the Homeric hero Achilles, he had since youth compared himself with Heracles, and he often appeared on coins wearing a lionskin to show this connection. In Egypt he was proclaimed as the son of the Egyptian god Ammon, and there are later coins that show him with the horns of Ammon, and occasionally wearing both the lionskin and horns. Later after his campaigns in India, he added Dionysus to his range of gods. After his death, the Successors often used his face on their coins to stress the legitimacy of their rule, and depicted him as one of the gods he had emulated in life. (Left: akg-images. Right: TopFoto)

mixture of both. Command of a conquering army in any case made for convenient travelling. At Siwah, the oracle was said to have hailed Alexander as the son of Zeus, with whom the Egyptian deity Ammon was identified.

On return to Memphis, he reorganized the political administration of Egypt, replacing Persian officials with Egyptians, but he left the garrisons of Pelusium and Memphis under the command of his own officers. Modest reinforcements meanwhile reached him from the Aegean area: 400 Greek mercenaries sent by Antipater and 500 Thracian cavalry. Hegelochus, Alexander's victorious commander in the north-east Aegean, had also arrived in Egypt, bringing

The Temple of the Oracle at the Siwah oasis, built some time in the 6th century. Alexander visited the temple in 331, having apparently followed birds across the desert. (TopFoto/ImageWorks)

with him prisoners; but Pharnabazus, the Persian admiral captured at Chios, had escaped.

UPRISING IN GREECE

When Alexander returned to Tyre, after his lengthy period in Egypt, he learned of serious unrest in the Peloponnese. There the Spartan king Agis III, who had begun his dealings with the Persian leaders in the Aegean very soon after Alexander's departure from Europe, openly resisted Macedonian power. In a bold move he defeated the army of Corrhagus, thus forcing Antipater himself to lead an army to the south. Nor was Agis' force inconsequential: he had collected 22,000 men from the neighbouring states of Elis, Arcadia and Achaea, and with these he now laid siege to Megalopolis. Antipater was, however, preoccupied with affairs in Thrace, where the military governor of the region, Memnon, was in open rebellion. However, Memnon quickly came to terms with Antipater, thus freeing him to deal with the Greek insurrection. Furthermore, the fact that Memnon later brought reinforcements to Alexander in the east suggests that the king did not regard his actions as treacherous.

The Macedonian army confronted Agis at Megalopolis in the summer of 331 – certainly the entire rebellion had been suppressed before the battle of Gaugamela was fought. The contest was a renewal of the bitter struggle between Macedon and the Greeks, who had still not accepted the suzerainty of the former. Although he fell on the battlefield, Agis did not sell his life cheaply; nor did the 5,300 other Greeks who perished in the battle. Alexander, when he learned of the engagement, dismissed it as insignificant. Plutarch said that 'Alexander even added a joke when he was told of the war waged by Antipater against Agis. "Men," he said, "it appears that while we were in the process of vanquishing Darius, there was a battle of mice over there in Arcadia."' (Plutarch, *Life of Agesilaus*, 15) But the contest had left 3,500 Macedonians dead, and until it had been decided Alexander's activities in the east were suspended in uncertainty.

THE BATTLE OF GAUGAMELA

Alexander had now completed the first phase of his grand strategy. He had firmly secured the whole of the east Mediterranean seaboard, and in summer 331 he again marched eastward in pursuit of Darius, reaching Thapsacus on the Euphrates in August. Darius' forces, under Mazaeus, had held the crossing of the Euphrates against the Macedonian advance guard, but they fled on news that Alexander himself was approaching. Numbering 3,000 cavalry in total, they could not prudently have done otherwise.

After crossing the Euphrates, Alexander did not march on Babylon, which might have seemed the next obvious target, but instead turned northwards, hugging the foothills of the Armenian mountains, where foraging was easier and the heat less oppressive. But he probably already suspected – as his scouts soon confirmed – that Darius was waiting for him on the other side of the Tigris, ready to fall on his rear if he turned southwards. At the same time, from the intelligence he had gained, it appeared that the Persians intended to block his passage if he attempted to cross the river. In fact, at the higher point where he ultimately crossed, the Tigris was undefended. That did not mean the crossing was easy, for his men were in danger of being swept away by the rapid current, and it was necessary for the army to stop and rest after the river had been crossed.

The Tigris was not the only natural hazard to face Alexander at this time. An eclipse of the moon provoked agonized superstition among the Macedonian soldiers, which could have ended in mutiny. However, the Egyptian seers whom Alexander had taken on his march east out of respect for their learning served him well. They knew how lunar eclipses were caused, and their knowledge of astronomy was supplemented by an at least equal knowledge of human nature, so instead of trying to explain the movements of the sun, moon and earth, they declared the eclipse to be a good omen signifying Alexander's victory, which reassured the army.

OPPOSITE

A romantic depiction of Alexander's triumphant entry into Babylon after Gaugamela by Charles Le Brun. (akg-images/ Erich Lessing)

Four days after crossing the river Tigris, Alexander's scouts sighted Persian cavalry in the distance. On being informed, Alexander drew up his army in order of battle and, thus deployed, advanced slowly. Later intelligence revealed that the Persian force was but an advance party, no more than 1,000 in number. Leaving his army to continue its slow advance, Alexander rode on ahead with his Royal Squadron and a detachment of light Paeonian horsemen. The Persians fled at his approach, but he gave chase, killing some of the enemy and capturing others. From these prisoners, he learned much concerning the strength and movements of Darius' army and of the various contingents that formed it. The Persian Empire, even after Alexander had detached from it Asia Minor, Egypt and the Levant coast, was still vast, and its military potential was formidable.

DARIUS' PLANS

While Alexander was in Phoenicia and Egypt, Darius, once his attempts to win a negotiated settlement had failed, marshalled another army. If there was anything that the empire had in abundance, it was manpower; though, as Darius would learn, mere numbers of men would not suffice against a brilliant tactician like Alexander. The army at Gaugamela did contain several contingents that had faced the Macedonians before. Syrians, defeated at Issus but steadfast in their loyalty to Persia, stood shoulder to shoulder with Persians, Babylonians and Medes, who formed the nucleus of the Great King's strength. Nevertheless, the composition of Darius' army was radically different from the army routed at Issus. Bessus, satrap of Bactria in the north-easterly Persian dominions, led an army from this region, which also included a unit of Indians. Other contingents were of Asiatic Scythians, Arachotians, Hyrcanians from south of the Caspian and their eastern neighbours the Areians under the satrap Satibarzanes. Also recruited were Persian Gulf tribesmen, Medes and associated peoples, forces drawn from the regions of Susa and Babylon, with Mesopotamian Syrians under Darius' trusted commander Mazaeus. The total numbers reported amounted to 40,000 cavalry, 1,000,000 infantry, 200 scythed chariots and a few elephants, perhaps 15 in number, contributed by Indians from west of the Indus. This total, however, probably reflects theoretical strength rather than the force fielded, which would have been considerably smaller.

The Persian army had encamped near Gaugamela (literally 'The Camel's House'), a village beside the river Bumodus 75 miles west of Arbela. Recognising his fault at Issus, Darius had chosen a wide plain for his battlefield, where cavalry could be deployed and chariots used to advantage. The Persian king had even given orders that the ground in this area should be levelled where it was uneven in order to facilitate chariot tactics. As he had done at Issus, Darius prepared the

battlefield, littering it with obstacles and traps for the unsuspecting enemy, though these were revealed by deserters and their effectiveness negated.

THE FINAL CLASH

As soon as Alexander knew that Darius was waiting for him, he halted his advance and made a camp, fortifying it with a ditch and stockade. Here he left all his baggage and pack animals, together with camp followers, non-combatant troops and prisoners, then by night led his fighting men forward, in battle order, with little equipment but their weapons. His purpose was to confront the enemy at dawn. The camps of the two armies were about seven miles apart. A range of hills still separated them, and they were not visible to each other.

Alexander had set off with his battle force about the second watch of the night, probably a few hours before midnight. After he had covered about half the distance between his camp and the enemy he found himself just over the crest of the intervening hills. Here the Persian positions were within view, vividly illuminated by their watch-fires.

BATTLE OF GAUGAMELA: PHASE 1

1. Alexander led the Companion cavalry obliquely in column while the infantry advanced in line of battle.
2. Bactrians and Scythians tried to envelop and contain Alexander's move on their flank.
3. Menidas, with mercenary cavalry, tried to break through the Persian left.
4. After Menidas was repulsed, Aretas attacked the Bactrians and Scythians.
5. Aretas opened a gap. The Companions attacked in successive waves: they broke through and scattered the enemy.
6. Persians launched chariot attacks.
7. Chariot attacks broken up by archers and Balacrus' light troops.
8. Confronted with the collapse of his left wing and the threat of the advancing pike-phalanx ahead, Darius fled towards Arbela.
9. Parmenion's cavalry wing was fighting on the defensive.
10. Alexander's central infantry moved forward.
11. Gap opens between infantry and Parmenion's cavalry.
12. Persian and Indian cavalry penetrated the gap, then fanned out to attack Macedonian base camp and surround Parmenion's cavalry.
13. The two left-wing phalanx units were halted in their efforts to stem the Persian break-through and support Parmenion.

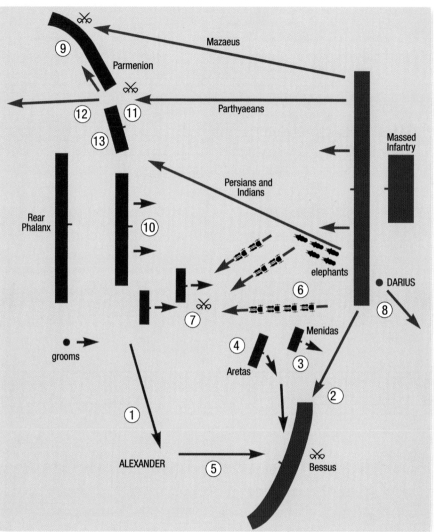

The hills on which the Macedonians had halted must have been virtually treeless, and Alexander now deployed his army for battle. He held a council of war with his officers, and it was decided to bivouac where they were, still deployed in line of battle.

Taking with him a body of Companion cavalry and light-armed troops, Alexander rode down to reconnoitre Darius' chosen battlefield in the plain below by moonlight. However, he must have kept his distance from the enemy lines, for it was no part of his plan to engage in night operations.

In fact, when he returned to the Macedonian positions, Parmenion is said to have suggested that he should make a night attack and take the Persians off their guard. Alexander replied flippantly that it would be a pity to steal a victory in this way. He usually invited the opinions of his officers but took his own decisions without feeling obliged to account for them. Certainly there were always incalculable factors in a night attack. Also, although Alexander often surprised his enemies by a rapid night march, he seemed to prefer to do his actual fighting in daylight.

The Persians apparently did fear that he would make such a night attack, and having built no camp, remained throughout the hours of darkness drawn up under arms in their battle formations. The Macedonians were also without a fortified camp, but the hillside they had halted on offered natural defence, certainly impossible for Darius' chariots to manage, and they felt sufficiently secure to eat and rest.

The Persian battle order is known with some precision, for Darius' written instructions were afterwards captured. The left wing, facing Alexander himself on the Macedonian right, was held by Bactrian cavalry with Asiatic Scythians and Arachotians. The Persians themselves were stationed in the centre. Here, in accordance with usual practice, the king with his royal entourage took up his position. The right wing was held by troops from Syria, Mesopotamia and the Persian Gulf. An advance force screened the left wing. This force was composed of Scythian cavalry, 1,000 Bactrians and 100 scythed chariots. The elephants, with 50 chariots, were posted in front of Darius himself. Greek mercenaries, with Persian troops stationed on either side, were also drawn up in front of him in the central sector. These were the only forces that could be relied upon to face the Macedonian phalanx. Alexander's army numbered about 40,000 infantry and 7,000 cavalry.

Although the often-seen 'phalanx drift' led to the envelopment of the enemy left, there remained the danger that the enveloping force might lose contact with its own centre and leave a gap, which the enemy could easily exploit. In Alexander's tactics, this danger became a calculated risk. He was always alert to the threats involved and took measures to offset them. In the first place, the right-wing cavalry, which he commanded in person, was completely under his control and could be recalled, even in heady moments of victory and pursuit, to succour the hard-pressed central phalanx. Second, the phalanx was organized to some extent as a self-contained and self-reliant unit, able to maintain its position and function until help could arrive.

In none of Alexander's battles were these tactical calculations more evident than at Gaugamela. Knowing that the Macedonian phalanx was virtually certain to be

CHARIOTS AT GAUGAMELA

At Gaugamela, Darius attempted to disrupt the Macedonian phalanx by driving scythe-bearing chariots into their ranks. This tactic was countered by the phalanx in a number of ways, as instructed by Alexander. According to Diodorus, 'he ordered the infantry of the phalanx to join shields as soon as these went into action against them and to beat the shields with their sarissae, creating such a din as to frighten the horses into bolting to the rear, or if they persevered, to open gaps in the ranks such that they might ride through harmlessly' (17.57.6). Arrian's account says 'the chariots were no sooner off the mark than they were met by the missile weapons of the Agrianians and Balacrus' javelin-throwers, who were stationed in advance of the Companion cavalry; again, they seized the reins and dragged the riders to the ground, then surrounded the horses and cut them down. Some few of the vehicles succeeding in passing through, but to no purpose, for the Macedonians had orders, where they attacked, to break formation and let them through deliberately.' Arrian goes on to say that the chariots and drivers drove through the alleys created by the phalanx and were finished off by the troops stationed at the rear. He also implies that there was no significant harm done to the Macedonians. Diodorus, however, shows this was not the case and intead severe wounds were inflicted by the chariots. (Christa Hook © Osprey Publishing Ltd)

isolated while he and the cavalry were operating on the far right, he took particular measures to safeguard its position. First he supported it with a rear duplicate formation, which in the event of encirclement could face about and receive the enemy from the reverse direction. He also arranged that the phalanx should be able to extend its line or close ranks at the last minute before battle was joined, and to protect it – at least while this operation was being carried out – he posted curving screens of Agrianians and Macedonian archers on either of its flanks.

In some ancient accounts, it appears that Alexander overslept on the morning of the battle, and that his officers, realizing his need for rest, hesitated to wake him. At any rate, the actual fighting seems to have begun when the sun was well up. The two armies advanced towards each other slowly in line of battle and both sides made cautious and calculated preliminary manoeuvres.

The wide plain completely favoured Darius, giving him every opportunity to exploit his superior numbers. The Persian host far outflanked Alexander's army on either side, but Alexander, determined as always to retain the flanking advantage, led his cavalry off continually towards the right. The Bactrian and Scythian cavalry kept pace with him, extending their line in the same direction. These manoeuvres meant that both sides were drawn away from the central ground that Darius had specially levelled for use by his chariots, and there was a danger that the chariots would be unable to operate as planned. The king therefore sent orders that his left wing, taking advantage of numbers and greater frontage, should contain Alexander's lateral movement by an enveloping sally, and these orders were duly carried out.

Finding himself thus obstructed, Alexander launched an attack into the middle of the enveloping troops, using for this purpose the Mercenary Cavalry under Menidas. Scythian and Bactrian troops counter-attacked, but Alexander sent in his Paeonian horse with other mercenaries and temporarily routed them. Even then, reserves of Bactrians arrived and rallied the fugitives. They restored the position, and an evenly contested cavalry action resulted, in which Alexander's men suffered serious casualties. They were fighting against great odds, and the Scythians in particular were heavily armoured. However, one wave of Macedonians after another was thrown into the fight and the enemy formations were eventually broken up. It may be that Alexander's flanking moves were often in the form of a feint and that his attack was timed to catch the enemy in the process of re-forming to meet the challenge, at a moment when organized response would be most difficult. Tactics of this sort probably opened the battle at Gaugamela, though their success was not immediate.

At this point, Darius threw in his scythe-wheeled chariots. They proved a fiasco, in much the same manner as those which had fought for Artaxerxes at

OVERLEAF
Early 17th-century painting of the battle of Gaugamela by Jan Brueghel the Elder. (akg-images/Erich Lessing)

Cunaxa. As Xenophon recorded, on that occasion, the Greek troops under attack had simply opened their ranks and allowed the chariots to hurtle through them, pelting drivers and horses with missiles as they passed. Alexander's archers and javelin-throwers, who had been stationed forward to protect the cavalry from such an attack, used similar tactics, in some cases seizing the horses' reins and dragging down the drivers. Chariots that passed through unharmed were ultimately isolated and rounded up by the Macedonian hypaspists and grooms. Such at least is Arrian's account. Other historians present a more gruesome account of the effect produced by the scythes. But at Gaugamela, the impact of the chariot attack was in any case certainly not decisive; nor does it seem to have much influenced the course of the battle. The chariot had become a symbol of Oriental vanity, for its effectiveness had already been challenged by infantrymen at the end of the Bronze Age, and it remained a splendid anachronism, but no match for cool minds and brave hearts.

Darius, as soon as the chariots had spent their force, or even while they were still in action, made a further attempt to contain Alexander's movement on his left. For Alexander, once his Bactrian and Scythian adversaries had been thrown back, continued to lead his cavalry outward in column.

In a new attempt to block his way, Darius dispatched Persian cavalry from the central sector of his extensive army. This left a gap in the centre, a fatal weak point, and it no doubt presented the opportunity for which Alexander had been watching – perhaps the false move he had sought to provoke. At once he changed direction and galloped left. Converging with the right-hand units of his own central infantry, he then led them straight into the gap with blood-curdling war-cries, making straight for the spot where Darius himself was stationed. Very soon, the Macedonian phalangites were following up.

Darius fled, as at Issus, so setting the example for his army. It may even be said that he lost the battle by his flight. Meanwhile, Aretas, Alexander's redoubtable cavalry officer, had finally broken up the Persian troops engaged on the Macedonian right wing, and on this sector of the field the Macedonians were entirely victorious. Rout, pursuit and slaughter followed.

On the Macedonian left, however, and in the centre, events had followed a very different course. Only the extreme right-hand unit of phalangites had been able to follow Alexander in his headlong attack on Darius. The rest had halted in order to sustain their comrades on the left wing, who were in difficulties. A gap inevitably appeared in the phalanx, and into this gap Persian cavalry and men of the Indian contingent now poured. They did not attempt to take the phalanx in the rear, but penetrated deeply, riding straight on, across country, to attack the Macedonian baggage camp. Even allowing for the Persian general

BATTLE OF GAUGAMELA: PHASE 2

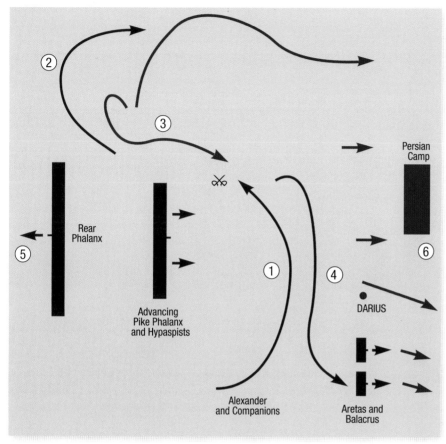

1. *Parmenion appealed to Alexander for help. Alexander led his Companions to relieve him.*
2. *Mazaeus' attack on Parmenion's wing faltered, and Parmenion took the offensive.*
3. *Persians and Indians who had penetrated to Parmenion's rear attempted to withdraw but collided with Alexander. They were annihilated as a force.*
4. *Alexander, learning of Parmenion's rally, resumed pursuit of Darius.*
5. *Other Persians and Indians reached the Macedonian base camp, about five miles distant. Alexander's rear phalanx followed them, and dispersed the raiders.*
6. *Parmenion captured the Persian camp. Alexander pursued Darius.*

advance in the morning, this must have been at least four or five miles west of the battle. Invading the camp, they cut down the non-combatant troops who had manned it and liberated the Persian prisoners who now joined in the attack on their former guards.

Apart from those who attacked the camp, some of the Persian cavalry that penetrated the gap in the Macedonian phalanx must have fanned out and threatened Parmenion's left wing from the rear and flank. The danger coincided with an enveloping move launched by the Persian right-wing cavalry, and Parmenion's horsemen found themselves menaced by a battle on two fronts. In this desperate situation Parmenion got a message to Alexander on the other side of the battlefield urgently requesting help.

The rear phalanx, which had been specially posted and briefed to deal with an enemy breakthrough of this kind, faced about, raced back to save the camp and at the same time posed a threat to the Persian cavalry that had turned against Parmenion's wing.

As at Issus, it was a mark of Alexander's control and discipline that he was able to lead his men back from the easy and rewarding pursuit of a routed enemy into the heat of battle. For this is what is implied in his swift response to Parmenion's appeal. But a confused situation now resulted. In the central plain Alexander collided with the fleeing Persian cavalry, who, as their position deteriorated, were attempting to withdraw. A fierce, congested and chaotic

These warriors are characteristic of the Scythians at the time of Alexander's campaigns. The Scythians had their own independent kingdom north of the Black Sea and proved dangerous opponents for both the Persians and the Macedonians. They also provided some of the best mercenary light cavalry in the ancient world, fighting at various times for both Darius and Alexander. (Angus McBride © Osprey Publishing Ltd)

cavalry fight was the result. The effect was certainly to delay Alexander in providing help for Parmenion. However, the Companion cavalry eventually dispersed the enemy, cutting them down or driving them out of the way. Those who survived galloped away from the battlefield.

Ultimate victory

Alexander's relief operation, coupled with that of the rear phalanx, removed the menace to Parmenion's right, and the Macedonian horse were now better able to cope with the enveloping movement launched by Mazaeus, the cavalry commander on the Persian right wing. Mazaeus had indeed, as he pressed forward, lost touch with the king, and he was for a long while unaware of Darius' flight and of the collapse of the Persian army on the left and in the centre. The news, when it reached him, inevitably caused him to waver. His attack now lost impetus. From his own point of view, there now existed the danger of encirclement. It could only be a matter of time before the Macedonians, already in possession of the central ground, wheeled in his direction. Apart from that, the massive, variously derived Oriental host commanded by the king of Persia was not psychologically conditioned to prolong the battle after the flight of the king himself.

By the time Alexander approached Parmenion, the most serious threats to the Macedonian left wing had been removed. It was no longer necessary for Alexander to attack Mazaeus, because the Thessalian cavalry, after a heroic resistance under heavy pressure, were now able to take the offensive themselves, and Mazaeus' troops were giving way before them. Alexander turned once more to the pursuit of Darius, and the whole Macedonian army moved forward on the heels of its routed enemy.

The Persian centre had by no means relaxed its flight. Alexander pursued the fugitives until dusk, then crossed the river Lycus and rested his men until midnight. The pursuit was then resumed. Darius, for his part, never stopped to rest. Parmenion, who in his own sector had lagged only a little behind Alexander in the pursuit, now occupied the Persian camp. The Macedonians' own baggage camp had been saved and the raiders killed or routed, but the seizure of the Persian baggage train with its elephants and camels would have amply compensated them for any losses suffered. Alexander hoped to capture Darius in the town of Arbela, 75 miles east of the battlefield, but he was not to be found. His abandoned treasure and possessions were seized by Alexander, including – as at Issus – his chariot and weapons. As at Issus, it may be said that Alexander failed to capture Darius through his refusal to abandon the centre and left wing of his army in their difficulties. His caution seems appropriate given that history

Alexander charging Darius in his chariot on a late 4th-century amphora. (The Art Archive/Musée Archéologique Naples/Alfredo Dagli Orti)

tells us of other ancient battles where the victorious wing of an army rode in disorganized and reckless pursuit, only to leave the enemy securely established as victors on the central battlefield.

Casualty figures for the battle are variously reported by ancient historians, most of them hard to credit. According to Arrian, Alexander lost only 100 dead among his soldiers but over 1,000 horses, half of these having been ridden by the Companions. Persian losses are recorded as about 300,000 dead and an even greater number captured. Most of the casualties would have occurred in the course of the flight and pursuit after the battle.

At Gaugamela Alexander faced the Persian army on a wide plain that gave Darius little opportunity to bring his superior numbers to bear. Darius reacted to the beginning of what he thought was Alexander's flanking manoeuvre, remembering its devastating effect at Issus, but Alexander threw wave after wave of cavalry against the Persian cavalry sent to envelop him. Whether this was an adaptation of his original flanking manoeuvre, or whether it was a feint to allow him to attack while the enemy was reordering, it was audacious. When Darius continued to guard against the feared Macedonian cavalry charge to the extent that he caused a gap in his centre, Alexander turned round his cavalry and struck, hard and fast, at the weak centre. This characteristic, rapid snatching of a possibly momentary advantage could only be taken by a commander at the very centre of events, and Alexander yet again led his men to victory.

Darius fled north-eastward into the mountains of Media, guessing correctly that Alexander would immediately turn his attention to the great central cities of the empire, which lay to the south: Babylon, Susa and Persepolis.

ALEXANDER TAKES PERSIA

As Darius fled, his army dispersed to their territories, as was the custom. Those who commanded the garrisons and guarded the treasures in the empire's capitals made formal surrender to Alexander. Mazaeus surrendered Babylon, together with the *gazophylax* ('guardian of the treasures'), Bagophanes. Alexander entered Babylon in great ceremony, and the ancient city now publicly turned its resources over to the new king. What the Alexander historians depict as a spontaneous welcome was in fact ritual surrender, enacted many times in the past – in ceremony for the legitimate heir to the throne, as well as in earnest for a conquering king. In return, Alexander appointed Mazaeus satrap of Babylon, though he installed a garrison in the city and military overseers to ensure the loyalty of the new governor and the population.

Despite Gaugamela's ranking as one of the decisive battles of world history, the fact is that it was only decisive for the Persian side. For Darius it was the final nail in the coffin; Alexander, on the other hand, could have survived defeat in northern Mesopotamia and still held the western portion of the empire. Victory, however, belonged to the Macedonians, and the might of Persia was shattered. Babylon had no hope of resisting, and Susa, too, avoided pillage by embracing the conqueror. Again the defecting satrap, Aboulites, was retained and once more a Macedonian garrison was imposed. With Darius still at large, Alexander introduced military reforms to strengthen the army and the command structures. Reinforcements continued to arrive, even as the avenging army moved ever closer to its ultimate goal: Persepolis.

THE PERSIAN GATES

The satrap of Persis, Ariobarzanes, had mustered a sizeable force, and with 25,000 defenders he blocked the so-called 'Persian' or 'Susidan' Gates in the Zagros mountains in an attempt to stall the Macedonians until the treasures of Persepolis could be removed. In fact, Ariobarzanes was only facing a portion of the Macedonian force: the slowest elements and the baggage train were following

OPPOSITE
The reconstruction of the Ishtar Gate at Babylon. (akg-images/Bildarchiv Steffens)

the Royal Road into Persis under the command of Parmenion. Alexander led the more mobile contingents through the mountains to the Persian Gates. It was January and there was snow on the ground. A first attempt to pass through the gates seems to have ended disastrously with the Macedonians having to abandon their dead. Alexander then circumvented the satrap's position. The Macedonians braved the perils of terrain and winter snow, and led by captive guides, they approached Ariobarzanes' force from the rear. Ariobarzanes' troops were slaughtered in the pass and it was now a relatively simple matter to bridge the Araxes, whereupon Tiridates surrendered both Persepolis and its treasure to the Macedonians.

PERSEPOLIS

The symbolic importance of the capture of Persepolis – the very meaning of the Greek form of the name Persepolis, 'City of the Persians', enhanced its actual associations with Xerxes and the great invasion – dictated its fate: pillage, rape

MAZAEUS

Mazaeus was satrap of Cilicia, and later of Syria and Mesopotamia in the time of King Artaxerxes III. Under Darius III he probably fought at Issus, although there is no mention of him. In 331, he was ordered to prevent Alexander's crossing of the Euphrates at Thapsacus, but had insufficient numbers to do more than harass the bridge-builders. Upon Alexander's arrival, Mazaeus withdrew and rejoined Darius, who was now following the course of the Tigris north. At Gaugamela, Mazaeus commanded the Persian cavalry on the right wing and led a charge of dense squadrons together with the scythed chariots. He then sent a squadron of Scythian horsemen to capture the Macedonian camp, while he himself exerted pressure on Parmenion and the Thessalian cavalry on the Macedonian left. Eventually Mazaeus was overcome by the tenacity of the

Thessalians and the demoralizing news of Darius' flight. It is likely that the Alexander sarcophagus depicts Mazaeus' valour at Issus, which strengthens the argument that it was constructed for Mazaeus, rather than Abdalonymus. Mazaeus fled from the battlefield to Babylon, which he promptly surrendered to the Macedonians. In return he was installed as its satrap, the first Persian to be so honoured by Alexander.

The Alexander sarcophagus also depicts a notable Persian engaged in a lion hunt with Alexander and other Macedonians; one of the Macedonian riders may be Hephaestion. If this depicts a historical event, then it could not have occurred before late 331, and the most likely Persian with whom Alexander might have hunted would once again have been Mazaeus. Mazaeus remained in office and served his new master loyally until his death in late 328.

and massacre ensued. The palace too fell victim to the victor's wrath, but only after the treasures had been removed and shipped to Ecbatana. Then, whether by design or through a spontaneous urge for revenge, it was put to the torch. One version attributed the burning to an Athenian courtesan, Thaïs, who was to become the mistress of Ptolemy, the later king of Egypt.

The destruction of Persepolis was symbolic rather than total, for it continued as the capital of the province during the age of the Successors. At this point,

however, it illuminated the difficulties faced by Alexander. For one thing, the destruction of Persepolis could be taken to signify the completion of the war of vengeance, the attainment of the stated goal of the expedition. Therefore the allied troops would naturally assume that it warranted their demobilization. Still, Alexander could remind them that as long as Darius lived, the mission had not been completed.

Conversely, the destruction of the palace and the maltreatment of the citizens undermined Alexander's propaganda, which had at an early stage sought to portray him as the legitimate successor of the Great King. Rightly had Parmenion advised against such action, reminding Alexander that he should not destroy what was now his own property. Nevertheless, what may have caused resentment in Persia could well have been received with a degree of satisfaction in Babylon and Susa, even Ecbatana, all of which had been overshadowed by the advent of the Achaemenid dynasty and the growing power of Persepolis.

CHANGES TO ALEXANDER'S ARMY

On the road to Susa, passing through the fertile province of Sittacene, Alexander's army was met by a large reinforcement from Macedon under the command of Amyntas and consisting of 6,000 Macedonian infantry, 600 Macedonian cavalry, 600 Thracian cavalry, 3,500 Trallians, and mercenaries to a total of 4,000 infantry and 380 horse. Alexander halted the army and carried out the first of a series of thorough re-organizations. He also took the opportunity to introduce some purely administrative reforms, and to promote officers of ability to the vacancies created by the campaigns so far.

The large number of reinforcements, even after replacing losses and releasing men from service, allowed Alexander to expand the infantry. Curtius seems to be talking of the hypaspists when he says that the lochoi were grouped into chiliarchies which had not existed before. New officers were appointed on the basis of military virtue: eight names follow, including Philotas and Hellanicus, so it seems that the number of lochoi was raised to eight. It also seems that a seventh taxis was added to the pezhetairoi. The following year Alexander left 6,000 Macedonian infantry (four taxeis) at Ecbatana to guard the treasure, but took the hypaspists and the taxeis of Coenus, Craterus and Amyntas with him in the pursuit of Darius and the Hyracanian campaign. Seven taxeis are also mentioned as being present at the Hydaspes.

The cavalry was also re-organized. Each ile was now divided into two lochoi of two troops each, and officers were appointed to command on the basis of ability after a close scrutiny of the military conduct sheets. This reform was probably instituted to ease administrative efficiency, as the ile was rather a large force of

Whether Alexander and his men intended to burn Persepolis down will never be known, but it is obvious that they focussed their attentions on the palace of Xerxes to avenge his destruction on Greek temples back in the 5th century. In this photograph of one of the surviving parts of his palace, deliberate hammer damage to the face of the king can clearly be seen. (Werner Forman Archive)

horses, grooms and riders for one man to administer. From this date on, the cavalry was administered by century (*hekatostuas*), which becomes interchangeable with lochos in the cavalry.

More major changes occurred when the army reached Ecbatana. The Thessalian cavalry and the allied forces, both infantry and cavalry, were disbanded and sent home. Many, however, remained with the army as mercenaries, and in the later campaigns, much more use was made of mercenaries and Asian troops.

During the early part of 330, in preparation for the arduous campaigns lying ahead in the mountains and deserts of Iran and central Asia, the pezhetairoi started to lose their armour. A stratagem described in Polyaenus (4.3.13) tells us that Alexander re-equipped his soldiers with the half-cuirass (*hemithorakion*) instead of the cuirass, after they had fled, in order that they would not turn their backs on the enemy again. The incident referred to must be

Alexander's first, unsuccessful attempt to storm the Persian Gates, and the information should be accepted as genuine, even if the reason given for the change is incorrect. During the Hyrcanian campaign, Coenus' taxeis is described as 'the lightest armed of the Macedonian phalanx'; 'the lightest armed of the phalanx' are mentioned a year later in operations near Maracanda; and in 326 in the advance to the Aornos Rock 'the lightest but at the same time the best armed' men are selected from taxeis other than that of Coenus. So it seems that other taxeis, or ranks of other taxeis, may have also started to use lighter equipment.

INTO CENTRAL ASIA

Before moving north again through Media in pursuit of Darius, Alexander placed governors over the territory he had recently conquered. These included Persian administrators, and one may discern a new policy here, a foretaste perhaps of those war aims of universal citizenship that he would later embrace when the mere destruction of an enemy seemed no longer to justify the time, trouble and suffering involved.

At the beginning of 330, Darius retained only one of the four capitals of the empire, Ecbatana (modern Hamadan). It was a convenient location, from which

CALLISTHENES THE HISTORIAN

Callisthenes of Olynthus was, according to some accounts, the nephew of the philosopher Aristotle. He joined Alexander's expedition as the official historian, and if – as appears to be the case – he sent his history back to Greece in instalments, he was at the same time historian, propagandist and war correspondent. He also tutored the young men of the Macedonian court. His travels with Alexander took him to exotic places and he was able to speculate on natural phenomena as well as describe the course of the war, for he appears to have theorized about the source of the Nile. It was his literary training that led him to depict Alexander as a latter-day Achilles, and it would not be wrong to class him with the numerous flatterers who swelled the king's ego and entourage. But, although

he likened the receding sea near Mount Climax in Pamphylia to a courtier doing obeisance (proskynesis) to the Great King, he nevertheless resisted Alexander's attempt to introduce the Persian court protocol in 328/327. This caused him to fall out with the king, and when some time later a conspiracy was uncovered involving the Royal Pages, Callisthenes was easily implicated. Convicted of complicity in the conspiracy of the pages, Callisthenes was incarcerated and died some months later. The Peripatetic philosophers, the followers of Aristotle, never forgave Alexander.

Callisthenes' history of Alexander is now lost, although it was thought that he was the author of the *Romance of Alexander*; the author of that work is still sometimes known as Pseudo-Callisthenes.

ALEXANDER'S ROUTE TO BABYLON

1. Alexander crosses the Hellespont and sacrifices at the site of ancient Troy, in keeping with Panhellenic aspects of his campaign.
2. Battle at the Granicus river. Alexander defeats a coalition of satraps (334).
3. Gordium. Alexander cuts the Gordian knot (spring 333).
4. Battle of Issus. November 333. First battle against Darius III. The Persian King's mother, wife, daughters and son are captured.
5. Siege of Tyre. January to August 332.
6. Siege of Gaza. September to October 332.
7. Alexander is crowned as Pharaoh of Egypt at Memphis.
8. Alexander goes to the oasis of Siwah, establishing Alexandria *en route*. He is recognized as the 'Son of Amun'.
9. Alexander crosses the Euphrates at Thapsacus.
10. Battle of Gaugamela, northwest of Arbela. Second battle against Darius III. 1 October 331.
11. Mazaeus surrenders Babylon to Alexander and is retained as satrap of Babylonia.

he could receive reports of Alexander's activities in Persia and at the same summon reinforcements from the upper satrapies. Furthermore, it lay astride the Silk Road, the great east–west corridor that ran south of the Elburz mountains and the Caspian and north of the Great Salt Desert. Unfortunately, many of the king's advisors warned against awaiting Alexander in that place, and they urged Darius to withdraw in the direction of Bactria, which lay beyond the Merv oasis, just north-west of modern Afghanistan.

This plan was adopted by Darius, but only when it was too late to elude Alexander, who resumed hostilities once the mountain passes were free of snow. The Great King's column was much too cumbersome: the royal equipment that offered the necessary comforts, and the covered wagons that sheltered the concubines on the journey, made slow progress through the Sar-i-Darreh or Caspian Gates, even though they had been sent in advance of the army. Only

40,000 native troops and 4,000 Greeks remained with Darius, and deserters – many of them prominent men – drifted back towards the Macedonian force that was, every day, shortening the distance between the two armies.

In the remote village of Thara, the chiliarch, Nabarzanes, and Bessus, the satrap of Bactria, challenged Darius' leadership. Aided by other prominent figures, they arrested the king, only to murder him soon afterwards. His body was left by the side of the road in the hope that when Alexander encountered it he might break off the pursuit. Nabarzanes himself attempted to rally support in Hyrcania and Parthia; Bessus continued towards Bactria and Sogdiana, accompanied by 600 horsemen and intending to usurp the throne.

Alexander had covered some 450 miles (720km) in three weeks: with a larger force he had pushed east from Ecbatana to Rhagae (that is, from Hamadan to Rey, on the edge of modern Tehran), a march of roughly 250 miles (400km), in 11 days; after a five-day rest, he took a much smaller, mounted force another 200 miles (320km) after Darius. He came upon Darius' body late on the sixth day of pursuit. Alexander arranged a royal funeral for the murdered man. Bessus himself had, for the present, eluded him, but the Macedonian army had scattered in the chase and the daily arrival of high-ranking Persian deserters made it necessary to take stock before turning to deal with the usurper.

Some Persians were installed as satraps – Phrataphernes in Parthia, Autophradates amongst the Tapurians – while others remained in Alexander's entourage, awaiting suitable employment and reward. Two dangerous men were pardoned, Nabarzanes and Satibarzanes. The former ought to have considered himself lucky to escape execution. Instead, he contrived to regain control of Parthia and Hyrcania; ultimately, however, he was arrested and killed. The latter was reinstated in his old satrapy of Aria (in the Herat region of Afghanistan), though a detachment of 40 javelinmen under Anaxippus was sent with him to his capital of Artacoana. Satibarzanes promptly murdered his escort and openly rebelled, encouraged perhaps by reports of Bessus' usurpation.

Only two days after learning of Satibarzanes' treachery, Alexander was in Artacoana, from which the rebellious satrap had fled. But when Alexander replaced him with another native ruler, Arsaces, and moved on to subdue Afghanistan, Satibarzanes returned with the aim of reimposing his rule. In this he failed, and he was killed in single combat by the Macedonian cavalry officer Erigyius.

The problem of war aims now became acute. In his satrapy of Bactria, Bessus was proclaiming himself King of Kings under the name Artaxerxes V, and fomenting revolt in central Asia. But before making any northerly advance, Alexander pursued the Greek mercenaries who had served under Darius and forced their surrender when he overtook them in Hyrcania, south of the Caspian

Alexander comes across the dead Persian king, in a Persian manuscript illustration. (ISI)

sea. During his campaigns in the north-east of the Persian Empire, there were conspiracies among his men, mainly in reaction to Alexander's ideal of an empire of mixed Asiatic and European nationality. He executed Philotas, the son of his once-trusted second-in-command Parmenion, and then as a precaution arranged the execution of Parmenion whom he had left in charge of the Median garrison. In a drunken brawl he later killed Cleitus, who had saved his life at the Granicus. In fact, Alexander often now appeared as a tyrant, a role in which many ancient historians of later centuries saw him. Nevertheless the rank and file of his army still followed him devotedly.

Alexander moved south and came upon the Ariaspians, who lived near Lake Seistan. These supplied his army, just as 200 years earlier they had aided Cyrus the Great of Persia and earned the title Euergetai ('Benefactors'). From there the Macedonians followed the Helmand river valley, the course of which took them in the direction of Arachosia. A new settlement was established at Alexandria-in-Arachosia (near modern Kandahar), one of many such foundations in the area.

Taken from figures on the Alexander sarcophagus, these are reconstructions of a javelinman (left), a senior ranking soldier and an allied Greek infantryman, all serving in Alexander's army. (Angus McBride © Osprey Publishing Ltd)

In 329, Alexander entered Bactria, crossing the Hindu Kush via the Khawak Pass and reaching Qunduz. On his approach, Bessus' nobles sent word that they were prepared to hand the usurper over; stripped naked, in chains and wearing a dog-collar, Bessus was left by the roadway to be picked up by Alexander's agent, Ptolemy. But those who had betrayed him fled, wary of submitting to Alexander and determined to maintain their independence in one of the most remote regions of the empire.

Ancient historians differ on how Bessus was killed. Curtius Rufus says he was crucified in the place where Darius III had been killed, Plutarch suggests that he was torn apart in Bactria after a Macedonian trial, whereas Arrian states that he was tortured and then decapitated in Ecbatana. Bessus had done more than simply murder Darius: he had challenged Alexander's claims to the kingship. Claims to legitimacy have little force, however, unless backed by military action, as Darius' illustrious forefather and namesake had discovered in the years from 522 to 519. That king's imperial propaganda, inscribed in three languages on the rock face of Bisitun, proclaims how he became king through the will of

Ahura-Mazda; but it took the might of his armies and the public execution of his opponents to confirm the god's will.

As Alexander reached the north-eastern limit of the empire, a new uprising began in Sogdiana, spreading south to Bactria. The years of Alexander's fighting in the north-eastern provinces of the Persian Empire are recorded by historians in some detail, though with many discrepancies. We hear of battles and of treachery, rapid marches and river crossings, the scaling of cliffs and the capture of daunting mountain strongholds, with feats of arms in the course of which Alexander was more than once wounded. At this time more than any, the sum of effort and hardship suffered by the conquering army seems great and out of all proportion to any useful purpose served.

However, by dint of war and diplomacy, Alexander subdued the intransigent population. He secured the whole territory by planting garrisons of Macedonian and Greek soldiers throughout it.

The Scythians north of the river Jaxartes were a constant menace. They had once lived in the lands the Persians later controlled, and there was also a danger that they might make common cause with any resurgent movement in the north-east provinces themselves. Before leaving the area, Alexander had to leave outposts of war-weary men to hold the frontier of the Jaxartes and the town he had founded there – Alexandria-Eschate (Alexandria the Farthest, modern Khojend).

At Samarkand, Alexander married Roxane, the daughter of a Sogdian nobleman. The wedding is depicted as a love match, which may be true, but the political implications did not escape Alexander either. By means of a wedding ceremony, the Macedonian king helped to terminate the lengthy guerrilla war that he had been unable to bring to an end militarily. Philip II had used political marriage to great advantage in his time; after seven years of campaigning, Alexander too had come to appreciate its usefulness.

It is difficult to determine how much the marriage to Roxane influenced Alexander's thinking about the benefits of intermarriage with the Persians, and the forging of a Eurasian nation with a Graeco-Asiatic culture. Some ancient writers mention other marriages between Macedonians and barbarian women at this time, but these may anticipate the great mass-marriage ceremony at Susa in 324. It is certain, however, that soon after marrying Roxane Alexander attempted to introduce the Persian custom of obeisance (*proskynesis*) at his court. This met with fierce resistance on the part of his Macedonian generals and courtiers, and the king reluctantly abandoned the scheme.

arti pour recieuer son corps iusques
tant que les dernieres furent
assez · Toute celle nuit passa sans
rmr en grant commotion de son
urage ne la lendemain nestoit
fusioieux pour ce quil nauoit
re de nauir auec ce quon ne vou
t dreschier aucune ponts sur la

piames de feurr sur lesquel
transnageirent la riuier et a
qui passoient les premiers se
toient en battaille tandie qi
austres trauersoient · En cest
mer le v.e iour expsa son o
sautre riue · ▬▬▬▬▬▬▬
Comment sritamenes py

13

THE INVASION OF INDIA

The political marriage of Alexander and Roxane had brought the guerrilla war in Bactria and Sogdiana to an end, but the fighting was to continue. The Macedonian army now turned its attention to the last corner of the Achaemenid Empire. Here three provinces remained: Parapamisadae, which lay beyond the passes of the Hindu Kush east of the city of Bactra (Balkh, near Masar-e-sharif); Gandhara (now part of northern Pakistan); and Hindush (Sindh), the valley of the Indus. Once through the Hindu Kush, Alexander advanced into the Bajaur and Swat regions, moving relentlessly towards the Indus, where an advance force under Hephaestion and Perdiccas had constructed a boat-bridge across the river, leading into the territory of Taxiles.

On the march, Alexander had encountered fierce resistance from the Aspasians and Assacenians. The chief city of the latter was Massaga, located in the Katgala Pass and defended by a woman, Cleophis, the mother (or possibly widow) of the local dynast Assacenus. He had died only shortly before Alexander's arrival at the city, probably in an earlier attempt to stop the Macedonians en route. It was Assacenus' brother, Amminais, who conducted the actual defence, with the help of 9,000 mercenaries, but legend chooses instead to focus on the queen, who negotiated the surrender of the city and retained her throne by dazzling Alexander with her beauty. Her story must be read with caution, since her name and conduct are reminiscent of the famous Egyptian queen, Cleopatra VII. The first historian to mention her may, indeed, have written in the Augustan age, when Cleopatra herself had gained notoriety.

Some of the Assacenians fled to a seemingly impregnable mountain known to the ancients as Aornus (probably Pir-sar, though some have suggested Mount Ilam). Here, just as he had done in his siege of Arimazes, Alexander overcame the rugged terrain, this time herding many of the terrified natives to their deaths as they attempted to descend the steep embankment overhanging the Indus. By capturing the place, the king could claim to have outdone his mythical ancestor, Heracles, who had been driven off by an earthquake.

In crossing the Indus, Alexander was pitching his ambitions even beyond the confines of the old Persian Empire. At this point, if any, Alexander's men could be expected to show those symptoms of mutiny that were later to frustrate him. But the army, reassured by legends of the god Dionysus' visit to India, followed their leader over the Indus without demur.

Alexander crossed into the territory of Taxiles. Taxiles' real name was Amphi, but he is known in Arrian's history as 'Taxiles', which was probably a title derived from his capital city. Taxiles ruled the region between the Indus and Hydaspes (Jhelum) rivers and he gave Alexander a lavish reception in his capital at Taxila (near modern Islamabad). He was at the time hard pressed by his enemies – Abisares to the north (in the Kashmir) and Porus, rajah of the Paurava, to the west. In exchange for support, he accepted a Macedonian garrison and an overseer, Philip son of Machatas. But Taxiles remained nominal head of the territory.

Porus meanwhile had urged Abisares to lend aid against Taxiles and the Macedonian invader. Instead, he made perhaps token submission to Alexander, content to await the outcome of events. When Porus went down to defeat, Abisares sent money and elephants, but argued that he could not come in person on account of illness, an old trick of rulers confronted by those more powerful.

Alexander understood that in making a friend of Taxiles, he had assured himself the enmity of Porus. Accordingly, intent upon a new war, he now marched east again towards the river Hydaspes, beyond which Porus was mobilizing his army.

Alexander's army in India

It was perhaps when the army entered India that the sarissa first reached its enormous length, giving the phalanx greater capability to fight elephants and their drivers. The cuirass had now been abandoned and normal equipment now consisted of shield, sword, javelin and sarissa, held in the left hand at first, then transferred to the right after the javelin had been thrown.

The army in India must have presented a strange sight. Before the campaign, Alexander had issued the hypaspists with silvered shields, the cavalry with gilded bits, and the rest of the infantry with gilded and silvered equipment. This sumptuousness was mixed with shabbiness. Eight years had passed since Alexander had led his army across the Hellespont, and his men had covered thousands of miles. The lines of supply had started to break down. At first Persian tunics had to be worn, then re-cut Indian ones; cuirasses and other armour wore out and had to be discarded. The morale of the troops was severely undermined by the presence of Porus' elephants, and when rumours circulated that an army of 4,000 elephants waited beyond the Hydaspes, there was mutiny. This fear of elephants was probably the main consideration which induced Alexander to re-distribute armour to the infantry shortly afterwards.

ANCIENT INDIAN ARMIES

Armies of the different Indian states obviously differed in appearance and weaponry. Most had a combination of infantry, cavalry, chariots and war elephants.

The archer was the most common type of infantryman in the Indian army that faced Alexander. He was equipped with a large and powerful bow, as long as the archer was tall, and fitted with a hemp or sinew string that could be drawn to the ear. Arrows were very long, of cane or reed and flighted with vulture feathers. Arrow-heads were usually of iron, sometimes of horn and, according to some Greek sources, could carry poison. Arrian says that the Indian bow was very powerful, no shield or cuirass being able to stop its arrows. Some of Alexander's officers maintained that it was too heavy to aim accurately, however, and the effects of Indian archery at the Hydaspes appear to have been negligible.

There seem to have been several different types of sword employed by the infantry, and one can assume that some of the infantry were designated as swordsmen, though it was noted by Nearchus that Indian infantry were not eager for close combat. Armour was minimal, if worn at all. Other infantry were equipped with javelins; they may sometimes have been formed up in front of archers. They are likely to have had shields with which to protect themselves and the archers, but no armour.

War elephants were expensive to obtain and maintain, so not all Indian states had the necessary resources to be able to use them, but for those who could, they were valuable as 'mobile fortresses'. They served the Indian cavalry and infantry either as a refuge behind which they could retreat or as a base from which they could sally forth. Both Diodorus Siculus and Curtius compare the elephant line to a walled city with towers raised at intervals. Arrian says that the Indian infantry companies projected for a short distance into the spaces among the elephants. Diodorus compares the infantry to curtain walls between towering elephants. (Richard Geiger © Osprey Publishing Ltd)

BATTLE OF HYDASPES

Porus determined to face Alexander and Taxiles at the crossing of the Hydaspes near modern Haranpur. When Alexander reached the Hydaspes, he found King Porus' substantial army ranged against him on the opposite bank. In ancient times, it often happened that battles were fought at river crossings: not only was a river a defensive moat, it was also a water supply for the troops encamped on its banks. The Hydaspes in any case was not a mere torrent or mountain stream, nor even a river of moderate size that could be forded easily at suitable points. At this time of year in particular it was a full-flowing navigable waterway: there would be no repeat of the charge at the Granicus.

Nevertheless the two armies were perfectly visible to each other across the broad waters, which were, in early summer, swift and turbulent. The numerical strength of Porus' army is variously recorded by different ancient historians, and modern accounts do not always agree in the interpretation of the figures. The main body of the Indian army seems to have numbered between 20,000 and 50,000 infantry, between 2,000 and 4,000 cavalry, anything from 85 to 200 elephants and from 300 to more than 1,000 chariots. It is additionally reported that Porus' brother was present with a force of 4,000 cavalry and 100 chariots. Margins of difference are therefore considerable, and the best estimate is a mid-way figure.

Alexander led the Asiatic troops, except for a force of 5,000 Indian allies, from further west, but the core of his army was still that body of Macedonian infantry and Companion cavalry with which he had crossed the Hellespont, and the army with which he faced Porus was probably no more than 40,000 strong. He had always found that such a number gave him strategic and tactical mobility, and he had proved that it was capable of defeating in battle Asiatic forces of any size that could be brought against it.

With the Hydaspes in flood, there was, of course, no immediate possibility of fording the river. Alexander gave out publicly that he was content to wait for the autumn months when the water would run very much lower. No doubt he intended that such a pronouncement should come to the ears of the enemy – but it is quite evident that he had laid other plans.

Porus strongly guarded all possible ferry crossings, and his elephants became extremely useful in this role, for they would certainly terrify any horses that confronted them, making a cavalry landing from rafts or barges quite impossible. But Alexander was, as ever, resourceful. Before moving up to the frontiers of Porus' territory, he had dismantled the boats and galleys he had used on the Indus. The smaller craft had been broken into two parts, the 30-oar galleys into three parts; the sections had then been transported on wagons overland and the whole flotilla reassembled on the Hydaspes. From the first, these boats had been

STRATEGY AT THE BATTLE OF THE HYDASPES

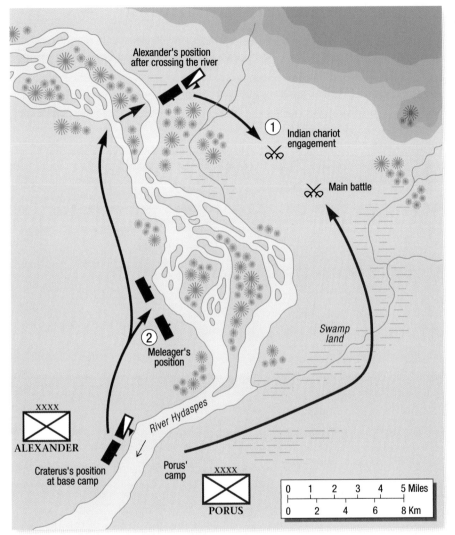

Alexander's position after crossing the river

① *Indian chariot engagement*

Main battle

② *Meleager's position*

Swamp land

River Hydaspes

XXXX

ALEXANDER

Craterus's position at base camp

Porus' camp

XXXX

PORUS

| 0 | 1 | 2 | 3 | 4 | 5 Miles |
| 0 | 2 | | 4 | 6 | 8 Km |

1. The preliminary Indian chariot attack.

2. Craterus and Meleager held the line of the river and immobilized the Indian troops that might otherwise have been led off to confront Alexander. Craterus and Meleager then crossed the river when Alexander had been victorious.

able to navigate the river unmolested, the Indians having made no attempt to deny them the use of the midway channel.

During the weeks that followed, Alexander moved his cavalry continually up and down the river bank. Porus, to forestall the concentration of Alexander's troops at any single point, dispatched forces to march level with Alexander's men on the opposite bank, guided by the noise that the Macedonians were deliberately creating. Any place at which a crossing seemed contemplated was immediately guarded in strength by the Indians. Alexander's movements were however, mere feints. No attack materialized and eventually Porus relaxed his vigilance. This, of course, was Alexander's intention. The Macedonians were now in a position to make a real attack. Any sound of their movements would inevitably be discounted by the enemy as another false alert.

As they moved up and down the riverbank, Alexander's cavalry had been reconnoitring for suitable crossing places, reporting back to Alexander. He now selected one, and made plans to cross the Hydaspes by night. He left his officer Craterus in the area where the Macedonian army had originally encamped, together with the cavalry unit this officer normally commanded, as well as attached units of Asiatic cavalry and local Indian troops to the number of 5,000, plus two units of the Macedonian phalanx.

Alexander himself set out for the chosen crossing place with a similarly mixed but stronger force. It included the vanguard of the Companion cavalry and the cavalry units of his officers Hephaestion, Perdiccas and Demetrius. These units were hipparchies of greater strength than the squadrons he had used in Asia Minor. He also led Asiatic troops that included mounted archers, and two phalanx units with archers and Agrianians.

The purpose of leaving a substantial force at the base camp was to disguise Alexander's movements from Porus. It was imperative that the Indians knew nothing of the crossing until it was accomplished. His orders to Craterus were that if Porus led away only part of his army to meet this emergency, leaving a force of elephants behind him, then the Macedonians at the base camp should remain where they were, covering the enemy on the opposite bank. However, if Porus abandoned his position entirely, either in flight, or to face Alexander, then Craterus and his men might safely cross. In fact, the main danger to the Macedonian cavalry was from the elephants. Once these were withdrawn, the river might confidently be crossed, no matter what other Indian troops remained.

Night operations

The point selected as a crossing place was about 18 miles upstream from the base camp. Here, on the opposite bank, was a headland where the river bent, covered with luxuriant undergrowth, and in the river alongside it rose the island of Admana, also densely forested and so providing concealment for the proximity or presence of cavalry. Along the Macedonian bank Alexander had already posted a chain of pickets, capable of communicating with each other either by visual or audible signals. Similar to his previous practice, Alexander had allowed the enemy to become accustomed to the shouts and nightly watchfires of these outposts.

BATTLE OF THE HYDASPES: THE RIVER CROSSING

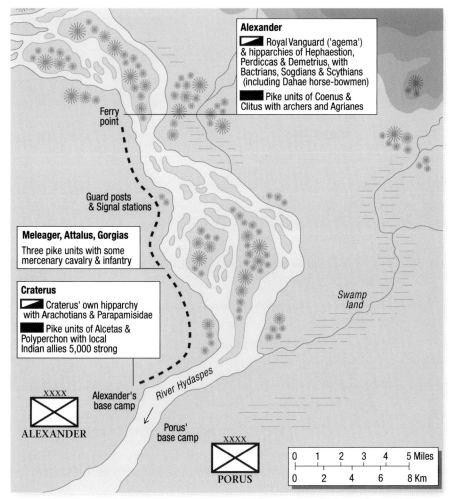

Alexander

Royal Vanguard ('agema')
& hipparchies of Hephaestion,
Perdiccas & Demetrius, with
Bactrians, Sogdians & Scythians
(including Dahae horse-bowmen)

Pike units of Coenus &
Clitus with archers and Agrianes

Ferry
point

Guard posts
& Signal stations

Meleager, Attalus, Gorgias

Three pike units with some
mercenary cavalry & infantry

Craterus

Craterus' own hipparchy
with Arachotians & Parapamisidae

Pike units of Alcetas &
Polyperchon with local
Indian allies 5,000 strong

Swamp
land

River Hydaspes

XXXX

ALEXANDER

Alexander's
base camp

Porus'
base camp

XXXX

PORUS

0	1	2	3	4	5 Miles
0	2		4	6	8 Km

Screened by such diversions, Alexander's march was made in great secrecy. It followed an inland route, possibly a short cut. As the Macedonians marched through the night, they were overtaken by a thunderstorm and heavy rain. Though they cannot have enjoyed it, the storm must have rendered their movement imperceptible to the enemy.

At the crossing place a ferry fleet had been prepared in advance. Many of the ferries were rafts floated on skins that had been transported empty to the spot, then stuffed with chaff and sewn up to make them watertight. Alexander had previously used this technique for ferrying troops on the Danube and on the Oxus. Alongside these waited the 30-oar galleys carried overland from the Indus.

Close to the river bank, at an intermediate position between the base camp and the ferry point, he stationed three of his officers, Meleager, Attalus and Gorgias, each in charge of his own infantry unit, with attached cavalry and infantry detailed from the mercenaries. Like Craterus, this force was ordered to cross only when it saw that the enemy on the opposite bank of the river was committed elsewhere. The crossing was to be made in three waves, probably because there were not enough ferries to permit a transit in one body.

At dawn the storm subsided. As the ferry flotilla, led by Alexander and his staff in a galley, moved out into the river, it was initially out of sight of the opposite bank. But as they went further across the river they were obliged to break cover, and enemy scouts galloped off to report their approach.

Alexander's men now ran into unforeseen difficulties, as the bank that had seemed to be the mainland opposite in reality belonged to another island. A deep but narrow channel separated it from the land beyond, and men and animals barely managed to ford the fast-flowing current – sometimes with little more than their heads above water. Emerging at last from this second crossing, Alexander was able to marshal his troops unmolested by the enemy and without difficulty on the opposite bank. Though the ancient sources vary, it seems that he now advanced along the river to face Porus' army, marching in semi-deployed formation. The Companions, with all the best cavalry, were massed in front of the infantry, and ahead of these were 1,000 mounted archers serving as a screen and equipped to deal with elephants at long range. The main cavalry, about 5,000 in number, were provided with a flank guard of archers under the command of Tauron, who was ordered to keep up with the horses as best he could.

Behind the cavalry marched the hypaspists under Seleucus. The main phalanx, marching in battle formation, was guarded by Agrianians and javelin-throwers on both its flanks. The position of the other cavalry not in a forward role is not recorded; either they must have followed at this stage in the rear, or guarded the left flank of the hypaspists.

Arrian suggests that Alexander was willing, if the occasion arose, to challenge Porus' whole army with just his cavalry, but this can hardly have been the case. Apart from anything else, the whole object of Alexander's tactics was to avoid putting his cavalry up against elephants. He must have led his mounted troops forward simply to repel any cavalry or chariot attack against the disembarkation point. Indeed, the ferry operation was not complete, even after the landing of his main body. He had not been able to transport the whole force in a single crossing, as the infantry with which he first disembarked numbered about 6,000, certainly a smaller number than that with which he had set out from base camp.

The Indian reaction

When news of the crossing reached Porus, he did not believe it had been made in strength, and he thought that a mobile force, dispatched under the leadership of his son, would be enough to cope with the situation. He could, after all, see Craterus' men still encamped opposite him on the other side of the river, and he imagined that these represented the Macedonian main army, just as Alexander had hoped. The detachment sent against Alexander numbered only some 2,000 cavalry and 120 chariots. (These at least are the figures recorded by Alexander's officer Ptolemy and accepted by Arrian.) The chariot force was in any case immediately routed, with a reported loss of 400 killed – among whom was the young prince. Horses and chariots were mainly captured.

Porus now realized that he would have to march against Alexander with the greater part of his army. However, Craterus' troops, already preparing to cross the river in force, could not be disregarded, and the Indian king left a small body of men to guard the riverbank, with some elephants, which he hoped would be enough to daunt any oncoming Macedonian cavalry. He himself moved with his main army against Alexander. His army numbered about 4,000 cavalry, 300 chariots, 200 elephants and 30,000 infantry. Much of the country over which he marched was muddy and difficult, but finding a sandy plain that would give his cavalry freedom of manoeuvre he halted, and made ready for battle.

The Indian front line was composed of elephants, stationed at intervals of approximately 100ft (30.5m). Behind the elephants and in the intervals between them were more infantry, guarded on their exposed flanks by cavalry and further screened by war chariots at each end of the whole front. When Alexander came within sight of the Indian battle array, he halted and allowed his infantry to rest, while the cavalry patrolled around them.

Before going into action against Porus, Alexander reshuffled the leadership of his own army. His senior officers were variously assignable, their individual competence not limited to one arm of the fighting forces. Coenus was appointed to command of Demetrius' cavalry, Demetrius being perhaps retained as second-in-command. Seleucus remained in charge of the hypaspists. But the leaders of the pike phalanx were now Tauron and Antigenes. It is easy to see how such changes might become desirable at this stage. Crossing a river and fighting a battle are very different operations and so might reasonably call for changes of leadership.

Porus enjoyed an overwhelming superiority in infantry numbers, but Alexander had the advantage in cavalry. The issue was whether the Macedonian cavalry would be engaged by the Indian elephants and thrown into confusion, or whether such a confrontation could be avoided. Alexander avoided it.

OVERLEAF
A 17th-century painting by Charles Le Brun of Alexander and Porus, after Porus' defeat at the Hydaspes. (akg-images/Erich Lessing)

The diagram shows 200 elephants stationed at 100ft (30.5m) intervals. The arrangement, in four ranks, is conjectural.

BATTLE OF THE HYDASPES: THE ELEPHANT LINE

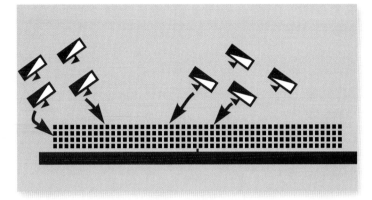

He opened the battle with an attack by his horse-archers, which produced considerable disorder in the enemy's left-wing formations.

Porus' chariots had been marshalled on both wings ahead of his cavalry. The chariots on his left must have borne the first impact of Alexander's mounted archers. They presumably presented large targets to the attackers, for each chariot is reported as carrying six men, only two of whom bore shields.

It seems that the Indian king now had second thoughts about the deployment of his army, for an attempt was made to lead his cavalry out in front of the chariots. But Alexander, with his Companion cavalry, fell upon the Indian left-wing horsemen while they were still advancing in column and before they had time to deploy into line of battle. The whole of Porus' left wing was now forced on the defensive.

On the other side of the field, the right-wing cavalry of the Indians did their best to save the situation. They swept across the central plain to counter-attack against Alexander's flank. Any opposing horsemen on the left flank of the Macedonian infantry must have been too few or too far off to discourage the Indian manoeuvre. But Alexander's officer Coenus, acting on a pre-arranged plan, now detached himself from the other Companions and led his cavalry in a circuitous ride – presumably at a gallop – to emerge on the tail of the counter-attacking Indians in their transverse career across the battlefield. It cannot be excluded that in order to carry out the operation Coenus actually passed to the rear of the advancing Macedonian infantry before the enemy observed his approach. He certainly came into view suddenly and unexpectedly, when the Indian right-wing cavalry was already almost at grips with Alexander's Companions.

The Indians were now threatened with battle on two fronts. They reacted by dividing their forces and facing in two directions simultaneously, against Alexander and against Coenus. This meant re-forming. But Alexander suddenly wheeled inwards and charged them as they were in the middle of their manoeuvre. Without attempting to withstand the full onslaught of the Companion cavalry, they fell back for cover among the elephants.

The defeat of Porus

The elephants now proved their value, moving forwards against the oncoming Macedonian infantry, despite showers of missiles from Alexander's archers and javelin-throwers. They savagely mangled the phalanx, trampling men underfoot or attacking with tusk and trunk with an effectiveness which must have been partly due to military training. Taking heart from the elephant charge, the Indian cavalry now made a final sally against Alexander's cavalry, but they were driven back once more among the elephants. The battle at this stage was rather unusual, for the cavalry of both sides, instead of being distributed on either wing, was concentrated as a dense and confused mass in the centre of the field.

The attack of the elephants soon lost its momentum: the drivers were vulnerable to javelins and arrows, and the Macedonians were in a position to give way before them as they charged, then renew their attack as the elephants tired, using sabres to attack their trunks, and axes to cut off their feet. The elephants were soon wounded and maddened to a point at which they were out of control, even where they had not lost their drivers. It was a common experience of ancient warfare that when frightened elephants became out of control, they could do as much damage to their own masters as to the enemy. Porus' elephants at the Hydaspes were no exception: the cavalry, penned in an ever-contracting space among the elephants, jostling and huddling, were trampled and crushed. The Indian infantry, deprived of any support from cavalry, chariots or elephants, were no match for the Macedonian phalanx as it came on against them with shields locked together.

At last, when all arms of Porus' forces were exhausted, Alexander's cavalry and infantry moved in, surrounding and capturing the elephants, which had now been reduced to a stationary role, trumpeting and bellowing in pathetic protest. In this action, the Indian cavalry was annihilated as a fighting force, and those of Porus' men who found a merciful gap in the encircling enemy lines took to flight. However, flight did not save them all, as Craterus and the other Macedonians posted on the west bank now crossed the river and intercepted the exhausted fugitives. In the battle and the pursuit that ensued, 3,000 Indian cavalry were reported lost, 20,000 infantry were killed, and all the chariots were wrecked. The surviving elephants became the booty of the victors.

TACTICS AT THE HYDASPES

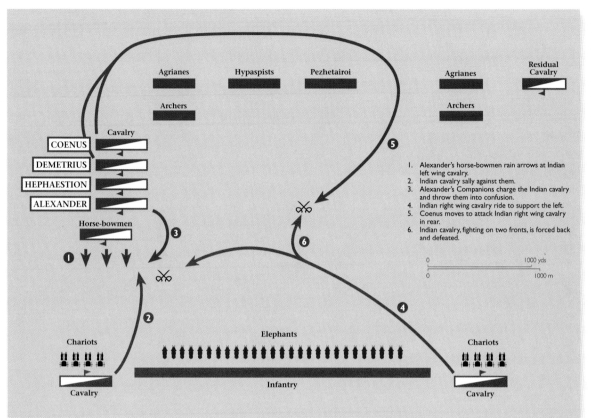

1. Alexander's horse-bowmen rain arrows at Indian left wing cavalry.
2. Indian cavalry sally against them.
3. Alexander's Companions charge the Indian cavalry and throw them into confusion.
4. Indian right wing cavalry ride to support the left.
5. Coenus moves to attack Indian right wing cavalry in rear.
6. Indian cavalry, fighting on two fronts, is forced back and defeated.

Porus, a gigantic man, mounted on an elephant and protected by a stout corselet, had, unlike Darius, continued fighting until the end. Only when he was wounded did he abandon the struggle. Alexander sent his ally, Taxiles, to pursue Porus and invite his surrender, but Porus, from the back of his elephant, threatened Taxiles with a spear and drove him away. A second ambassador was sent, whose relations with Porus had in the past been happier. The Indian king was finally induced to dismount from his elephant and parley with Alexander, who, full of admiration for a gallant enemy, and probably also aware of diplomatic considerations, granted him the honourable terms he demanded and concluded an alliance with him. It had not always been so: Alexander had often been less than generous in his treatment of stubborn adversaries in the past. The greater challenge lay, however, in the attempt to bring about lasting peace between the Indian rivals. Curtius claims that an alliance between Taxiles and Porus was sealed by marriage, the common currency in such transactions. But the arrangement was never entirely satisfactory. Though Taxiles was perhaps more to be trusted than Porus, Alexander needed the latter for his upcoming campaigns in the Punjab.

Alexander at the Hydaspes was at his most cunning, splitting his forces then creeping upriver and making a secret crossing at night. In doing so, he caused Porus to split his forces before the battle, weakening and confusing him. When battle was joined, though cautious of using his cavalry against the elephants, he deployed them against the enemy left wing as usual; however, he had clearly planned for every eventuality, as can be seen with Coenus' mad gallop to appear in the rear of the attacking Indian right-wing cavalry as they dashed to counter-attack Alexander's cavalry. Soon Alexander had the Indian army fighting on two fronts, and as at Gaugamela, he swooped in with a cavalry charge when the Indians had to re-form to meet the Macedonians. Though this is not as clear an example of Alexander's tactical brilliance as elsewhere, his opening moves were highly characteristic, as is his quick thinking during the battle to take advantage wherever it appeared.

Beside the Hydaspes Alexander founded two new towns, Nicaea and Bucephala, the latter named after his warhorse, which had died of old age. He rested his men for a month, and about this time received reinforcements of Thracian troops drafted by his governor in the Caspian area. Hearing of disaffection in Assacenia, he dispatched troops to restore the situation. But Alexander was now defied by a second king called Porus. This second Porus soon fled from Alexander's advance, but Alexander eagerly pursued him, crossing the Acesines and Hydraotes rivers. This brought him into conflict with the tribe of the Cathaei. Having subdued them, he marched to the river Hyphasis (Beas).

THE JOURNEY BACK

THE LIMITS OF CONQUEST

Beyond the river Hyphasis lay the populous and little-known subcontinent of India proper. Arrian suggests that Alexander had hopes of reaching the 'Ocean Stream', which the Greeks believed encircled the landmass of the world. However, on the banks of the Hyphasis, the war-weary Macedonians, battered by the elements, their uniforms literally rotting off their bodies, called a halt. Alexander yearned for further adventure and conquest, this time in the valley of the Ganges. The soldiers, however, went on strike and even the bravest and most loyal of Alexander's officers spoke on their behalf. The king sulked in his tent, but the men remained obdurate. There was nothing to do but turn back.

Behind this traditionally accepted view of the end of Alexander's eastward march, there may be another, more complex story. After all, why would an experienced and shrewd military leader like Alexander allow reports of extraordinary dangers, or numerous enemies and exotic places, to come to the attention of soldiers whom he knew were demoralized and tired? If the fantastic report of India beyond the Hyphasis was 'leaked' to the Macedonian soldiery, it was because Alexander wanted them to hear it. All this may have been a face-saving gesture by a king who was just as tired as his men, but for whom it would have been unheroic to decline further challenges. Instead, the responsibility for ending this glorious march into the unknown was placed squarely on the shoulders of the common soldier. The stubbornness of his troops alone robbed Alexander of further glory. This was the accepted tradition, and this is how it has come down to us. Further evidence of Alexander's duplicity can be found in the fact that he ordered the men to build a camp of abnormal size, containing artefacts that were larger than life, in order to cheat posterity into thinking that the expeditionary force had been superhuman. Curtius states that Alexander had 12 altars erected to commemorate the expedition, then ordered the camp fortifications to be extended and over-sized couches to be made and left behind, in order to 'leave to posterity a fraudulent wonder' (9.3.19).

OPPOSITE
Dionysus on a leopard. Mosaic from Pella, 4th century. When Alexander reached India he began to emulate Dionysus as well as Heracles.
(TopFoto/HIP)

RETURN TO THE WEST

The army was returning to the west – but not directly. It was not necessary to cross the Hyphasis in the quest for ocean. Alexander knew full well that the Indus river system would lead him there, and he had transported boats in sections for

ENDURING ALEXANDER'S CAMPAIGNS

Alexander led his men from the Balkans to the Indus, across desert wastes and some of the world's highest mountain passes. It has been calculated that the infantryman who campaigned with Alexander in Europe in 336–334 and then joined the Asiatic campaign had covered 20,870 miles (33,587km) by the time Alexander died in Babylon in 323, an average of 1,605 miles per year. For many this was not the end of it; for example, the argyraspids marched from Cilicia to Egypt and back (if they did not first make a detour to Media) and then campaigned with Eumenes in Mesopotamia, Persia, and on the Iranian plateau, thus adding at least another 5,000 miles to a journey that was destined to leave their bones scattered throughout distant lands. Alexander's route to Bactria and then to India took them twice over mountain passes that approached or exceeded 12,000ft (3,658m). Many of Alexander's veterans could claim to have crossed the Euphrates and Tigris rivers, the Oxus and Iaxartes, the Indus and three of its tributaries, as well as the Nile. In addition to these natural obstacles, they had also faced the seemingly impregnable fortresses of Tyre and Gaza, the Rocks of Ariamazes and Sisimithres, and Aornus on the edge of the Indus, all of which combined natural and man-made positions with armed defenders. Disease and wounds carried off many, and settlements in central Asia were dotted with colonists who included those men unfit for

battle (apomachoi). Sometimes their stay was temporary, and they later rejoined the army, but for many it was a bleak and unwelcome 'retirement'. The speech of the taxiarch (now promoted to hipparch) Coenus son of Polemocrates delivered at the river Hyphasis, indicates the cumulative effects, physical and moral, of the campaigns that Alexander's soldiers had undertaken:

Whatever mortals were capable of, we have achieved. We have crossed lands and seas, all of them now better known to us than to their inhabitants. We stand almost at the end of the earth [and] you are preparing to enter another world ... That is a mission appropriate to your spirit, but beyond ours. For your valour will ever be on the increase, but our energy is already running out. Look at our bodies – debilitated, pierced with all those wounds, decaying with all their scars! Our weapons are blunt; our armour is wearing out ... How many of us have a cuirass? Who owns a horse? Have an inquiry made into how many are attended by slaves and what anyone has left of his booty. Conquerors of all, we lack everything! And our problems result not from extravagance; no, on war have we expended the equipment of war. (Curtius, 9.3.7–11)

Alexander's campaigns

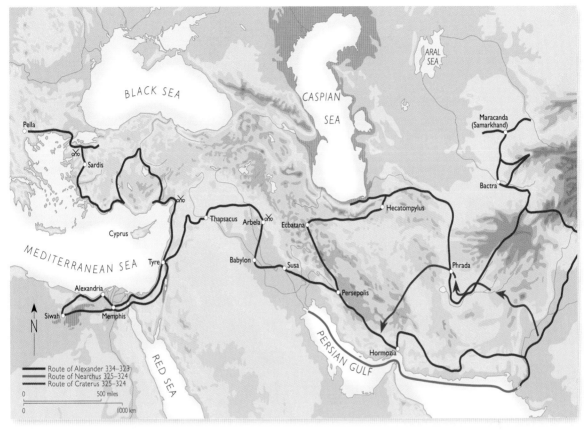

Route of Alexander 334–323
Route of Nearchus 325–324
Route of Craterus 325–324

0   500 miles
0   1000 km

the very purpose of following the river to its mouth. On the way, he subdued warlike tribes, troublesome neighbours for his new vassal, Porus. Among these were the Mallians, a tribe of the Indus valley who had sympathized with the Cathaei.

Disregarding his own safety and forgetting that the Macedonians' enthusiasm for war was no longer what it had been, Alexander was the first to scale the walls of the Mallians' main city and jump inside. Only a few bodyguards accompanied him. When the troops saw that their king was trapped, they scrambled up the ladders, overloading and breaking them. Inside the walls, the king was showered with arrows; one officer, Abreas, died rescuing him, the other two rescuers, Peucestas and Leonnatus, were later promoted and decorated. Alexander was rescued, but he had an arrow lodged deep in his chest, and once the troops poured over the battlements, they took vengeance, killing every man, woman and child in the town.

Miraculously, Alexander survived, though for a good portion of the journey downriver he was all but incapacitated. By the time he reached the Indus delta he had recovered, and from here he sailed out into the Indian Ocean and conducted sacrifices at the limits of his empire, just as he had done at the Hellespont in 334.

Military and political considerations had led him to dispatch Craterus and his main army on a homeward march through Arachosia and via the city of Alexandria (Kandahar) that had been founded there. Alexander himself was now bent upon exploration and discovery. He assembled his remaining troops and an accompanying fleet at Pattala at the head of the Indus delta, preparatory to a double homeward expedition made concurrently by land and sea.

It was planned that Nearchus' fleet would sail alongside Alexander's land forces as they moved westwards. However, the fleet was delayed by the monsoon, and soon lost contact with Alexander's forces. The fleet sailed along the coast, eventually passing through the Straits of Hormuz and entering the Persian Gulf; it was a journey fraught with hardship, deprivation and danger.

The crews were often terrified by the unfamiliar conditions of the Indian Ocean, which included such unknown phenomena as tides and whales. Some vessels were lost during the journey.

The land forces suffered more horribly. Led by Alexander, they struggled through the Gedrosian desert. At first they trailed luxurious spoils acquired in their eastern wars, as well as women and children. But soon they ran short of food and water. Curtius describes the march:

> Their provisions exhausted, the Macedonians began to experience first shortage of food and eventually starvation. They rummaged about for palm roots (that being the only tree growing there) but, when even this means of sustenance ran out, they began to slaughter their pack-animals, sparing not even their horses. Then, having nothing to carry their baggage, they proceeded to burn the spoils they had taken from the enemy, spoils for which they had penetrated the furthest reaches of the East. (9.10.11–12)

Although tortured by thirst, the army met disaster in a torrent bed, where a meagre trickle of water had encouraged them to pitch camp. A sudden cloudburst over distant mountains turned the little stream into a raging flood without warning, and many of the women and children drowned. There were considerable casualties both among people and animals during the march. The sick and exhausted were left to lie where they fell; none had the strength to help

CRATERUS

Craterus began the expedition as a taxiarch, a commander of pezhetairoi. He served as the second-in-command on the left wing, under the direct authority of Parmenion, whom he was being groomed to replace. Craterus was an officer of unswerving loyalty to Alexander, and his promotions squarely reflected his abilities. As the campaign progressed, Craterus exercised more frequent independent commands. During Alexander's return through the Gedrosian desert, Craterus led the slower troops and invalids through the Bolan Pass towards modern Kandahar. On the way he apprehended rebels, whom he took to the king for execution.

In 324 Craterus was sent to replace Antipater as viceroy of Macedon. This order was pre-empted by Alexander's death and the outbreak of the Lamian War. In 321/320 Craterus returned to Asia and did battle with Eumenes near the Hellespont. He was thrown from his horse and trampled beneath its hooves, an ignominious end for one of Alexander's greatest generals.

HEPHAESTION

Hephaestion, son of Amyntor, had been a close friend of Alexander since boyhood. They had been at Mieza together as teenagers, where the heir to the throne was educated by Aristotle. Romanticized accounts compared the two with Achilles and Patroclus. Whether they were lovers, as many modern writers have asserted, is not entirely clear, but Alexander certainly promoted Hephaestion's career despite the fact that he seems to have possessed poor leadership qualities and little military skill. He was nevertheless a gifted organizer, and Alexander left many matters of logistics – supply, transport of equipment, bridge-building and the founding of settlements – to him. By the time the army reached India, Hephaestion's promotion had brought about friction with other officers, especially Craterus. At one point the two came to blows in front of their respective troops and Alexander had to intervene. Although he chided Hephaestion because he failed to recognize that 'without Alexander he would be nothing', he remained devoted to his lifelong friend. In October 324, Hephaestion died of illness, and the king was inconsolable. According to Plutarch he gave orders that as a sign of mourning the manes and tails of all the army horses should be shorn, the battlements of neighbouring cities demolished, Hephaestion's doctor crucified and all music banned. Alexander planned an elaborate funeral including a pyramid. The project was never completed, although the lion of Hamadan is said to have been part of the plan. Many have tried to link the deaths of Alexander and Hephaestion, especially as Alexander died within eight months of Hephaestion's demise. (akg-images)

or carry them. When a violent wind obliterated all landmarks and erased the tracks with sand, Alexander's guides, unable to read the stars, failed him. In this emergency, Alexander took charge personally and, using his sense of direction, led his desperate men back to the sea, where a fresh-water spring was discovered under the shingle beach. Sustained by a succession of such springs, they marched along the shore for seven days. Although Alexander stood up to the hardships as well as any man, and indeed it was on this march that he displayed some of his most noble qualities, the march was an unmitigated disaster.

Alexander eventually made contact with Craterus inland, in Carmania (Kerman). Craterus brought pack-animals and elephants and the remainder of the march was made in comparatively civilized conditions.

At the entry of the Persian Gulf, Nearchus' men had fallen in with a Greek-speaking straggler from Alexander's army, and Nearchus ventured north with a small party to meet Alexander. After an emotional meeting, however, land and sea expeditions continued on separate lines. Nearchus sailed up the Persian Gulf, first to the mouth of the Euphrates, then to the Tigris, finally rejoining Alexander at Susa. Reports of the time taken by this voyage differ wildly. But it seems most likely that Nearchus sailed from the mouth of the Indus at the end of the south-westerly monsoons in October 325 and reached Susa in spring 324.

When Alexander returned to Susa in 324, he celebrated mixed marriages on a grand scale. Alexander himself married Stateira, daughter of Darius III, and Parysatis, daughter of Artaxerxes III. Another of Darius' daughters, Drypetis, married Hephaestion, and nearly a hundred other noble Persian women were given as brides to Macedonian officers. An even larger number of common soldiers took barbarian wives, but this was probably just a way of legitimizing common-law unions that had existed for some time. These marriages were part of Alexander's plans for an empire which was a fusion of culture, nation and race. The marriages appear to have been unpopular with the aristocracy, and after Alexander's death most appear to have repudiated their Persian wives.

Comet furet foules in victo

15

THE DEATH OF THE CONQUEROR

CONSOLIDATION AND FUSION

The wars of Alexander had resulted in the conquest of an empire and the imposition of a Graeco-Macedonian ruling class upon a diverse population that had hitherto been united under Persian control. Greek was now to replace Aramaic as the official written language of the East, although local tongues would endure – just as regional culture and religion would not be wiped out by the mere change of rulers. But the success of the expedition must be measured by the effectiveness of the process of consolidation rather than the speed of conquest.

In fact, the Macedonian conquest was far from complete, as some areas were only partially subdued and others were bypassed intentionally in a bid to come to grips with the Persian king and to strike at the nerve-centres of the Achaemenid Empire. Pockets of independent or recalcitrant states remained throughout the East: Pisidia, Cappadocia and Armenia are notable examples from the northwestern region; the Uxians, who had collected payment from the Persians who crossed their territories, and who had been chased from the invasion route by Alexander, were again asserting their independence in the age of the Successors.

Now Alexander was back in the heart of Persia there was much work to be done to consolidate his conquests and mould his new empire. However, first he had to deal with immediate issues. His attempts to introduce the Persian court ritual of proskynesis and obliging his officers to marry Persian wives had not pleased his court, but it was the integration of large numbers of barbarian troops into the Macedonian army that gave offence to the soldiery. The army mutinied at Opis on the Tigris, complaining that they were being supplanted by foreigners. These complaints Alexander countered with soothing words, but the ringleaders of the mutiny were seized, chained and thrown into the Tigris. Ten thousand veterans, many of them injured, were sent back to Macedon under the command of Craterus, who was himself in poor health. Some of them would

OPPOSITE

This illustration from a 15th-century French manuscript of Curtius' history of Alexander shows Alexander's war elephants. (The Art Archive/ Bibliothèque Municipale Reims/Gianni Dagli Orti)

An illustration of the funeral procession of Alexander the Great. (Prisma/Ancient Art &Architecture Collection Ltd)

indeed reach their homeland, but only to fight again. Others would not advance beyond Cilicia before becoming embroiled in the wars of the Successors.

In Alexander's absence there had also been much evidence of corruption at the heart of his newly established empire. Harpalus, left in fiscal control, had been guilty of grave irregularities and absconded to Greece. Alexander's first impulse was to follow him and arrest him, but welcome news came that he had been murdered by his own subordinates.

When Alexander the Great died, his notebooks (*hypomnemata*) included grandiose plans for the conquest of North Africa and the circumnavigation of the Arabian peninsula, though in truth there was much left to be done in areas that had formerly been subject to, or else a thorn in the side of, the Persian kings. The presence of would-be overlords who were even more alien than the Achaemenids served only to strengthen the determination of these areas to resist. Some regions rebelled in Alexander's lifetime, incited by the very Persian officials whom he had appointed as satraps and hyparchs.

The border provinces in the east were disrupted by both the presence of hostile elements on the fringes and a reluctance on the part of their Greek garrison troops to remain there. Upon the premature news of Alexander's death – after the attack on the Mallian town in the Punjab – the Greeks of Bactria and Sogdiana, some 10,000 in number, had entertained hopes of abandoning their outposts and marching back to the West, an undertaking that would have exceeded by far the accomplishment of the more famous Ten Thousand three-quarters of a century earlier. The first attempt in 324 was thwarted at the outset; the second, immediately after Alexander's death, resulted in the slaughter of the majority of these troops through the treachery of Peithon, to whom the suppression of the revolt had been entrusted.

It is possible that as well as plans for North Africa and the Arabian peninsula, Alexander was also considering expeditions west, as near Babylon in 324 he received embassies from Libya, Carthage, Spain and Gaul. But he was not destined to set out on any more expeditions or conquer any more nations, for in 323 he died following a sudden fever.

ALEXANDER'S DEATH

After sailing on the marshes of the Euphrates waterway near Babylon, a region where malaria was endemic, the king returned to the city. One evening he was invited to a drinking party at the home of Medius of Larisa. While drinking, he suddenly experienced a pain in his chest, 'as if he had been pierced by an arrow or a spear'. He soon returned to his own quarters and his health deteriorated

PTOLEMY

Ptolemy is probably the best known of Alexander's commanders to the modern reader, yet in 323 he was far from being the most noble, influential or most accomplished of the king's generals. Born in the 360s, he was older than many of the young generals and he may not have held his first command until late 331 at the Persian Gates. During the campaigns in what are now Afghanistan and Pakistan, he came into his own as a military commander; he had also been a member of the Bodyguard since 330. When Alexander died, he received the satrapy of Egypt, which he put on a sound administrative and economic footing. Thereafter it was impossible to dislodge him, and he ruled there until 283, sharing the throne with his son Philadelphus in the period 285–283. At some point he wrote a *History of Alexander*, which is now lost but

which was used as a principal source by Arrian. (akg-images/Erich Lessing)

steadily. Nevertheless, he slept, bathed and continued drinking, at least for a while. He developed a fever, which became more severe, and not long afterwards he began to lose the ability to speak. By the time the men had learned of his predicament, he was no longer able to address them, but could only make physical gestures of recognition. On 10 or 11 June 323, he was dead. He had not yet reached his 33rd birthday.

The cause of Alexander's death will always be a topic for debate. He could have succumbed to typhoid, cholera or malaria. More dramatically, he could have been poisoned, the victim of a conspiracy by a number of his generals. The story of his murder is almost certainly a fabrication dating from the wars of the Successors, and no doubt used to political advantage at the time. It is also possible that he was the victim of depression and alcoholism. This is the most difficult to prove, since we cannot psychoanalyze him or determine to what extent his drinking affected his health. The Macedonians were notoriously heavy drinkers, by ancient standards at least, and there are tales of drinking contests in which the winner does not live long enough to enjoy the prize. However, the stories of Alexander's alcoholism are suspect as well: they were probably invented, or at least embellished, by writers like Ephippus of Olynthus, with the aim of discrediting the king.

The loss of a dearly loved king was bad enough, but the uncertainty of the future was increased by the fact that no provisions had been made for the succession and numerous controversial policies had recently been set in motion – including the proclamation of Alexander's Exiles' Decree, which enabled all Greek exiles to return to their native cities, disrupting the politics of the Greek

PERDICCAS

Perdiccas was one of several of Alexander's young and talented officers who vied for power after the king's death. In 336, he was a member of Philip II's hypaspist bodyguard; it was unfortunate that the king's assassination happened when he was on duty. Alexander had promoted him to the rank of taxiarch and as such he led one of the brigades of the pezhetairoi. Probably in 330, he became a member of the Bodyguard, and soon afterwards he commanded a hipparch of the Companion cavalry.

He appears to have worked well with Hephaestion, but others found him difficult to deal with. After Hephaestion's death, he was undoubtedly the most influential of the king's officers, and after Alexander's own death Perdiccas was the logical person to assume control in Babylon. However, he had made too many enemies and his ambitions made him the object of suspicion and hatred. In 320 his invasion of Egypt failed and he was murdered by his own officers.

world, and the orders that Craterus should relieve Antipater of his command in Europe. Grandiose and expensive plans had also been laid, both for the erection of monuments – including the massive funeral pyre for Hephaestion – and for military expeditions. It soon became clear that, although the conquests had come to an end, the war was about to be prolonged; for the struggles between Alexander's generals were destined to be more bitter and more destructive than those against the Persian enemy.

Alexander had never made adequate provision for the succession, nor did he name an heir or even an executor of his will. It was not the first time that his life had been threatened by sickness or wounds, and on these former occasions he had shown no inclination to name a successor. Death in battle had threatened him continuously, but he had never apparently fixed his thoughts on the question of who would inherit the empire he had created. Perhaps Alexander, from his deathbed, had designated Perdiccas as regent by handing over his signet ring. But some modern scholars have questioned whether this gesture was ever made, assuming that it was part of the propaganda devised by Perdiccas or his military heir, Eumenes of Cardia. If the story is false, then Alexander died without making any indication of what should happen to his empire, suggesting that either he did not wish to indicate a successor, or he was indifferent. He may have realized that there was no one legitimate, strong heir who could hold together his empire; he was thus resigned to the fact that it would be fought over by all those strong enough to compete for a piece of the prize.

THE STRUGGLE FOR SUCCESSION

Thus history moves from the age of the brilliant conqueror to that of his Successors (*Diadochoi*). Alexander had always kept his officers on a fairly equal footing, perhaps to increase his own security; once he had freed himself from the clutches of older generals and their factions, he was not eager to create powerful new rivals. Instead, he balanced one appointment with another, encouraging a certain amount of rivalry

This tetradrachm was issued by Demetrius Poliorcetes after the death of his father, Antigonus, at Ipsus in 301. Demetrius often chose coin designs that reflected the naval basis of his realm; on this coin the sea-god Poseidon wields a trident, and the legend reads 'of King Demetrius'. (The British Museum/HIP/TopFoto)

and even open confrontation. As a result, the army too was divided, each section favouring its own commander or combination of commanders. An even greater divide existed between the cavalry and infantry. In short, a peaceful and effective transfer of power was all but impossible.

Philip Arrhidaeus, Alexander's half-brother, was in Babylon at the time of Alexander's death. The son of Philip II and his wife Philinna of Larissa, Arrhidaeus was mentally defective and unable to rule. Alexander had been very fond of his half-brother and took him on his campaigns, both to protect his life and ensure he would not be used in any challenge for the throne. Now Alexander was dead, Arrhidaeus was a political asset to anyone who could claim to be his guardian. Also, at the time of his death, Alexander's wife Roxane was pregnant. A conflict broke out over whether Arrhidaeus should be made king as the closest living relative of Alexander, or whether they should wait and see if Roxane's child was a boy. A compromise was struck: Arrhidaeus was made Philip III, and when Roxane's son was born, he joined his uncle as king, with the name Alexander IV. Neither could rule, so Perdiccas was regent. Both of these kings were murdered during the ensuing struggles for power.

In these early stages, the aim for Alexander's generals was to exercise authority on behalf of the inept or illegitimate candidates for the throne, or else to defy such authority in a bid to carve out a portion of the empire for themselves. In the latter group, we find Ptolemy, who from the first chafed at the thought of serving under a fellow officer, and Peithon, a former Bodyguard. The supporters of the kingship were men like Perdiccas, Aristonous, Eumenes and probably Craterus. Between 323 and 321 (or 320), preparations were made to convey the king's body from Babylon to the oasis of Siwah, where he would rest in the lonely embrace of his divine father Ammon. This never happened, as Ptolemy decided to take possession of the late king's corpse to justify his independence. Meanwhile, the centrifugal tendencies were encouraged or repressed by the various factions within the officer corps, as each pursued either a course of separatism or the fruitless attempt to preserve the integrity of the empire.

SELEUCUS I NICATOR

Seleucus fought alongside Alexander throughout his campaigns from Asia Minor to India. After Alexander's death he gained the satrapy of Babylonia, and in the ensuing wars took Media, Susiana and Persis, then campaigned in the eastern satrapies out to Bactria and the Indus region. Victory at Ipsus gave Seleucus north Syria and Cilicia, and victory over Lysimachus in 281 won him Asia Minor. He then launched a campaign to take Macedon, but was assassinated.

Seleucus married a Bactrian princess, Apame, who became mother to his heir, Antiochus. After this marriage, the Seleucids pursued a policy of dynastic marriage alliances with non-Greek dynasties. Seleucus ruled with his son as co-regent to secure the succession and continuance of the line. In his actions after Alexander's death in securing and then maintaining his empire, Seleucus is shown to be one of the ablest of the Successors. (Roger-Viollet/Topfoto)

Amongst the first to contest the prize were the officers who had been raised at the Macedonian court and educated along with Alexander at Mieza. They were also the first to die. Some admittedly endured and established dynasties that would rule the so-called Hellenistic kingdoms – Seleucus, Lysimachus and Ptolemy – but others, like Antipater and Antigonus Monophthalmos, were grizzled veterans in 323. The former did not long survive the king. Antigonus, however, lived until 301, when he perished on the battlefield of Ipsus. Not many of the companions of Alexander crossed the threshold of old age, and of those who did, few died in their beds. Ptolemy son of Lagus, better known as Ptolemy I Soter of Egypt, proved a rare exception.

Alexander's failure to indicate a successor ensured that the empire was in danger of collapse following his death. Although his death did not mean the empire was unsalvageable, events soon made it so. Matters were made worse by the army's continued hostility to Alexander's plans to integrate Persians into the military and the command structure. Some changes would have to be made if the multicultural empire was to become a cohesive whole. This included a shifting of the government to a more central location – probably to Babylon, though some have disputed this claim – since it would be impossible to rule the East from Pella.

Consequently, the Diadochoi, starting from a position of disadvantage and weakness, could scarcely be expected to succeed. Posterity remembers them as lesser men who jeopardized the whole for the sake of individual gain, whose pettiness and personal rivalries squandered all that Alexander had won and who sacrificed countless lives in the process. This verdict is rather unfair: premature death had saved Alexander's reputation and ensured his greatness. His generals were left to clean up the mess, to attempt to consolidate the conquered empire, without enjoying any of the authority of the man who had created it.

The wars of the Successors lasted until the late 280s, when Lysimachus was killed in the battle of Corupedium and his conqueror Seleucus was assassinated by an opportunistic and ungrateful son of Ptolemy Soter, known to posterity simply as Ceraunus ('The Thunderbolt'). Then the Successor kingdoms came to be ruled by the offspring of the conquerors: the Hellenistic kingdoms had been formed.

The Antigonids (descendants of Antigonus Monophthalmos) ruled Macedon and dominated the affairs of the south by garrisoning the so-called Fetters of Greece – Demetrias (near modern Volos), Chalcis and Acrocorinth. In 197, at Cynoscephalae, Philip V was defeated by the Romans in what is called the Second Macedonian War; a Third Macedonian War, in which Philip's son Perseus succumbed to the army of L. Aemilius Paullus, effectively brought Antigonid rule to an end.

In Egypt the Ptolemaic dynasty enjoyed a period of prosperity in the third century, especially under its 'Sun-King', Ptolemy II Philadelphus, but by the late second century it was in decline and threatening to destroy itself from within. An unpopular and weak ruler, dubbed Auletes ('the Flute-Player') by the Alexandrians, survived only with Roman aid, as did his daughter, Cleopatra VII, who linked her fortunes first to Julius Caesar, then to Mark Antony, and thus attained a measure of greatness. Ultimately, however, these associations brought her infamy and the destruction of her kingdom.

The most extensive and diverse territory – that is, the bulk of Alexander's empire – was ruled by the descendants of Seleucus Nicator. Already in his reign the eastern satrapies were ceded to Chandragupta. However, as Mauryan power declined India was again conquered by Greek-speaking kings who were the successors of Alexander's governors and garrisons in Bactria and Afghanistan. Coins inscribed in Greek and Indian scripts provide evidence of some 40 Indo-

Greek kings during the third and second centuries. In the time of Seleucus' successor, Antiochus I, the Galatians entered Asia Minor and settled around Gordion and modern Ankara, posing a threat to the Hellenes of Asia Minor, who gradually turned towards the dynasts of Pergamum. The third man of this line, Attalus I, gave his name to the dynasty, which sought the friendship of Rome as a means of protecting itself from the Antigonids in the west and the Seleucids in the east. There were indeed short-term advantages but, in the long run, Roman protection entailed loss of freedom in matters of foreign policy. In 133, when Attalus III died, he left his kingdom to the Romans, who converted it into the province of Asia.

The struggle between the Successors for possession of Alexander's empire carried on for years. This tombstone marked the grave of Menas, killed in the battle of Corupedium in 281, where the army of Seleucus Nicator defeated that of Lysimachus. (akg-images/Erich Lessing)

The Seleucids themselves had been crippled by the War of the Brothers in the second half of the third century. A brief reassertion of Seleucid power under Antiochus III proved short-lived, for in 189 that king met with decisive defeat at the hands of the Romans. The subsequent Peace of Apamea deprived the Seleucids of their lands west of the Taurus Mountains and imposed a huge indemnity upon them. From this point onwards, it was a story of steady decline. Pressured by the Parthians in the east and threatened by a revived Ptolemaic kingdom to the south, the Seleucids embarked upon a series of civil wars between rival claimants to the throne. By the middle of the first century, they had ceased to exist, having been crushed by the competing forces of Roman imperialism, Parthian expansion and Jewish nationalism.

ALEXANDER THE GREAT?

There is no question that Alexander was a great military commander. Building upon the army and tactics his father had introduced to Macedon, he became a fearsome opponent. He never lost a battle, and most of his victories were stunning successes ending with the enemy fleeing the field in disarray. Often leading from the front, he employed and adapted tactics never before seen by the Persians, and was a bold and decisive leader in the face of the enemy. He used his intelligence and education to trick opponents with his strategies, as at the Hydaspes; he would split his forces to achieve his ends, as at the Persian Gates, and was flexible in his leadership to follow up any advantage that he gained in battle, as at Gaugamela. To compare one of his dynamic and flowing battles with the staid, ritualistic hoplite warfare, played out only on level ground and only in season, seen in Greece until a few decades previously, is to see two different worlds. Philip II had started to transform the Macedonian army, but Alexander completed the change to a well-trained standing force with strong heavy infantry, cavalry able to deliver complex tactical manoeuvres at the necessary moment, and allied troops integrated and exploited for their strengths. That there were foreign influences on the development of the Macedonian army is clear, but the outcome was unique to Macedon, and Alexander's successes with the army he had created changed the face of ancient warfare.

Also testament to his greatness as a commander was the loyalty he inspired in his men. At the Granicus, Cleitus disregarded his own safety to save Alexander from the Persian spear, and when Alexander endangered himself jumping into the Mallian town unsupported, his men rescued him, then took vengeance on the people who had wounded their beloved leader. The Macedonians and their allies followed him thousands of miles, mostly on foot, through desert heat, winter snow, foreign mountains and endless plains. After a decade of campaigning, on

Alexander holding court in China, an illustration after a Persian manuscript made in the Middle Ages or later. The romance and legend of Alexander the Great was recounted endlessly in Islamic art and literature from southern Russia to the gates of India. (Ann Ronan Picture Library/HIP/TopFoto)

the other side of the world, Alexander's remaining men did eventually refuse to go any further, but that he had held the army together, motivating them to carry on until that point, is quite remarkable. There are also hints in the sources about the consideration and care he gave his men, sending the newly wed men home from Asia Minor for the winter, letting them share in the plunder after battles, visiting the wounded and commemorating the dead. Though he punished them when they displeased him, and regularly put them in danger, he seems to have been a father-figure to his men, wanting them to look up to him and follow him willingly, rather than through compulsion.

Although the three great battles fought between Alexander's army and Persian forces are the best-known elements of Alexander's campaigning, Alexander was also very successful at siegecraft. He had quite a different attitude to siegecraft from his father's, rarely resorting to treachery or betrayal. Alexander's siegecraft is especially characterized by the spectacular siege of Tyre, which, although a long-drawn-out affair, impressed the ancients because of its technical aspects. The sieges of Tyre and Gaza highlight Alexander's ability to visualize large-scale operations and his willingness to carry them through to completion. His perseverance is also clear at Managa in 327, and at the Rock of Aornus. There was no place for the passive blockade in Alexander's dynamic style of siege warfare. Although he occasionally adopted the strategy of encirclement, this was never an end in itself. For example, during the campaign against the rebel Sogdian towns in 329, Alexander instructed Craterus to encircle the strongest one, Cyropolis, with a ditch and palisade. This contained the rebels there, while he recovered the other towns. Returning to Cyropolis, he began a battering attack then infiltrated the town along a dry watercourse.

His success as a besieger has been attributed to the possession of superior siege machinery. Following on from his father's use of engineers, Alexander employed engineers to develop siege machinery during his campaigns. Alexander's frequent deployment of artillery was probably made possible by the technical advances of his father's engineers. The development of the torsion catapult must have been a slow process of trial and error, and the stone-projectors seen at Halicarnassus and Tyre cannot have been particularly powerful. The massive and complex machinery often deployed by Macedonian armies must have been expensive to manufacture and troublesome to transport. After the fall of Miletus, Alexander had his siege train carried to Halicarnassus by sea, and the artillery used at Gaza was shipped from Tyre. Transfer by land must have been more difficult, but his siege towers were designed to be disassembled, permitting Alexander to use machinery in the mountainous terrain of the Hindu Kush.

Of course, many factors determined whether siege machines should be used, not least the strength and situation of the defences, and Alexander was also perfectly willing to launch an assault without the support of heavy machinery. as at Thebes in 335. Similarly, the machinery assembled for attacking the main town of the Mallians in 326/325 did not arrive quickly enough for Alexander, so he stormed the place without it, and at Sangala, although he had machines ready to batter the town wall, his men instead undermined it and crossed over the ruins by ladder.

Alexander was an innovative and bold leader in military matters, but whether he was a great ruler is a rather different question. He never had a chance properly to rule his empire, and so how he would or could have done so will never be known. The challenges of such a newly created, extensive and disparate empire would surely have been large, but as the man – the god – who had conquered the empire, he arguably would have had more success than the mere mortals who had to follow his act. His education at the hands of Aristotle and others gave Alexander skills which he wielded with confidence in creating his persona as ultimate king and conqueror. He was the avenger of Persian wrongs against Greece, until, as ruler of the Persian Empire, this became inappropriate, after which time he began to portray himself as the heir of Cyrus. He modelled himself on Achilles, he claimed to be the son of Ammon, and he identified himself with the god Heracles. His benefaction to cities was also in keeping with the behaviour of a god, and his fantastic deeds must have made him the equal of many gods. At Siwah, even before Gaugamela, he asked the oracle which gods to honour when he reached the Ocean, the edge of the world, not only showing his self-confidence and ambitions, but also his piety, probably genuine, towards the gods he claimed as family.

THE LEGACY OF ALEXANDER
The Hellenistic era

Alexander died as ruler of a huge empire that stretched from continental Europe to the Indian sub-continent. Though it was split up among the Diadochoi, his conquests had long-term cultural effects. To secure his empire, and because he believed that culture and government meant cities in the Greek style, he had founded settlements throughout his campaigns. There are 70 towns or outposts scattered across Asia which it is claimed were founded by Alexander, many of them named for him, including Alexandria in Egypt, Iskenderun in Turkey, Iskandariya in Iraq and Alexandria on the Indus (Alexandria Bucephalous) in Pakistan. These may be his most lasting contribution to history. By means of these towns and his court, Alexander introduced Greek speech and customs to Asia. In many areas of Alexander's empire Hellenistic civilization flourished, affecting art, architecture, religion and philosophy. Greek became the lingua franca of the civilized world, learnt by all those who wanted to succeed, employed by the Romans for their intellectual discussions, and found in Indo-Greek inscriptions and Hebrew scriptures.

The act to follow

A man who had achieved as much as Alexander, as quickly as he had, at such a young age, was an inspiration to other ambitious individuals, who tried to emulate his achievements, or use any real or imagined connection to the great man to help them with their own ambitions. The Successors all realized the importance of connecting themselves to Alexander. Perdiccas moved to become regent so that he was ruling on behalf of the legitimate royal heirs to Alexander. Ptolemy took possession of the king's corpse, and instead of sending it to Siwah as apparently agreed, put it on display in Memphis, then Alexandria, where it was still available to be viewed 300 years later. In the empires they had carved out for themselves, all the Successors issued coins with Alexander on them, and coins of themselves in poses reminiscent of Alexander.

The Romans particularly admired Alexander, and many wanted to associate themselves with him. Julius Caesar is said to have wept at the sight of Alexander's statue, and bemoan that he had not even begun to equal Alexander's deeds. Pompey the Great actually found and wore Alexander's cloak, while Augustus travelled to Alexandria to lay a wreath on Alexander's coffin. Later, the emperor Caligula took Alexander's armour from his tomb, and wore it himself.

This fanciful illustration shows Alexander exploring the sea in a glass diving bell with a cat and a rooster. It is from a 15th-century manuscript of Le Livre et la vraye histoire du bon roy Alexandre, *now in the British Library. Legends and myths of Alexander have been rife throughout the 2,000-plus years since his death. (akg-images/Erich Lessing)*

Legends and stories

Alexander the man will never be fully understood, his plans for further conquest and his aims for his spear-won empire lost in the distant past. Modern historians view him in many different ways, and will continue to do so because the available information is not able to answer the many questions that even the briefest consideration of his life provokes. The primary texts, written by men who actually

Colin Farrell starring as Alexander the Great in the 2004 film Alexander. *(TopFoto)*

knew Alexander, or who gathered information from those present, are all lost, apart from a few fragments. Contemporaries who are known to have written accounts of his life include Callisthenes, Ptolemy, Aristobulus, Nearchus and Onesicritus. Other influential works include those of Cleitarchus and Timagenes. In the absence of these, we have access to five main surviving accounts of Alexander's life which are based on these primary sources, by Arrian, Quintus Curtius Rufus, Plutarch, Diodorus Siculus and Justin.

Arrian, a native of the Bithynian city of Nicomedia in Asia Minor, wrote his *History of Alexander* in the first half of the 2nd century AD. A military man himself, he modelled himself on Xenophon. Arrian's history is usually taken to be the most trustworthy account of Alexander, because he used the contemporary sources of Ptolemy and Aristobulus. This, along with his detailed and consistent style, means that he has been highly valued by scholars. Diodorus Siculus wrote his account of Alexander in the last half of the 1st century BC. He used Cleitarchus, who had compiled an account of Alexander based on first-hand accounts around 300. Diodorus is often regarded as an uncritical compiler of earlier historians, though this may be overly harsh. Plutarch also used Cleitarchus, as well as other sources, in his *Life of Alexander*. His *Life* is biography, and included moralizing tendencies and anecdotes. Despite this, both Plutarch and Diodorus are useful as counterbalances to Arrian's sometimes sanitized and certainly court-centred history. Dating from around AD 200, Justin's *Epitome of the Universal History of Pompeius Trogus* is an abridgement of an earlier 'universal history' by Pompeius Trogus, a native of southern Gaul. It seems to stem from the same tradition from which Diodorus and Plutarch also borrowed. Curtius was a rhetorician who wrote a history of Alexander in ten books in the mid-1st century AD for Roman readers. Based at least partly on Cleitarchus, the first two books of the history do not survive, and sections are missing from some of the other books. Curtius was not a critical historian, and in his desire to entertain and focus on Alexander's personality, he elaborates, omits and dismisses chronology, though he does not invent, except for speeches and letters inserted into the narrative. Due to the writers' use or valuing of different sources and confusion over certain details, the histories vary in both details and the main elements of Alexander's life. The story, or tradition, that the writer was trying to tell or perpetuate and the genre for which he was writing also have an effect, and all the extant sources contain a certain amount of re-telling, if not sections of pure fantasy.

Fascination with the person of Alexander started while he was still alive, fanned by the myths and stories that he and his court started and encouraged – such as his tryst with the queen of the mythical Amazons – and shows no sign of stopping now. The exotic, colourful backdrops, the monumental battles, the fortitude and perseverance of his men, thousands of miles from home, the court scandals, and the uprisings and conspiracies at the end of his reign: all have proved fertile soil for legends and myths over the centuries.

Throughout Europe, Alexander is a legendary hero, appearing in many folk tales in Greece and elsewhere. A few centuries after his death, the *Romance of Alexander* was written, or edited together from the more legendary material about him. This text was revised and expanded throughout antiquity and the Middle Ages. In late antiquity translations were made into Latin and Syriac. From these, versions developed in all the major languages of Europe and the Middle East, and it was one of the most widely read works of pre-modern times.

Just like the Achaemenid kings before him, Alexander is mentioned in the Bible. A prophecy in Daniel refers to a king of Greece conquering the Medes and Persians and then having his kingdom split into four. A brief resumé of his life also appears in the first Book of the Maccabees.

In much of south-west and central Asia, he is also a hero, known as Iskander or Iskandar Zulkarnain; however, the Zoroastrians remember him as 'the accursed Alexander', the conqueror of their empire and the destroyer of Persepolis. The *Shahnama* of Firdowski, one of the oldest books written in modern Persian, is a book of epic poetry written in about AD 1000. Alexander's story follows a mythical history of Iran, and he is described as being the son of a Persian king and a daughter of Philip, a Roman king. He may appear in the Koran as 'the Two-Horned One', although this has been long debated; and the *Iskandarnama* combines Persian traditions of the Macedonian king with those from the *Romance of Alexander*.

Alexander has continued to feature in culture and literature right up to the present, inspiring works of art and sculpture down the centuries, many modern works of fiction, music, Hollywood films, television programmes and computer games. His ability to fascinate and perplex shows no sign of fading. The name of Alexander the Great lives on.

GLOSSARY

Achaemenids	Ruling dynasty of the Persian Empire established by Cyrus the Great.
Age of the Successors	The period following the death of Alexander during which his officers fought for control of the empire.
Agema	a Guard comprised of hypaspists.
Akontistai	Javelinmen.
Antilabe	Hand-grip on the back of a shield.
Archihypaspistes	Commander of the hypaspists.
Argyraspids	Literally, 'silver shields', an elite force comprised of veteran hypaspists.
Asthetairoi	A sub-group of pezhetairoi; the term is subject to debate, but could be a term for elite battalions, for battalions recruited in Upper Macedonia, or for those who fought in a position closest to the king. The asthetairoi may have been better equipped or trained to fight next to the hypaspists.
Baivarabam	A Persian unit of 10,000 men, equivalent to the Greek myriad.
Baivarpatish	The leader of a baivarabam.
Basilike Ile	Royal Squadron of the Macedonian Companion Cavalry.
Bathos	'Deep order' in Alexander's army.
Chiliarchy	Four lochoi, totalling 1,024 men.
Dathaba	A unit of ten men in the Persian army. Ten of these units comprised a sataba.
Dekas	Originally a file of ten men, later expanded to 16 men.
Delian League	The alliance formed by Athens and other city-states in 477 to wage war on the Persians.
Diadochoi	Successors of Alexander the Great.
Dory	The usual hoplite spear, about 8ft in length.
Doryphoroi	Literally, 'spear-bearers'. Another term that may be applied to hypaspists when they are equipped as traditional hoplites.
Ektaktoi	Supernumeraries. They did not fight in the ranks but conveyed commands to the men in the lochoi. In Alexander's army of the Hellespont in 334, one ektaktoi was allowed to each dekas as an attendant in charge of baggage.

Exomis	Short-sleeved tunic worn by Greek and Macedonian soldiers.
Hamippoi	Infantrymen who fought on foot among the cavalry.
Hazarabam	A Persian unit of 1,000, equivalent to the Greek chiliarch.
Hazarapatish	The leader of a hazarabam.
Hetairoi	Macedonian Companion cavalry, companions of the king.
Hipparch	The leader of a hipparchy.
Hipparchy	A cavalry brigade comprised of two, three or four ilai.
Hoplite	Literally 'man-at-arms', the citizen soldier of the Greek city state.
Hyparchoi	Persian rulers of administrative units smaller than satrapies, although the term may also be used interchangeably with 'satraps'.
Hypaspitai, hypaspists	Literally 'shield-bearers', the elite infantry guard, hand-picked for their strength and bravery.
Hypaspitai basilikoi	'Royal hypaspists', hyspaspists of an aristocratic background and often former Royal Pages. If they had a precise function in battle, it is unknown.
Hyperaspisantes	Hypaspists who held up their shields to protect the king, and probably carried somewhat larger shields than the usual pelte.
Hyperetes	An aide in the Macedonian cavalry.
Ilarch	(pl. ilai) A squadron commander.
Ile	A cavalry squadron of 200 men in four tetrarchies, the building block of the Macedonian cavalry force. The basilikon ile was the Royal Squadron of the Companion Cavalry.
Kardaka	Non-Persian, non-Greek troops of the royal Persian household, or possibly royal mercenaries.
Kausia	A slouch hat.
King's Peace, The	The peace imposed by the Persian king Artaxerxes II in 386.
Kopis	Longer, curved sword used by cavalrymen.
League of Corinth	The federation of Greek states formed by Philip II in 338, of which he was head.
Linothorax	A corselet made of layers of linen, with elongated wings.
Lochagos	The commander of a lochos, later of a syntagma.
Lochos	(pl. lochoi) A group of dekas organized 16 by 16, totalling

	256 men.
Medism	Sympathy with the Persians, also known as the Medes.
Melophoroi	Literally 'apple-bearers'. The 1,000 spearmen of the Immortals, known as such from the golden apples that constituted their spear-butts.
Peace of Callias	The formal peace treaty negotiated between the Delian League and Persia in 449. After this peace, Persia left Greece alone for 30 years.
Peloponnesian League	The defensive alliance between Sparta and other city-states of the Peloponnese. The League would act if one of its members was directly threatened.
Peltasts	Lightly armed troops, usually equipped with a dagger, a javelin, the pelte from which their designation derived, and perhaps a sword, but with little or no armour.
Pelte	A small shield with which a peltast was armed.
Pentakosiarchy	Half a chiliarchy, 512 men.
Pezhetairoi	Heavy infantry, armed with sarissai and perhaps a sword as well.
Phalanx	Literally 'battle-formation'. Usually refers to heavy infantry formation.
Phalangites	The infantrymen who made up the phalanx.
Pilos	Conical helmet.
Polis	(pl. poleis) Greek city, city state, and the city's body of citizens.
Prodromoi	Literally 'scouts', the term usually applied to the Thracian cavalry squadrons of the Macedonian Army, but occasionally to other auxiliary cavalry also. As the name implies, their role was to scout ahead of the advancing army.
Proskynesis	The Persian custom that required individuals to approach the throne on their knees as a mark of respect. On his return to the west, Alexander attempted to introduce this custom at his own court. It was decidedly unpopular.
Psiloi	Light infantry.
Pteruges	The 'wings' of the corselet, hanging down below the waist.
Pyknos	'Close order' in Alexander's army.
Sarissa	(pl. sarissai) A spear between 15 and 18 feet (4.5–5.5m) in

	length.
Sarissophoroi	Literally 'sarissa bearers'; the term is used interchangeably with prodromoi after Alexander's crossing of the Hellespont, suggesting that the scouts were now armed with a longer spear or sarissa.
Sataba	In a hazarabam, in the Persian army, a unit of 100 men.
Satrapy	Province of the Persian Empire, ruled by a satrap.
Sparabara	In the Persian army, the shield men of the archer-pair.
Strategos	'General'. The term is also used for the military governor of a conquered region.
Synaspismose	Formation with locked shields.
Syntagma	The later name for a lochos.
Takabara	Persian infantry armed with spear and taka shield.
Tara	Individual shields carried by Persian archers for use if the shield wall was broached.
Taxiarches	Leader of the taxis; when the army was divided into divisions, the general also acted as taxiarch.
Taxis	(pl. taxeis) A unit of six lochoi, totalling 1,536 men.
Thorax	A corselet.
Toxarch	The leader of a company of 500 toxotai.
Toxotai	Archers.
Trireme	Greek galley powered by three banks of rowers.
Xyston	A cavalryman's lance, made of cornel wood.

BIBLIOGRAPHY

ANCIENT SOURCES

Arrian, *The Campaigns of Alexander* (trans. A. de Sélincourt) (Harmondsworth: Penguin Classics, 1971)

Curtius Rufus, Quintus, *The History of Alexander* (trans. J. C. Yardley) (Harmondsworth: Penguin, 1984)

Diodorus Siculus, *Library of History, VIII* (trans. and ed. C. Bradford Welles) (Cambridge, Massachusetts: Harvard University Press, Loeb Classical Library, 1963)

Justin, *Epitome of the Philippic History of Pompeius Trogus, Books 11–12: Alexander the Great* (trans. J. C. Yardley) (Oxford: Clarendon Ancient History Series 1997)

Plutarch, *The Age of Alexander* (trans. Ian Scott-Kilvert) (Harmondsworth: Penguin Classics, 1973)

MODERN WORKS

Adcock, F. E., *The Greek and Macedonian Art of War* (Berkeley: University of California Press, 1957)

Boardman, J., Hammond, N., Lewis, D. and Ostwald, M. (eds.), *The Cambridge Ancient History Vol. 4: Persia, Greece and the Western Mediterranean c.525 to 479 BC* (Cambridge: Cambridge University Press, 1988)

Borza, E. N., *In the Shadow of Olympus: The Emergence of Macedon* (Princeton, New Jersey: Princeton University Press, 1990)

Bosworth, A. B., *Conquest and Empire: The Reign of Alexander the Great* (Cambridge: Cambridge University Press, 1988)

Bosworth, A. B., *Alexander and the East: The Tragedy of Triumph* (Oxford: Clarendon Press, 1996)

Bosworth, A. B. and Baynham, E. J. (eds.), *Alexander the Great in Fact and Fiction* (Oxford: Oxford University Press, 2000)

Briant, P., *Histoire de l'Empire Perse de Cyre à Alexandre* (Paris: Fayard, 1996)

Cook, J. M., *The Persian Empire* (London: Dent, 1983)

Engels, D. W., *Alexander the Great and the Logistics of the Macedonian Army* (Berkeley: University of California Press, 1978)

Errington, R. M., *A History of Macedonia* (trans. C. Errington) (Berkeley: University of California Press, 1990)

Fuller, J. F. C., *The Generalship of Alexander the Great* (New York: Da Capo, 2004)

Green, P., *Alexander of Macedon, 356–323 BC: A Historical Biography* (Berkeley: University of California Press, 1991, rev. ed.)

Hammond, N. G. L., *The Genius of Alexander the Great* (London: Duckworth, 1997)

Heckel, W., *The Marshals of Alexander's Empire* (London: Routledge, 1992)

Holt, F. L., *Alexander the Great and Bactria: The Formation of a Greek Frontier in Central Asia* (Leiden: E. J. Brill, 1988)

Lane Fox, R., *Alexander the Great* (London: Penguin, 2004, rev. ed.)

Marsden, E. W., *The Campaign of Gaugamela* (Liverpool: Liverpool University Press, 1964)

Olmstead, A. T., *History of the Persian Empire* (Chicago: University of Chicago Press, 1948)

Pearson, L., *The Lost Histories of Alexander the Great* (New York: American Philological Association, 1960)

Roisman, J. (ed.), *Brill's Companion to Alexander the Great* (Leiden: Brill, 2003)

Stewart, A. F., *Faces of Power: Alexander's Image and Hellenistic Politics* (Berkeley: University of California Press, 1993)

Wilcken, U., *Alexander the Great* (New York: W. W. Norton, 1967)

Wood, M., *In the Footsteps of Alexander the Great* (London: BBC Books, 2004)

INDEX

References to illustrations are
shown in bold.
All dates are BC.

A